LONG TIME GONE

LONG TIME GONE

William Lee Brent

▼▼▼

TIMES 𝕿 BOOKS

RANDOM HOUSE

Author's note:
While this is a work of nonfiction,
some names have been changed.

All rights reserved under International and Pan-American Copyright
Conventions. Published in the United States by Times Books, a division
of Random House, Inc., New York, and simultaneously in Canada by
Random House of Canada Limited, Toronto.

Library of Congress Cataloging–in–Publication Data

Brent, William Lee
    Long time gone: a Black Panther's true-life story of his
hijacking and twenty-five years in Cuba / William Lee Brent.
    —1st ed.
        p.   cm.
    Includes index.
    ISBN 0-8129-2486-X (acid-free paper)
    1. Brent, William Lee, 1930–   —Homes and haunts—Cuba.
2. Afro-Americans—Biography.   3. Cuba—Social conditions—1959–
4. Hijacking of aircraft—Cuba.   5. Hijacking of aircraft—United
States.   6. Black power—United States—History—20th century.
7. Black Panther Party—Biography.   8. Afro-Americans—Cuba—
Biography.   I. Title.
E185.97.B816A3   1996
972.9106´4´092—dc20
[B]

Printed in the United States of America on acid-free paper

9 8 7 6 5 4 3 2

First Edition

Book design by Chris Welch

*To my mother, Cora Mitchell, who made every
conceivable sacrifice to guarantee the survival
of the two children she brought into this
troubled and uncertain world;
To my sister, Elouise Rawlins, and her children—
some of whom I have never seen;
To my wife, Jane McManus, who has supported,
nurtured, and inspired me for nearly a quarter of a century;
To all who fight against evil, injustice,
hatred, and intolerance throughout the world,
and to all my brothers and sisters
who have fallen in the never-ending struggle
to make our planet a better place to live*

ACKNOWLEDGMENTS

Nobody writes a book alone. Many people contributed to the development, writing, and publishing of this one, some with timely suggestions and practical ideas, others by sharing their literary knowledge and skills in ways that helped make the writing easier and less pretentious. I thank them all. I am especially grateful to my wife, Jane McManus, for her faith in my ability to write a book. She unstintingly supported, encouraged, and inspired me in my task of bringing this prose portrait of my life to completion.

To Steve Wasserman, editorial director of Times Books, my sincere thanks for his insistence that I write this book in the first person, his faith in my ability to do so, and his invaluable editing advice and suggestions on the final draft.

My editor, Tom Miller, read the original draft manuscript in 1987 while doing research in Havana for his book *Trading with the Enemy*. His knowledgeable criticisms caused me to rewrite the entire thing. Since that time he has helped me by patiently and firmly correcting my errors of fact as well as form. I thank him as a friend.

I am also grateful to my literary agent, Frances Goldin, for delicately nudging me in the right direction, and for the expert way she has handled all the technical and legal elements involved in contracts and publication.

Thanks also to the hundreds of authors whose books have evoked my emulation and inspired me to write.

And especially my infinite gratitude to the Cuban government for granting me political asylum and giving me the opportunity to discover a new, more rewarding lifestyle. And to the Cuban people, who took me into their hearts and let me share the unique experience of participating in the ongoing process of their revolutionary development.

CONTENTS

Out of the night that covers me,
  Black as the Pit from pole to pole,
I thank whatever gods may be
  For my unconquerable soul.

In the fell clutch of circumstance
  I have not winced nor cried aloud;
Under the bludgeonings of chance
  My head is bloody, but unbowed.

—WILLIAM ERNEST HENLEY,
from "Invictus" (1875)

LONG
TIME
GONE

1

CHILDHOOD

SOMEONE WAS HAM-
mering on my cell
door. I wiped the
sweat from my face, sat up on the bunk, and looked around the
semidark cell. "What the fuck?" I muttered.

"Hey, you," the guard yelled through the port. "Come over
here. Come here." I pushed myself up off the bed and walked
cautiously over to the door. Hey You shoved a hunk of stale
bread and a tin cup of lukewarm coffee with milk through the
opening, then quickly closed the panel and locked it.

I placed the food on the nightstand, splashed cold water on
my face, and sat down on the edge of the bed to wait for the rest
of my breakfast. It took about an hour before I realized bread
and coffee with milk was all the breakfast I would get.

I ate only half the bread and took just a few sips from the cup.
I'll save the rest for later, I thought. I reached for my cigarettes—

damn, only one left. I crumpled the pack, put it on the table, and lit up. How the hell do you ask for cigarettes and matches in Spanish? I wondered. Hoping for a breeze and some relief from the oppressive tropical heat, I walked over to the louvered slits that served as a window in the outside wall. While trying to figure out what to do about getting cigarettes, I remembered an old saying I'd heard as a child: "The squeaky wheel gets the grease." I walked back and started pounding on the cell door. The panel slid open immediately and a stern-faced guard glared in at me. I held up the empty matchbook and cigarette pack, pointed to each of them in turn, and repeated, "Cigarettes, matches." The guard nodded understandingly and closed the panel. A short while later the panel slid open. The guard thrust a pack of Cuban cigarettes and a box of safety matches at me, closed the panel, and disappeared. I opened the pack, marked *Populares,* lit up one of the strong-smelling cigarettes, and inhaled deeply. My lungs caught fire. I felt as if I'd inhaled a cigar. Jesus Christ, I thought. I can see I'm just going to love this place. Yesterday I had awakened to a delicious home-cooked American breakfast. I'd had my choice of cigarettes and anything else I wanted. Now I was an international air pirate sitting in a foul-smelling Cuban jail smoking cigars disguised as cigarettes. I wondered if the man upstairs was trying to tell me something. "Welcome to the revolution, motherfucker," I said aloud.

▼

SOME PEOPLE CAN RECALL INCIDENTS FROM THEIR INFANCY IN great detail. I have trouble remembering people's names. Memories of my early childhood are interwoven with sadness, darkness, fear, and pain. There were few moments of genuine happiness; most of the time I felt defenseless and alone. Thanks to the patience and indulgence of my mother and other family members, however, I have managed to dispel some of the darkness, understand and live with the loneliness, and deal with most of my fears.

During my adult years, through stories told by older blacks hanging out on the streets, sitting around the pool hall, or reminiscing in a jail cell, and especially through talking with my mother, who gave me graphic verbal descriptions of her life in the South before and after her marriage, I've managed to get a good picture of events and conditions that helped shape my life.

Franklin, Louisiana, snugly nestled between New Iberia to the north and Morgan City to the south, is roughly one hundred miles west of New Orleans. My mother, Cora Mitchell, was born in 1915 in that largely black farming community on the banks of the Mississippi River. Some blacks owned small parcels of land, but the big landholders were white. The village itself boasted a small wooden church that always needed repairs, a bare-bones general store that gave credit, and a train station with a ticket office, telegraph key, wall-to-wall mosquitoes, and a WHITES ONLY sign in the waiting room.

Cora was an adolescent when her half-Indian mother died giving birth to one more unwanted child. Her mother's death left Cora at the mercy of her near-white father, Pete. Cora was a handsome, light-brown-skinned child, quick-witted, outgoing, and generous. Pete hated her because her skin was darker than his other children's and her hair was short and nappy. Unlike W. E. B. Du Bois, who in 1920 wrote, "I am a Negro; and I glory in the name! I am proud of the black blood that flows in my veins," Pete made it his goal in life to get away from black people and pass for white.

Pete wasted no time in packing up his unwanted daughter and shipping her off to her mother's brother, Uncle Money, who lived a few miles away. Money had a large family, but there was always room at his table for one more. They called him Money because he worked hard and didn't waste his earnings on foolishness. Money was deeply religious, and he ruled his household with a firm and loving hand. The adults in that family demanded complete obedience at all times and were quick to punish any hint of resentment or rebellion. Pouting or muttering under your breath could earn you anything from a head-knuckling to a good old-fashioned ass-whipping.

According to local superstition, cleanliness warded off evil spirits. So the entire house, including the front and back porches, received a daily scrubbing with lye water and pieces of red brick. My mother knew all the rules governing the behavior of young girls in southern households and she fitted readily into her new family. The housework—cleaning, cooking, ironing, looking after the toddlers—was divided among the girls according to their ages. All of them helped with the dishes, taking turns washing or drying. As for the boys, when they weren't working in the fields—weeding, fertilizing, chopping cotton, picking peanuts or corn—they cared for the farm animals, kept the woodpile up, fetched water, made repairs on the house, and harassed the girls.

Every home had at least one gun: a .22 rifle, a pistol of some kind, or a 12-gauge shotgun. So the men and boys spent a great deal of their time hunting. The quarry ranged from rabbits, opossums, and squirrels to wild pigs and turkeys. They also did a lot of fishing and gator hunting. A favorite way to hunt gators was to tie a rope around the waist of a five- or six-year-old boy (preferably a kid who couldn't swim, so he would flounder around and make lots of noise in the water) and throw him into a clear spot near the bank of the river. Once the gator broke cover and started for the struggling live bait, the boy was quickly pulled out of the water and the hunters opened fire.

Family clothes were washed weekly in large metal tubs, with scrub boards and strong homemade soap. Each family thought its own soap recipe was the best in town, but they all contained the same basic ingredients: lye, ashes, and animal fat. After the girls had finished the wash and hung the clothes on long rope lines in the backyard, they called one of their spinster aunts to inspect the work. If she decided the wash wasn't clean enough, she kicked the prop from under the entire line and strode triumphantly back into the house. Cheeks burning with silent rage, the girls quickly gathered the dirt-smeared clothing and started over again, hoping to finish before nightfall.

Sunday school was sacred, one of the few occasions when youngsters could dress up and wear shoes. Normally, schools for black children in most of the rural South were open for only a few months a year. Even then, not everyone could afford to attend. "Niggers don't need no schooling to chop cotton and cut sugarcane," went the common saying.

Cora had passed through parts of the first, second, and third grades, but most of her time was dedicated to domestic chores and working in the fields—hoeing and picking cotton shoulder to shoulder with the boys. The cotton season had two major stages. The first was the growing season, when the young plants that were unwanted had to be chopped out by hand. This work was restricted to adults and those children big enough to handle a hoe. The second stage was the picking season, when six-year-olds developed the picking rhythm that would mark them for the rest of their lives.

Summertime was when the merciless sun turned the dusty unpaved roads into fire-hot griddles. Not even cool well water could quench Cora's thirst as she and other children put in from twelve to fourteen hours a day. They picked about half as much as their elders and earned only pennies. These were the last of the Hoover years and the Great Depression was waiting just around the corner.

Professional pickers traveled all over the state and were paid by the pound for their work. The working conditions were terrible and the pay was low, but some of them, like Three-Bale Shorty and Two-Ton Willie, picked so much cotton they became famous for their ability in the fields. During the peak season, entire families took to the cotton fields in a collective effort to bring in more money. Teenage mothers, toddlers at their sides, filled their sacks and wrestled them to the weighing stands. Cora learned it all, and by the time she got married she could hold her own with the best of them.

At sixteen she married the Reverend Manson Brent. (She called him Mr. Manson and he called her Miss Cora.) Most of her relatives had predicted the marriage would fail, since Manson was widely known as a ladies' man who had already been married. Manson, a tall, handsome, one-eyed black man, was thirty-four. His knowledge of the Bible, his strong singing voice, and his popularity in the village allowed him to substitute occasionally for the regular preacher in the local Baptist church.

Manson had constructed a sturdy little house of pine, set up on concrete blocks well back from the banks of the Mississippi River to avoid seasonal floods. The house, like most of the others in the area, was a shotgun house—if you opened the front and back doors at the same time, you could see (or shoot) clear through it.

Manson worked hard, drank hard, and was very popular with the ladies. He was also very jealous. Mother later recalled how he'd lavished her with attention during their first year of marriage. They often got spruced up and made the long trek into town to window-shop and eat out. He bought her pretty dresses, black patent leather shoes, and a white, floppy-brimmed straw hat with a blue ribbon hanging down in back.

Her first pregnancy was very difficult, but she said nothing and continued working around the house and in the fields. One wintry November night, contractions started, and the pains became so strong she was forced to send Mr. Manson running through the cold, black night to fetch the midwife.

Kicking and screaming, I was forced from the warmth of the womb prematurely, on November 10, 1930. Mother hadn't yet turned seventeen, and the nation's worst depression was little more than a year old. She named me William after one of Manson's younger brothers, a field hand and ladies' man. Mother's eyes filled with tears as she cradled me in her arms and complained to the midwife because I was so small and skinny.

Bundling herself up for the walk home, the midwife took a snuffbox out of her pocket and deftly placed a pinch of the finely ground powder between her lower lip and her gum. At the door, she assured Mother, "If you keep him clean and warm, feed him regularly, and put your trust in God, everything will turn out just fine." Mother later told me how she'd worried over me and pleaded to God not to let me die. Also, how she'd breast-fed me, changed my homemade diapers religiously, protected me from the flies and mosquitoes, and snapped awake at my slightest sound or movement.

Within two weeks my happy little baby sounds let her know I would be all right. Mother was overprotective: she kept me close, sang to me, played with me, and took me with her wherever she went. My father paid little attention to me except to complain I cried too much.

Manson's attitude toward Mother changed drastically after my birth. He became suspicious of her friends and accused her of messing around. Mother felt trapped. Nothing she did pleased her husband. The food didn't have enough seasoning, there was too little or too much starch in his shirts, or the house was a mess.

I was little more than a year old when, between fighting and making up with Mr. Manson, Mother became pregnant again.

She had to tell him before she started showing, no matter how angry he got. She prepared his favorite meal: fried chicken, white rice, thick brown flour gravy, biscuits, lemonade, and sweet potato pie. After supper, she told him they were going to have another baby. My father sat looking at her for a moment, then grabbed his coat and stormed out the door without saying a word.

After Elouise was born, Manson began to make Mother's life a hell. Mother took his insults for another year because she hoped to prove her relatives wrong and she had no place to go.

What in the world am I going to do? she asked herself one day. I ain't got no job and no money, and with two little children hanging on to my skirts I sure can't go running back to Uncle Money begging him to take us in and feed us.

Suddenly she picked Ella up, grabbed me by the hand, and walked swiftly out of the house toward the Mississippi. She hurried along the bank until we came to a familiar, well-worn trail used by fishermen and swimmers. The trail branched off from the main path and gradually descended to the water. Mother had warned me about the snakes down there, so I lifted my feet carefully as she led me almost to the water's edge. Then I panicked and began pulling back with all my strength.

Mother had planned to walk into the river clutching Ella and me and let the swift current sweep all of us away. She'd lived as an orphan herself and didn't want her children to go through the same suffering. The plan failed because I fought her every effort to drag me into the dark, muddy Mississippi. I kicked and screamed so hard that Ella, sensing something was wrong, started struggling in Mother's arms.

Mother suddenly realized she was about to do something unforgivable. Overcome with guilt, she started crying too. Then she turned and walked resolutely back toward the house. I followed at a safe distance. It took a long time before I learned to trust her again.

A short time later, my father came home full of whisky, started an argument, and struck Mother in the face, knocking her to the floor. She glared up at him, her eyes burning with rage. Then she got up, threw a few things into an old suitcase, bundled Ella up in her arms, and strode out the door. I grabbed her skirt and ran along behind as fast as my legs would carry me.

I still have clouded, recurring dreams of my father weeping drunkenly and begging Mother not to leave.

Carrying Ella, and with me in tow, Mother picked her way along the dirt path leading to her Aunt Bey's house. A feeling of relief flooded over her and she hugged Ella close to her breast. Why didn't I do this before? she asked herself. Then, as she approached the door, she wondered how Bey would react.

Mother swallowed her pride and told her aunt what she had gone through since her marriage; she even described the near-tragedy at the river. She also told Bey how, when Manson got drunk and hit her, she wanted to kill him. So she'd packed up and left before something really bad happened.

Bey said Mother should have left Mr. Manson long before. Bey had no children, but she loved them and was happy to have us move in. Her smile made me feel warm and melty inside.

Bey's husband, Papa Jones, worked as a lineman for the railroad and was away for days at a time. Bey devoted herself to church work and domestic chores. She always hummed as she worked around the house, and sometimes her low, melodic voice would break out in her favorite hymn, "That Old Rugged Cross." She was an expert in green medicines; roots and herbs held no secrets from her. She could whip up a cure for what ailed you before you even knew you were sick.

Bey also set a mean table, especially on Sundays and holidays.

Her specialty, prepared in a large cast-iron pot on top of an old wood-burning stove, was Creole gumbo, with chicken, fish, shellfish, beef, pork, lots of spices, and a little okra to thicken it up. The aroma kept you hanging around the kitchen with your mouth watering while it was cooking, and humming and tapping your feet as you ate.

Mr. Manson came to the house on several occasions, pleading with Mother to come back home, promising to change his ways, and pretending to be concerned about Ella and me. Mother wanted nothing more to do with him and quickly sent him on his way.

Normally, no one had trouble finding work in the Cotton Belt, but the Depression changed everything. Cora found some work in the fields, but the employment situation got increasingly worse, with fewer jobs for men *or* women and less pay for everyone. Because of the oil boom in the neighboring state of Texas, talk of abundant job opportunities and good pay spread throughout the black agricultural communities in Louisiana. Bey was skeptical, but she agreed to write a letter to some relatives living in Beaumont and see if they would be willing to put the three of us up and help Mother get a job.

▼

A FEW WEEKS LATER, ON A BRIGHT SUMMER DAY, CORA OPENED another chapter in her uphill struggle to survive and prosper on her own terms. Tickets in hand, she gathered her meager belongings, what little money she'd saved, and us kids, and, before she had time to change her mind, headed for the train that would take us to Beaumont, 160 miles away. For two years, Bey had been my loving grandma. She and I couldn't stop crying when we hugged and said goodbye. I was almost five years old.

Aunt Emma and Uncle Percy Griffin met us at the station. Emma had a sweet, infectious smile. She showered us with hugs and kisses. Percy ignored us and busied himself loading our bundles into the car. I was immediately fascinated by the shiny, three- or four-year-old Ford V8 that Percy caressed with pride. He carefully packed our few things in the trunk, ushered us into the backseat, and crammed his thick, bull-like body behind the wheel. He drove us home without saying a word. The women kept up a constant chatter, exchanging family news. Ella slept all the way, while I glued my face to the car window, marveling in silence at the wondrous sights flashing by.

We had never lived in a house like Emma and Percy's. It was a modest one-bedroom wooden structure with a screened front porch and swing; a large, tastefully furnished living-dining room dominated by the highly polished wooden table at its center; and an immaculate kitchen with an enormous bowlegged wood-burning stove, running water, and built-in cabinets. The screened backdoor led to a flush toilet—the first one I'd ever seen—on the kitchen porch, then to a driveway and a garage. Percy laid down his first ground rules: "Never touch my car, don't slam the doors, keep the screens shut, and stay away from the swing."

The house was near the foot of a bridge spanning the freight yards, in a black neighborhood with paved streets and clean sidewalks. All the houses were blackened by smoke from the trains' coal-burning engines.

The freight yard inspired dreams of far-off places. Its center was a large building called the roundhouse, which had a rotating floor that connected with the tracks outside. A smell of soot and burnt oil permeated the air. I'd had my first train ride coming to Beaumont, and although I didn't know where these other trains were going, I longed to hop on one of them and find out.

We adjusted quickly to our new surroundings: the sound of train whistles that put us to sleep at night and woke us in the morning, the constant din of cars and trucks passing on the bridge overhead, the family next door holding prayer meetings late into the night, and the strangeness of it all. Some people set their clocks by the trains' coming and going. I remember Uncle Percy listening to the lonesome whistle of an outbound freight, looking at his watch, and saying, "There goes the seven-fifteen. Time for you children to be in bed."

What a difference between the big city and the poor country community we had just left behind! The people hadn't changed, though; they were still country at heart, with the same religious beliefs, superstitions, and prejudices they had held all their lives.

Mother quickly found a job with a young, middle-class white family who lived within walking distance. Robert and Helen Walden were nice people with a boy and a girl about the same ages as Ella and me. Mr. Walden, a lawyer, spent most of his time working, while his wife busied herself with looking pretty and buying fancy clothes. Mother would start at a dollar twenty-five a week, and if they liked her work she would eventually get a raise. Mrs. Walden had also promised to give her some old clothes for all of us.

Ella and I played games at home, but we made sure not to touch the swing on the front porch. Sometimes, when there were no hoboes around—Percy constantly issued ominous warnings against the hoboes who passed through the freight yards—we played with the other neighborhood kids in the shade of the bridge.

The games we played in Beaumont were the same ones we had played in Franklin and the basic rules were the same, too: Boys didn't play with dolls; girls didn't wrestle, play marbles, or hunt. I spent hours flying my kite and running footraces. Only the older boys could beat me. I also became a pro at playing marbles for keeps and had to run home on more than one occasion after winning from a poor loser.

Next to husband-and-wife, hide-and-seek—we called it hide-

and-go-get-it—was the most popular game for the older kids, because it usually ended in a forbidden sexual experience. Life, however, was not all fun and games. Beatings were common in poor black families, and sometimes parents got so carried away they couldn't stop. We could hear the kids next door being whipped every night. The girls on our block often came out to play with welts on their legs from the switchings they'd received the night before.

Eavesdropping on the adults while they sat around talking at night, I heard about other, more bizarre forms of punishment: forcing a child to kneel on crushed bricks until his or her knees were raw and bleeding; whipping a rebellious boy with a fence post, chains, or strands of barbed wire to show him who was boss.

Percy was in his early forties, only a few years Aunt Emma's senior, though his perpetual scowl made him seem much older. He seldom spoke to me or Ella, and, when he did, a beating usually followed. He made a mental note of all our wrongdoings—markings on the wall, he called them—and when he was ready to whip us, he ran down the whole list.

Seated in his heavily cushioned wooden rocking chair, he called us to him one at a time. "Drop your pants, boy," he would say. Then he'd pull me across his lap and hold me down by the back of my neck with one hand while he worked the thick razor strap with the other.

He punctuated the blows with verbal reminders. "You re-member when you tracked mud all over the kitchen floor after Emma had just finished scrubbing?" Thwap! "Mr. Johnson saw you playing on the railroad tracks the other day." Thwap! "I've told you a hundred times about throwing rocks but you keep on doing it." Thwap! Percy went on and on, reciting from his men-tal list as he delivered the slow, merciless strokes to our naked buttocks. He accented each blow with an admonishment: "Stop crying. It's too late for tears now. Quit squirming. You'll only make it last longer and hurt worse."

I always screamed as loud as I could, hoping someone would hear me and come and stop the beating. "I won't do it no more, Uncle Percy," I promised between screams. "I won't do it no more." Ella stood watching and listening, paralyzed with fear, knowing she was next. Breathing heavily and wiping sweat from his brow, Percy finished with me and turned his wrath on Ella.

I never understood how the neighbors could listen to our screams and not do anything about it. Aunt Emma always busied herself in the kitchen during the beatings, pretending nothing was happening. She tried to make it up to us later by washing our faces and plying us with whatever goodies she had on hand. She feared Percy as much as we did. Mother was always at work when the beatings took place. We told her about them in detail when she came home, but she couldn't do much more than ask Percy why he had beat us and why he made us take off our clothes.

"I beat them for their own good," he'd reply. "The Bible says spare the rod and spoil the child. I make them undress because skin grows back but you have to buy clothes and they are expensive."

"You know Percy got some funny ways," Mother told us later, "but he's your uncle and he loves you. So try not to make him feel he has to punish you while I'm at work."

The beatings were repeated often enough to make us more afraid of Percy than we were of Rawhead and Bloody, two characters we learned about from horror stories. He even frightened us more than the Black Headless Horseman, who chopped off the heads of disobedient children. We would have preferred to take our chances with the Devil's Dog, who ate you up before you had time to scream, than be at home alone with Percy.

Percy washed and polished his Ford V8 nearly every day. He

watched over it like a mother hen protecting her chicks. When-ever Ella and I came near it, Percy's threatening voice rang out: "You children stay away from my car, you hear me?"

One Saturday, after Percy had carefully washed and polished the Ford and gone into the house to spruce up for his night on the town, Ella and I decided to go around to the kitchen porch for a drink of water. We had to pass the car to get there. Just as we reached the front fender, I slipped and fell, banging my head on the ground. Dazed, I picked myself up by leaning on the front bumper of the sacred car.

Ella helped me into the kitchen, where we explained to Emma what had happened. Percy bathed, dressed, and walked out without speaking to anyone. Aunt Emma was attending to the bump on my head when Percy burst through the kitchen door screaming like a madman.

"I just finished washing and polishing my car and you didn't have nothing better to do than go out there and put mud all over it. I've told you a thousand times not to play around my car. Now I'm gone teach you a lesson you won't never forget."

Percy stalked out of the house. We could see him dragging a pile of moss and sticks into the garage. A short time later, he ap-peared in the kitchen with a burlap sack and a piece of rope thrown over his shoulder. Without a word he grabbed me by the arm and started dragging me out the door.

"What's the matter?" I screamed. "I ain't done nothing."

I broke away from Percy's grip and ran to the front of the house yelling at the top of my voice, "I sorry, Uncle Percy. I sorry. I didn't mean to do it. I fell down. It ain't my fault."

Percy caught up with me in the living room, twisted my arm behind my back, and began pushing me out the backdoor. "You got the devil in you, boy, and I'm gone smoke it out of you once and for all."

Ella pulled at Percy's sleeve and screamed, "You let him go.

You let my brother go. He ain't done nothing. You let him go."
Percy pushed her out of the way and dragged me to the garage
where a rope hung from the rafters over a small, slow-burning
fire.

My stomach tightened into a hard ball of fear. I screamed,
scratched, bit, and kicked with newfound energy. Percy had me
stuffed halfway into the sack when Mother stormed through the
garage door. She'd heard the screams a block away and come
running as fast as she could.

Percy froze. He dropped me and the sack and took a step
backward. "Let me explain," he said. "I wasn't gone hurt him
none. I was only gone to scare him is all."

Mother, breathing hard, reached into her purse and rested her
hand on the knife she always carried. She said nothing, but the
look on her face frightened me more than Uncle Percy had.

I threw my arms around her legs, buried my face in her skirts,
and pleaded, "Don't let him smoke me. I didn't do nothing."

Mother slowly removed her hand from her purse. She bent
down and took me in her arms. "Stop crying now," she said.
"He ain't gone smoke you. He ain't never gone touch you
again." Turning to Percy, she said in a clear, icy voice, "If you
ever lay hands on one of my children again, I promise God
you'll regret it."

Percy backed up another step, eyes bulging, mouth open. He
knew he'd gone too far. Mother took me by the hand and
walked me to the house.

▼

THE INCIDENT IN THE GARAGE FORCED US TO FIND ANOTHER
place to live. This time it was with Aunt Alice, who lived across
the tracks and four blocks away on Avenue A. Widowed and in
her late forties, Aunt Alice lived with her unmarried daughter
Vergie, a part-time waitress. Aunt Alice read her Bible daily and

attended all church functions. What marked her as a true Christian, however, was her generous and forgiving nature.

The women on Avenue A washed, ironed, sewed, and cooked for workers at the freight yards and the nearby rice mill. Most people on the Avenue raised animals or grew vegetables of some kind. You had to shoo away the ducks, geese, chickens, and pigs just to walk down the street. Everyone in the neighborhood had some kind of hustle, too. Some ran boardinghouses. Others rented rooms by the hour to lovers seeking a few minutes of pleasure. Gambling, prostitution, and selling home brew were common, especially on weekends. Violence was an everyday occurrence. Before my seventh birthday, I had seen at least two men with their stomachs cut open. It took hours for the police or an ambulance crew to show up, and when they did, they were hostile.

Oil-rich Beaumont, Texas, in the 1930s was a city of affluence and poverty. It was also a source of hope and promise. In spite of the Depression raging in other cities, Beaumont had work for everyone. Newcomers usually lived crowded together in hastily constructed, run-down wooden houses in areas like Avenue A. The streets were unpaved, and malaria-carrying mosquitoes bred in the stagnant water in potholes. High rents and low wages limited most people's chances to enjoy modern conveniences such as electricity, radios, telephones, indoor plumbing, and flush toilets.

Automobiles on the Avenue were owned by the established ministers, the local grocery store owner, the black slumlords, honky-tonk owners, and professional hustlers who lived much better than most of the working people in the community. Yet, any job at all paid more than any of us could make as field hands.

Mother was a young, good-looking "high yaller" woman who enjoyed male companionship. There was never a shortage of suitors, but she was very particular about her independence and about being treated as a person rather than just another woman. None of her relationships lasted very long.

She was a good worker. She always arrived early and worked late, and she took care of the Waldens' house as if it were her own. The children loved her. Mrs. Walden cleared out her closets regularly and gave all her throwaways to Mother. Some of the clothes had been worn only once before they were discarded.

Ella and I didn't mix with the other children on the Avenue at first. We played together in the house and backyard. Aunt Alice patiently taught us to read and write from her Bible. She also made us memorize the Lord's Prayer, say grace before meals, say our prayers at bedtime, and respect our elders whether they deserved it or not.

The soulful blues and upbeat dance rhythms cranked out on the neighbors' old Zenith gramophones enchanted me. Gradually I was drawn into the street life of the Avenue. I learned to count numbers on a pair of dice and a deck of cards, to tell the difference between craps and passes, and to be suspicious of everyone. The guiding rule on the Avenue was: "Believe none of what you hear and only half of what you see." The more open and trusting you were, the easier it was for people to deceive you. During my basic training on Avenue A, hardly a week passed without my getting at least one black eye or bloodied nose.

Not every kid my age on the Avenue got beat up or run home as much as I did. Ella was a couple years younger than I but a lot smarter; she got along with everybody. My best friend, Clarence, lived only two blocks away and he never had trouble with kids the way I did. I was quiet and withdrawn. I didn't make friends easily. Nor did I have the aggressive, pushy character some kids seem to be born with. I was afraid of violence and I hadn't learned to fight back.

By the time I was ready for grade school, I could read and print from the Scriptures, handle a deck of cards better than most kids my age, and roll a pair of dice like a pro.

"Boy," a neighbor lady once said to me, "you gone be one of two things when you grow up: a no-good, lying preacher, or a good-for-nothing whore-chasing, heartbreaking, thieving gambler." I think I preferred the gambler to the preacher, although I wasn't sure about the difference between them.

Adams Elementary and Junior High School was just across the tracks from Aunt Alice's house. In Beaumont, education for black children was mandatory, beginning with first grade.

Mother got me up and dressed early for my first day of classes. "Now you be a good boy and mind your teacher and don't forget to say 'yes ma'am' and 'no ma'am.' " She gave me a big hug and rushed off to work. Cousin Vergie must have felt me holding back as she led me across the tracks to the school. "Ain't nothing to be scared of," she said in her high-pitched, girlish voice. "You just behave yourself, do what the teacher tells you, and raise your hand when you want to go to the toilet."

The school yard was filled with noisy children, anxious parents, and severe-looking teachers. My lunch bucket was a beat-up Karo syrup can with a wire hoop handle and a push-on metal top. In it were a piece of cold corn bread, some leftover pinto beans and rice, and half an apple. I clutched the can between my feet as I placed my right hand over my heart and obediently repeated after the teacher: "I pledge allegiance to the flag of the United States of America, and to the Republic for which it stands, one nation, indivisible, with liberty and justice for all." I had no idea what I'd said.

After the pledge of allegiance, we filed into the classrooms. The kids in my class were mostly six-year-old beginners like me, but there were a few older ones who were starting late or had been kept back. The staff and the student body at Adams School were black. The staff's goals were to teach us backward country bumpkins to read, write, and do basic arithmetic—and beat our little asses if we got out of line or didn't memorize fast enough. The underlying goal was not to educate us so that we'd be able to compete in society. It was to instill fear and obedience to authority. To make us understand our place in the world and accept it without question.

My first day in class gave me a chilling glimpse of what I was in for. My teacher, Miss Mogley, called two boys up to her desk and let them have a good whacking across their knuckles for talking during class. (One of them started crying, and after class everybody called him a sissy.) She also sent notes to their mothers.

Gertrudis Mogley was a frail, pasty-faced spinster with watery gray eyes, a small pinched nose, and thin lips. She wore her stringy, straight black hair piled high up on her head like a crown of honor, and she flaunted her light skin like a cloak of superiority. She despised her black-skinned, nappy-headed charges and never missed a chance to belittle and humiliate us.

After the first week of classes I, too, came home with a note from the teacher. My head was bowed in shame. Miss Mogley had called me to the board to write my name. I got up full of confidence, printed WILLIAM BRENT on the board, and turned around.

Miss Mogley jumped all over me. She said what I'd done was *print* my name, not write it. Printing might be all right in the country, she said, but here in the city I had to learn to write like civilized people. The note she gave me to take home was more civil. I needed to learn to write instead of print, it explained. Parents' cooperation with the school's teaching methods (memorization, beatings, and insults) could make a great difference in how well a student learned.

Mother and Vergie decided Miss Mogley was right. They

would teach me. So, at home I learned to write a sentence and singsong my multiplication tables. At school, however, I was constantly in hot water. My letters invariably strayed below the lines. I couldn't recite the multiplication tables as well as some of the other kids, and when it came to dividing, I just froze. I knew the teacher was going to hit me and make me look like a fool before the entire class.

For many of us children on Avenue A, school was only a dress rehearsal for the roles we would play as we grew up in a world where poverty, physical abuse, and senseless violence prevailed.

One day, when I was about nine years old, I staggered up the back stairs and into the kitchen, where Aunt Alice was cooking dinner, with my head bleeding profusely and my shirt splattered red. My best friend, Clarence, had hit me in the back of the head with a rock while we were catching crawfish near the tracks. Then, when I chased him to his house, his mama locked the door and I couldn't hit him back.

Mother was furious. She went right over to Clarence's house and warned his mother that if anything like this ever happened again, she would break somebody's neck. Clarence insisted he was just playing and hadn't really meant to hurt me. Mother and Aunt Alice made me promise not to do anything to Clarence in revenge. But I was just aching to hit him back, and with a bigger rock.

The months flew by. I grew straight up, tall and skinny, like a weed. I also came down with every childhood ailment you could name: measles, mumps, chicken pox. I even had malaria. Aunt Alice insisted nothing would stop me until I'd completed the work the good Lord had cut out for me. I didn't know if the Lord had work for me to do or not, but I did know He, or someone, sure wasn't making it easy for me.

School taught me to fear and distrust my teachers and fellow students. The church preached equality for all men in the eyes of God. I was never comfortable in church because I sensed that everything the preachers were telling me was a lie. What I saw every day was a few of my people living high on the hog while most of us were hard pressed just to survive.

Years later, while reading *The Wretched of the Earth* by Frantz Fanon, I understood why. In the chapter on violence, Fanon explains: "The Church in the colonies is the white people's Church, the foreigner's Church. She does not call the native to God's ways but to the ways of the white man, of the master, of the oppressor." I had many years to go before reading Fanon, however, and still more before I began to understand what he had been talking about.

I missed school a lot because I was often sick, but by being around the house all day I learned to clean, wash clothes, iron, and even cook and bake. I was always curious and my mind never ran out of questions.

Ella was growing up too. She and I were constant companions. One day a cute little brown-and-white mongrel dog followed us home from the store. "Please, Mother, let us keep him," we begged. "We'll take care of him. He won't be no trouble at all. Please." Mother reluctantly agreed. We named the dog Wimpy and began the frustrating task of housebreaking him.

Mother left the Waldens and began working as a kitchen helper in a large whites-only restaurant downtown. It was work normally assigned to men, but the pay was exceptionally good and there was always plenty of overtime. After three months she'd saved up a nice sum and was looking around for a place of our own.

Winter had set in; it was freezing cold. One night, we'd all gone to bed early to save on heating fuel. It must have been about two in the morning when Wimpy woke me up by barking in my ear and clawing at the covers. I smelled smoke.

"Mother!" I yelled, and shook her awake. The room was dark and the smoke was getting thicker.

Mother grabbed her purse from under the mattress, wrapped the quilt around Ella and me, and hustled us outside. The night was icy cold and filled with screams from people scrambling to get out of the smoke-filled building. The far-off wail of sirens told us help was on the way.

The fire had started when a kerosene heater in an adjacent apartment exploded, but the flames remained confined. The firemen finally arrived and sprayed water everywhere, causing much more damage than the fire had. Fortunately, no one was hurt. Wimpy was the hero of the day.

One evening, Mother got all spruced up and just sat around talking until someone knocked at the door. She jumped up, patted her hair nervously, and threw the door open. A well-dressed young man about her age stood framed in the doorway. She introduced him as Mr. Walter. Mother and Mr. Walter had been seeing each other for several months.

Walter was tall, good-looking, and light-skinned. He had dark wavy hair and sparkling brown eyes, and his smile could charm a bird out of a tree. He worked at the rice mill and was known as a lady-killer.

Shortly after the fire, he and Mother rented a small house near Aunt Alice's, and the four of us moved in together. I was twelve years old.

▼

EVERYONE WARNED MOTHER THE RELATIONSHIP WITH WALTER would only lead to trouble, but she paid them no mind. She had the man she wanted and she was happy. Trouble did come a few weeks after we'd moved. It showed up early one Sunday morning in the form of an angry, overweight mulatto woman named Lucille, who claimed to be Walter's wife and the mother of two of his children. Lucille had sworn to kill any woman who tried to take Walter away from her. Mother was washing dishes when Lucille knocked on the front door.

"Is your name Cora?" an ominous-looking Lucille asked.

Mother nodded.

"Well, I'm Lucille," the woman said. She took a straight razor from her ample bosom and stepped into the room. "I come to teach you a lesson 'bout messing round wit other women's husbands."

Though caught off guard, Mother threw the dish towel in Lucille's face and shoved her backwards. I watched as Lucille fell against the wall, regained her balance, and lunged toward Mother with the open razor gleaming in the light.

Mother looked around for something to defend herself with. The only thing within reach was the sawed-off axe handle she used as a window prop. She grabbed it with both hands and swung at Lucille's head with all her strength. Lucille dropped like a felled ox. The razor slid across the floor. Mother brought the axe handle down on Lucille's hand and kicked her in the face. Lucille screamed, staggered to her feet, and stumbled along the hallway trying to escape Mother's blows. Wimpy nipped frantically at her heels.

The fat woman's desperate howls brought out the entire neighborhood. People watched in amazement as she crashed through the kitchen door, taking the screen along with her, and fell headlong down the back steps. She tried to crawl under the porch for protection but her huge buttocks got stuck, making an excellent target for Mother's merciless axe handle.

Blow after blow crashed down on that ample posterior before the neighbors managed to pull Mother off Lucille and back into the house. Then they pried the hapless woman from beneath the steps and led her, limping and sobbing, away from the Avenue.

"Cora," Vergie said later, "you sure put the fear of God in that bitch. We ain't never gone see her round here no more."

Mr. Walter denied having fathered children by Lucille and wrote her off as a deranged troublemaker.

I, meanwhile, had learned within the space of a few minutes that, no matter what the odds, if you fought back the bully didn't always have to win.

A few weeks later, I went to the store for some salt. On the way, I was unfortunate enough to run into Bobby, one of the neighborhood bullies, and his younger brother and their girl-friends.

Bobby was several years older than I and a hell of a lot bigger. I was desperately afraid of him and he knew it. "Where you think you going, Ambo?" he asked as he grabbed my arm.

"I ain't going nowhere," I said.

"I think you lying, Ambo," he said. "I think you going to the store, so you must have some money. Give it to me and I won't beat your little black ass."

"Well, you jus' gone have to beat my ass," I said, " 'cause I ain't got no money, and I wouldn't give you none if I did."

I tried to break away and run, but Bobby threw me down. He got on top of me and began hitting me with his fists while his brother and the girls screamed, "Give it to the little black bastard, Bobby. Give it to him."

I covered up and insisted I didn't have any money. Bobby hit me a few more times, then stood up and kicked me in the back.

"You better have some money for me next time I see you, or you gone get a lot worse. You hear me, Ambo?"

After they left I picked myself up, brushed at the dirt on my clothing, and watched Bobby swagger away with his girl rubbing up against him. I tasted blood, and my head throbbed with pain. The memory of Mother, Lucille, and the axe handle flashed through my mind and sent a strange thrill through me. I continued on to the store, got the salt, and walked slowly back home.

Aunt Alice cleaned me up. I looked at myself in her bedroom mirror: My eye was swollen shut and my bottom lip was more than twice its normal size. I remembered Bobby's threat and his friends' jeers.

I went outside and walked along the railroad tracks as I often did when I needed to be alone. Trying to think. Trying to figure out what I could do to protect myself.

As I approached the rice mill I saw an elderly black man with shabby clothes and a homemade backpack. He'd stopped to rest in the shade of a large chinaberry tree. "Ooooooowee," he said, "you must have had one hell of a fight, boy. Looks like you been in a brick fight and everybody had a brick but you."

I had to laugh, though laughing hurt my swollen lip. "It wasn't exactly what I'd call a fight," I mumbled.

"Well, come on over here and tell me 'bout it," he said, patting the ground next to him. I was glad to have a friendly stranger who was willing to listen, maybe offer some advice.

When I finished, he scratched his short white beard, cleared his throat, and asked, "Is the boy light-skinned or black?"

"He light-skinned," I said.

"Uh-huh. I figured he was. Well . . . sooner or later somebody got to tell you and it might as well be me. It ain't the money. He beat you up 'cause you black and he hates you. Most of them light-skinned niggers, or 'Negroes' as they like to be called, is worse than white folks 'bout their black-skinned brothers and sisters. The more you give in to 'em, the more they hate you. You could give him all the money in the world and he would still beat you up, if you let him."

"But I didn't let him," I protested. "He bigger than me and his brother was wit him."

"I know, boy," the stranger said, "and I also know trying to reason with his kind don't do no good at all. You got to make 'em respect you, or they just keep on beating you up, no matter what."

"But how can I? Bobby ain't the only one and they ain't all light-skinned either. Some of 'em is blacker than me and they a lot meaner too."

"It's all mainly 'bout hate, not money. Some of us hate ourselves 'cause we're black, and some of us hate other blacks 'cause they make us remember we are black. Nevertheless, it don't matter what color or how big they is, if you puts the fear of God in one of 'em, the others will think twice before they mess with you again."

I was no longer angry or afraid. I went back home, took a brown paper bag from the kitchen cupboard, and slipped quietly out the door. At a nearby trash pile I stopped and hefted several chunks of brick. One fit comfortably in my hand. I wrapped it in the paper bag and went looking for Bobby.

I found him on his knees, shooting marbles behind the outhouses. The stranger's words kept running through my mind. I tightened my grip on the paper bag with the brick inside, and brought it down on Bobby's head with all my strength. He tried to stand. I pushed him back down and straddled him. He covered up and I brought the now-bloody bag down on his upraised arms again and again. Bobby could only scream for help.

A neighbor rushed over, grabbed me from behind, and pulled me off the bully. "Boy," he shouted, "is you done gone crazy? You could have killed the poor child."

Covered with Bobby's blood, I broke away from the neighbor and ran back to Aunt Alice's. There's one motherfucker ain't never gone mess with me no more, I thought. I felt as if I were flying.

I became a hero overnight. The girls adored me. The bullies

called me crazy and stayed out of my way. I even began to get better grades.

I was about to turn thirteen when Mr. Walter decided to take me out for a Saturday night on the town. "Boy, I know you been sipping wine and beer over at Big Mama Jackson's, and diddling with them young gals round here. But it's high time we made a real man out of you. I'm gone git you some real whisky and some sho-nuff pussy."

Thrilled at the thought of hanging out with Mr. Walter on a Saturday night, I got all spruced up, doused myself with cologne, and stuffed two dollars in the top of my sock. We hitched a ride to the Greasy Spoon, a notorious honky-tonk on the outskirts of town. From blocks away we could hear the music blasting. People crowded around the door. We pushed through and squeezed into the last empty seats at a packed table.

I soon found myself holding a fruit jar of moonshine and listening to my first live blues band. They were playing some of the best blues I would ever hear in my life. I could feel the rhythm in every part of my body. I inhaled deeply, closed my eyes, and took a big drink from the fruit jar. Damn, I thought, this stuff is good. I took another sip and looked around at the fun-loving crowd, men and women enjoying themselves without restraint. I like this, I said to myself. I like this a lot.

Pretty waitresses skillfully wended their way among the rustic tables. I noticed Mr. Walter talking quietly to a light-skinned young girl dressed in a soiled floor-length pink gown. He pointed toward me and the girl nodded. Then she grabbed an empty chair and dragged it over to my table. She squeezed in beside me and smiled seductively.

"I'm Kissy." She dropped her hand in my lap and began to rub my inner thigh. "Walter told me to be nice to you." Kissy smelled of moonshine, sweat, and urine, but that didn't stop me from getting an erection. I didn't know what to think or what to do. Maybe she'd like a drink, I thought, and offered her the fruit jar.

She held it with both hands and took a big long drink. Then she turned and kissed me full on the lips. I was completely aroused now and ready for anything Kissy had in mind. I called the waitress over and ordered two more drinks. She set them on the rickety wooden table and scurried away.

"I feel like dancing," Kissy said.

"I don't know how to dance," I said bashfully.

"All you got to do is listen to the music and let your body do the rest. It's easy. Come on, I'll show you."

Kissy was right. Dancing was easy. Especially to slow, rhythmic blues like "Big Leg Woman," a sultry tune about the prowess of a woman with big pretty legs. Kissy took my hand and led me outside. We walked to the rear of the building. Our bodies came together. Kissy crushed my lips with hers and filled my mouth with her hot, wet tongue.

I was sure someone would see us, but I didn't really give a damn. Breathing heavily and wanting this girl with a passion my young body had never felt before, I grabbed her, swung her around against the wall, and raised her dress. She wrapped her arms around my neck, opened her legs, and moaned softly as I forced myself into her. We listened to the music and let our bodies do the rest.

I could barely get my eyes open the following day. Mother had to shake me awake and threaten me with an ass-whipping to get me out of bed. "Walter should have better sense than to keep you out drinking all night," she said. "I don't care how much your head hurts, we going to church this morning even if you have to crawl."

One Saturday afternoon while I was shooting marbles with my friends, I looked up to see Mr. Walter, doubled over and holding his right side, walking slowly toward the house. My stomach tightened into a hard knot. I jumped up and ran ahead, yelling, "Mother, come quick, something bad has happened to Mr. Walter!"

Mother rushed out of the house. "Oh, my God," she screamed.

Mr. Walter almost fell as he reached out and slung his right arm over Mother's shoulder. His left hand was glued to his right side, just below the rib cage. "Get the boy out of here," he commanded.

But I had already seen the blood. I knew someone had attacked my stepfather, and I was afraid and angry. Please don't let him die, I prayed. Please don't let him die.

Mr. Walter had stuffed the wound with handkerchiefs. I watched through the keyhole as he and Mother carefully replaced the handkerchiefs with bath towels. Mother kept insisting he see a doctor right away, but Walter paid her no mind. He would take care of the business at hand first, then go to a doctor.

Mother grabbed her coat and said she was going with him. Walter took his .38 Special from the drawer and loaded it. He told Mother she was to stay at home until he got back because this was no business for a woman and she knew it. He dropped a handful of shells into his pocket and walked slowly out the door.

Mother took Ella and me in her arms and hugged us so tight we could hardly breathe. "How come we always got to hurt and kill each other?" she asked.

Mr. Walter didn't die, and the man who cut him had the good sense to catch the first freight out of Texas. "I don't know why he cut me," Mr. Walter said from his hospital bed a few days later, "but he is one dead nigger if I ever catch up with him."

Months later, Mr. Walter and two of his closest friends were arrested, tried, convicted, and sentenced to prison for stealing and selling a load of rice from a freight car at the Beaumont rice mill.

Mother was destroyed. She felt the farther she got away from Beaumont, the better. She and Walter had often talked about going to California, where, rumor had it, there was work for everyone and a person could get rich in no time at all. The same story she'd heard about Beaumont. Now her man was in prison and there was nothing to keep her in the South.

"Look," she said to Aunt Alice, "California can't be no worse than it is right here. I've heard women can make just as much as men on them wartime jobs out there. They say you don't have to ride in the back of the bus or bow and scrape to white folks the way you have to do here."

Mother decided to take me with her to the Golden State and leave Ella with Aunt Alice until she found a job and got settled. The year was 1943. I was thirteen years old.

2
▼▼▼▼▼▼

CALIFORNIA

▼▼▼

COUSIN DARBY owned two houses in the predominantly black west side of Oakland. His main goal in life was to get rich as fast as he could, and he didn't care how he did it. He rented us a furnished room he had partitioned off from a larger one on the ground floor of one of his buildings. The rent was excessive, we shared the bathroom and kitchen with another tenant, and we had to pay part of the utilities. "I know it's not much," Darby said to Mother, "but you'll soon be making enough money to buy your own house."

I liked our new home just fine. There were streetlights outside, and all the streets were paved. In the house, we had electric lights, a gas stove with an oven, and a sink and shower with hot and cold running water. The flush toilet worked every time I used it.

Wartime shipyards in the Bay Area were booming; they hired anyone who applied for work. To southern farmhands accustomed to long hours and low wages, the working conditions were ideal and the salaries seemed like small fortunes. Everyone had a well-paying job or some kind of hustle; some people had both.

A few days after we arrived, Mother started working as a mechanic's helper on the day shift in an Oakland shipyard. While she was gone, I spent the hours admiring the neighborhood and getting to know my big-city relatives, who regarded me as a backwoods country boy.

"You can't imagine how big the shipyard is," Mother said when she came home from work the first day. "There are thousands of men and women, blacks and whites, from all over the country, working side by side. I think I'm going to like California."

At an age when I needed stability and guidance, I found myself struggling to adjust to a completely new environment. My first week in Oakland showed me what I had to expect. Four boys about my age, two blacks and two whites, surrounded me on the way to the grocer's and demanded my money. I pushed the largest boy out of the way, turned, and ran back to Cousin Darby's. The boys gave chase, but I easily outran them.

"Those young good-for-nothings are always causing trouble around here," Darby said. "You'd better stay out of their way 'cause they're real bad news."

I tried staying out of their way: taking a roundabout route to the store or to the ice cream parlor and movie house a block away. But there were gangs on every block.

"You gone just have to learn to fight back," Mother said. "You can't just keep running away all the time."

She was right, of course, but saying was a lot easier than doing. In Texas I'd only had to worry about one bully at a time. Now I had to deal with whole gangs, and I didn't know how.

One day, again while I was on my way to the store, the same gang I'd escaped from the first time jumped me. I fought back the best I could, but one scared kid against four hasn't got much of a chance no matter how hard he fights.

An older kid who lived on the same block had seen what happened. His name was Jimmy Dee, and he decided to give me a few tips on street fighting.

"Whenever they come at you in a gang," he said, "try to get 'em to fight you one-on-one. Pick out one you think you can beat. Talk loud, call him yellow, talk bad about his mother. Anything to make him fight you. Better still, just go upside of his head. Then he'll be afraid of you right from the start."

"Then what should I do?"

"What the fuck you mean, what should you do? You stay on his ass till they pull you off him or he runs away. Always wrap a handkerchief around your hand before you start fighting so you won't cut your knuckles on their teeth. And don't never hit 'em on the head, 'cause you might break your hand. You got to aim for the eyes and the nose. They can't fight if they can't see or breathe. Keep your hands up and your head down, get in close and knee 'em in the balls. If you fall or get knocked down, curl up and cover your face 'cause they sure gone stomp on you." Damn, I thought, the big city just might not be as good as it's built up to be.

Mother got me enrolled in the seventh grade at Tompkins Junior High School, a few blocks from the house. I went pretty much unnoticed for the first week of classes. At least I thought I had.

As I left the building one afternoon after school, I noticed a group of students hanging around the front gate. Not thinking it had anything to do with me, I continued walking toward the group.

"Excuse me," I said, and started through the gate.

A short, husky boy called Juju stepped out in front of me. "Excuse you for what," he growled.

"I want to get through the gate," I said.

"Well then, you either got to say please, or walk right over me."

I knew if I said please, I'd have to say pretty please, then pretty please with sugar on it, and in the end I'd still have to fight.

My right fist flew out as if it had a mind of its own. It caught Juju flush on the nose. He staggered backwards and fell. He then quickly curled up in a ball as I began kicking and stomping him.

Jimmy Dee ran up and pulled me off. "Hold it, man," he said. "You don't want to kill this fool."

"I don't want you fighting in the streets like some kind of animal," Mother said later. "You go to school to learn, not to fight with the other children."

"I didn't start it," I said, "and besides, you told me I had to start fighting back. If I hadn't hit him first, he'd have hit me."

Most of the kids in Oakland ran in gangs. They were always fighting in school, and if you didn't fight, the other kids just took advantage of you. Once I learned the turf rules, I had less trouble adapting to my new reality. It took a little time but I finally learned there were two kinds of schools out there: the Street School and the Regular School. If you didn't learn from the first one, you couldn't even get to the second.

Mother and the rest of the family always called me William. My new friends called me Bill. I liked Bill better. "The rest of 'em can call you whatever they wants," Mother said, "but I named you William and that's what I'm going to call you."

The student body and faculty at Tompkins were an ethnic salad. The teaching methods were different from those used in Beaumont: Beatings were done by the school principal and only with the written consent of a parent. The system of teaching by

rote gave way to one of comprehension, perception, and practice. Many of the teachers placed more emphasis on helping
slow students than on criticizing and humiliating them.

I had the habit of dropping my head and mumbling when I
talked to adults. My clothing and speech immediately identified
me as a freshwater country boy. On occasion, some kids in
school made fun of the way I dressed or talked, and this in-
evitably led to a fight. I didn't always win, because I think I
really felt inferior.

Several weeks after Mother started work, she took me downtown and bought me some blue jeans, white T-shirts, and a pair
of square-toed dress shoes with thick leather soles and heels.
These were known as stomping shoes, and if you kicked a
sucker on the knee or in the balls, he had to go down. Besides,
just wearing them intimidated a lot of fools and kept them from
messing with you.

The custom on the streets was not to wash your jeans, because they would lose their shape and color if you did. Jimmy
Dee never washed his, and when he took them off they could
stand in a corner by themselves. I couldn't wait to show off my
new clothes. The T-shirt fit like a glove, the jeans rode comfortably halfway down my buttocks, and my shoes shone like glass.

"You looking good, my man," Jimmy Dee said on the way to
school. "All you need now is a steady and you got it made."

I already had my eyes on a pretty little light-skinned fox in
my homeroom. I'd caught this girl, who was called Ginger,
looking at me several times, and I decided to hit on her and see
where she was coming from.

Ginger couldn't keep her eyes off me when I walked into the
classroom in my brand-new duds. I played it cool until she was
alone. Then I went over and introduced myself. Before I knew
it, we were holding hands and talking right through lunch. The

chemistry was perfect. Back in class, Ginger moved her stuff to a desk next to mine. After class we left the school arm in arm. I had found my steady.

Several of my teachers saw I really had an interest in learning, and they did their best to help me. In time, I lost my fear of the big city, the gangs, and the classroom. I passed seventh and eighth grades and changed girlfriends three times.

One of my classmates, a boy named Jim, delivered papers for the *Oakland Tribune.* "I have to get up at five in the morning," Jim said, "and sometimes it takes two trips, but I make over fifty dollars a month."

"Fifty dollars a month just for delivering newspapers? You think I could get a delivery job too?" I asked.

Mother didn't think too much of the idea, but she helped me buy a used bicycle. Jim helped me get a paper route. It took me a while to learn all the streets and to get the knack of folding the papers into triangular packets so I could throw them onto my customers' porches. But before long I could do my route just as fast as Jim did his.

My third school year, however, brought more changes and new problems. Mother was making more money now, and she decided to rent a larger place so Ella could come spend her summer vacation with us. She struck a bargain with a widower who owned a small house and was tired of living alone. She would pay less rent than Darby demanded and have more space. Mr. Walker, the owner, was more than glad to have us in the house.

Ella arrived to a tearful reunion with Mother and me. She brought letters and good wishes from friends and relatives in Beaumont. After a month she went back to Beaumont to finish junior high school.

Mr. Walker, meanwhile, decided to remarry, so Mother and I had to move again. We located a furnished studio apartment above a church, in the worst part of West Oakland, for less than she'd paid Mr. Walker. She still had to share the bathroom and pay her gas and lights, but the place had a little more privacy.

The neighborhood was run-down but only two blocks from school, and some of my friends lived just down the street. I thought it was great. My only worry was, since we now lived above a place of worship, I might have to start going to church on Sundays again. Mother didn't insist, but she did suggest that attending services once in a while wouldn't hurt me none.

Seventh Street, especially the two-block area near our new apartment, was the heart of the ghetto. Pimps, whores, and hustlers hung out in the shoddy bars. Cafés and cheap hotels lined the street. Jim and I admired the pimps' and hustlers' sharp clothes, the fine-looking women they hung out with, and, above all, the money they flashed around and the fancy cars they drove. Soon we started hanging out at the pool halls. Before long, we had joined with other young bloods who were intrigued by the street crowd. We began to cut classes, drink cheap wine, and smoke weed. All my paper route earnings went to the pool sharks and the weed dealers.

The main drug dealer on Seventh Street at the time was a brother called Too Money (short for too *much* money). Too Money dressed like a millionaire, drove a new Cadillac Coupe De Ville, and never went anywhere without his bodyguard.

One day, as Jim and I were engrossed in a game of eight ball, Too Money sauntered over to our table. "You two cats want to make some easy money?" he asked.

"Depends on what you call easy money," I answered.

"Easy money is money you don't have to work for. You just stand around and people bring it to you."

"Yeah," I said. "I wouldn't mind making some easy money."

"Okay, here's the deal," Too Money said. "I supply the merchandise. You sell it and keep part of the profits; the other part you bring to me. It's as simple as ABC."

"How much do we get to keep?" I asked.

"Well now . . . let's say I give you twenty seventy-five-cent items. You bring me ten dollars and keep five for yourself. I figure you can sell fifty, sixty items at school every day. Plus you'll have plenty of smoke."

"Can we think about it and let you know tomorrow?" I asked.

"Sure," Too Money said. "Think about it. You won't find a better deal nowhere on the street."

Twenty-five cents didn't seem like enough to Jim because we would be taking all the chances and Too Money would be taking most of the profits. But since Too Money always sold good weed, I explained, we could cut it with Asthmador and double our profits. (Asthmador was an over-the-counter medicine for asthmatics; it looked and smelled like weed.) We accepted Too Money's offer the next day. He gave us twenty joints apiece with a warning not to cross him or he would have his boys fuck us up.

We did a brisk business at school. Our real sales, however, came from parties and hanging out at bars and after-hours joints. I began spending more time on Seventh Street than in the classroom. I intercepted all the letters from the principal's office, but I couldn't stop the visits from the truant officers. In a desperate effort to bring me back into line, Mother beat me with anything she got her hands on: a broomstick, a belt, the ironing cord. Once, she even hit me with a skillet.

"Nothing does any good," she told Cousin Darby. "God only knows what he and them other boys do out there. I'm afraid he's going to steal something and get sent to jail."

I did spend some time in jail before long, but not for stealing or for selling dope. A group of friends from school and I went on a picnic in the all-white Berkeley Hills district. Before we could unpack our food, several young white boys started shooting at us with .22 rifles. We dropped everything and took off in the direction the shots had come from.

We chased two of the boys down and beat the living shit out of them. It didn't take a genius to realize we were in big-time trouble, so we gathered our things and hotfooted it out of the area.

The police were waiting for us at the bus stop. They took us to Juvenile Hall and charged us with everything from trespassing to unprovoked assault. Later, we were released into the custody of our parents. Without knowing what had really happened, Mother reproached me for hanging around with a bunch of thugs and getting into trouble.

At our hearing, the white boys admitted having shot their rifles in our direction, but, they claimed, "not at the colored boys; we didn't even know they were there." The judge believed them. He placed us on probation, with the warning that if any of us appeared before him again, he would take us out of circulation for a long time.

I couldn't understand why the judge convicted us instead of the white boys. It seemed to me kicking a few asses wasn't nearly as bad as shooting into a group of people on a picnic.

"It don't matter what part of the world you in," Cousin Darby said bitterly, "white folks is always white folks and niggers is always niggers. Always remember the laws are made to protect white folks, not niggers. Everybody knows it ain't right, but if you forget, they either put you in prison or they kill you."

The incident in Berkeley was my first real brush with the law. It only heightened my resentment of authority and laws in general. "I just hope you stop hanging around on the street," Mother said, "before they catch you stealing or selling dope and send you to the penitentiary, or shoot you down like a dog."

▼

THE EXPERIENCE SOBERED ME ENOUGH TO MAKE ME FINISH junior high. But after a couple of years of high school, I'd had enough of classrooms, teachers, and truant officers. So several friends and I decided to enlist in the Air Force.

I was only seventeen, so I bought a phony birth certificate for ten dollars and went to the local recruitment office. My scores were so low on the various tests they ran me through that the Air Force wouldn't have anything to do with me. The Army, on the other hand, welcomed me with smiles. I knew I should have stayed in school, but I thought the Army could help me get off the streets and make something of myself.

They put me on a train and sent me to Fort Knox, Kentucky, in the dead of winter. Louisville, about thirty miles from the base, wore a thick mantle of snow to welcome the new recruits. Tough-looking white sergeants separated us by race, herded us onto covered military trucks, and rushed us off to the base. I took an instant dislike to the icy winter weather. Damn, I thought, I can't remember ever having felt this cold.

Winter had invaded the base. Snow-laden trees stood silent guard along the ice-slick roadways. Snow covered the surrounding countryside like a giant white blanket. Desolation and dread awakened inside of me. This was a mistake, I thought, a bad mistake.

The trucks pulled up in the bleak compound of the 367th Armored Infantry Division, unloaded their cargo, and sped off into the distance. NCOs—noncommissioned officers—barked out orders, and the bedraggled recruits lined up in formation.

A huge man with a ruddy, pockmarked face and a built-in scowl called us to order. "Fall in!" he bellowed. "My name is Sergeant Theodore Culpepper. You will call me Sergeant, or Sir. I don't like recruits; they're nothing but spoiled mama's boys or else they're troublemakers. Well, Mama can't help you now, and we got a special place for troublemakers. From now on you will do what I tell you, how I tell you, and when I tell you. Otherwise, you'll wish you'd never been born. Is that clear?"

"Yes Sir, Sergeant, Sir," someone yelled out.

"He forgot to mention kiss-asses," I said under my breath.

Sergeant Culpepper called the roll and assigned everyone to a squad and a barracks. Later we went to the supply room to exchange our civvies for uniforms. Next, we stopped at the barbershop for our first GI haircuts.

In the welcome warmth of the barracks, Corporal Higgins gave us detailed instructions on how to make our beds, how to hang our uniforms, how to position our shoes under the bed, and how to arrange every article in our footlockers.

"We hold inspections every day," Corporal Higgins said, "sometimes more. You get a demerit for each item out of order, and you get one if your bed is improperly made. If any part of the barracks is not clean, the entire barracks is not clean, and you will have to clean it again until it passes inspection."

I don't think I'm going to like this place, I said to myself. As a matter of fact I already don't like it.

"Make sure all your clothing is stamped with your serial number," Corporal Higgins continued, "and always keep your footlockers locked because you have to pay for everything you lose. Not saluting or not saying 'Sir' to an officer or a noncom and talking in formation or after lights-out are demerits too."

Before we knew it, bedtime arrived. "All right, everybody," Corporal Higgins ordered, "knock it off. Time to hit the sack. And remember, no talking after lights-out."

Whispers, murmurs, and snickers reached my ears through the darkness. I had a feeling there was going to be trouble, so I quietly put my pants and shirt on and set my shoes at the ready beside my bunk.

"Hold it down," Corporal Higgins said loudly.

Silence held for a few minutes; then the whispers began again. "Hold it down," the corporal repeated, a trace of anger in his voice. More silence. Suddenly someone broke out laughing and others joined in. Without warning the lights went on, the command "TENNNNNNNSHUN" rang out, and NCOs rushed into the barracks from both entrances.

The recruits jumped out of bed and came to attention before their bunks. The smart ones managed to jam their feet into shoes.

"All right," said Sergeant Culpepper, "you want to play games, we'll play games. Fall out."

The surprised recruits reached for their clothing.

"NO. Fall out, and fall out now, just the way you are."

I don't believe this, I said to myself as I stepped out into the freezing cold. What in the world have I gotten myself into now. The others reluctantly followed, most of them dressed only in shorts and undershirts. Outside, Corporal Higgins called the roll and turned us over to Sergeant Culpepper.

"When I give the order I want you men to go back inside in an orderly fashion. You will have ten minutes before lights-out. You will maintain absolute silence or you will be right back out here. Are there any doubts?"

"No Sir, Sergeant, Sir," several people chorused.

Back in the barracks, we hurriedly went to the john and then climbed into bed. There was absolute silence the rest of the night. The next morning, several angry recruits swore they would personally kill anyone who talked after lights-out again.

In 1948, President Truman would issue an executive order calling for "equality of treatment and opportunity" in the armed forces. But in 1947, discrimination and bigotry flourished at Fort Knox. I knew racial segregation existed, but I had never had to confront it, one-on-one, until then.

The base was divided by race. Black companies and battalions received the same training as the white ones. Yet blacks lived and trained in one section and whites in another. We never bivouacked or used the shooting range together. At parades, the whites always went first and the blacks followed. To my knowledge, all the COs—commanding officers—were white, and so were most of the MPs.

On my first three-day pass to Louisville, white MPs made me and my friend Sergeant Jones show our passes five times within a few hours.

"What the fuck is this?" I asked Jones.

"Don't let 'em provoke you," Jones said. "They just itching to bust your head so they can have something to brag about."

Sergeant Jones's real name was Jesus Abraham Jones. He knew how to soldier but sometimes he just didn't give a damn. He'd made sergeant several times during his six years in the Army and had gotten busted for gambling or being drunk and disorderly each time. Everyone called him Sarge, just the same.

"The Army's a good place for people like me," he said. "The pay's good, I always know where my next meal's coming from, and I don't have to worry about rent or doctors' bills. Besides, I got no trade or skills; soldiering is the only thing I know."

"I don't understand how you can stay here and let these ignorant honkies fuck you over the way they do."

"We can run but we can't hide, young blood. They gone fuck us over no matter where we are. Here at least I'm on my home ground and I know what to expect."

I decided to settle down and try to soldier. I'm here, I thought, and didn't nobody send for me, so I might as well make the best of it.

I pulled guard duty in ankle-deep snow, plodded along muddy back roads on thirty-five-mile forced marches with rifle and a full pack, bivouacked in pup tents on soggy Kentucky hill-sides, and crawled through the mud in mock attacks on simu-lated Asian villages. I hated every minute of it. Every night I prayed, God help me think up a way to get out of the Army and the shit I've gotten myself into. I even thought about shooting myself in the foot or doing something equally stupid.

"Your girlfriends in town ain't seen you in weeks, boy," Sergeant Jones said, "and you always on detail or KP for one thing or another."

"Yeah," I said angrily. "No matter how hard I try, Sergeant Culpepper keeps me on his shit list. He won't give me a pass and I'm on KP so often people think I'm training to become a cook. I got to find a way out of this mess somehow."

"Well, if you thinking about going AWOL, forget it. You could wind up with a court-martial. They want you to do some-thing dumb so they can jail you and stay on your case for as long as you're in the Army."

"I'm not talking about no AWOL," I said. "I'm talking dis-charge. Like ... maybe a Section Eight—like they give to sol-diers with mental problems, or something. I can't take much more of this bullshit."

I asked the old-timers for their ideas. They all advised against trying for a Section Eight. "In the first place, it's hard to get, and second, it'll screw you up in civilian life," they said.

A sergeant from the super-bad all-black 84th Tank Battalion suggested I look through the GI Bill of Rights. I got a copy and began spending all my spare time with it. My efforts paid off. Eight months after I'd entered Fort Knox, I presented written proof that I had falsified my age to enlist in the service. I was granted a general discharge under honorable conditions. The Army gave me three months' back pay and a train ticket to Cal-ifornia. I was one happy young black man when I boarded the train for Oakland.

▼

WITH MY DUFFEL BAG SLUNG ACROSS MY SHOULDER, AND WEAR-ing a brand-new Army dress uniform with illegal T5 (technician fifth grade) stripes on the sleeves, I stepped joyfully off the train in Oakland. Perhaps as an ominous sign against my return, a squad car screamed away from the station just as I found a cab.

"What happened?" I asked the cabbie.

"Busted some cat they caught trying to steal suitcases," he replied. "Can I take you somewhere, Sergeant?"

I had him take me straight to the Triangle Pool Hall on Sev-enth and Pine. One of Too Money's dealers sold me two cans of Acapulco Gold, dynamite weed on the streets at the time. I stopped at the drugstore for two packs of Zig Zag cigarette pa-pers, then headed for home.

Ella had arrived from Beaumont to live with Mother and me. To make sure we all had enough space, Mother had rented a larger house near another busy freight yard.

I spent the evening telling Mother and Ella about my brief stay in the U.S. Army. "Would you believe Sergeant Culpepper had us crawling around the compound on our hands and knees picking up cigarette butts? His favorite saying was, 'I don't want to see nothing but shoe soles, assholes, and elbows.' I mean . . . the motherfucker was crazy. I think he sat up nights thinking of ways to punish us. Once he ordered me and two other dudes to dig a six-by-six with the spoons from our mess kits. We worked at it for a week and we didn't make a dent in the frozen ground."

"I knew you wouldn't like the Army," Mother said, "but it serves you right for sneaking off and joining up. Maybe now you'll settle down and finish high school."

I enrolled in Oakland's predominantly black McClymonds High School knowing it wouldn't work out. I'd become too jaded. I had no goals, no direction. My only ambition was to get rich and live high on the hog.

My brush with juvenile court had shown me there was no justice. My experience on the streets of Oakland and Louisville had taught me to admire hustlers and look upon working people as chumps. The segregation and abuse I'd had to live with in the Army had convinced me this was a white man's world in which I had no voice. I had reached the point where I didn't believe in anything or anybody.

Just as I'd expected, the teachers were indifferent, and the classes were boring. The whole regimen reminded me of Fort Knox except we didn't have to wear uniforms. I felt more grown-up than my classmates and soon fell back into my old habit of hanging out on the streets.

Before long, I began buying kilos and selling matchboxes and cans of weed. My street teachers taught me to shoplift, short-change, burglarize, pimp, strong-arm, and roll drunks. My home-away-from-home was the Triangle Pool Hall.

In time, the police as well as the truant officers began to hassle me, so I dropped out of school. I got a job as a sorter in an industrial laundry. The work was tedious and filthy: maggots in the laundry from the restaurants, and shit, blood, or vomit on the sheets from the hotels. Everything stank to high heaven. I stuck with it because the pay was good and because the swing shift, from four to twelve, gave me a chance to catch the nightspots in full swing and sell a little weed before going home to sleep.

As far as unorganized street hustling went, I did all right. I knew lots of people, dressed sharp, and always had money to spend and a good-looking woman on my arm. Everything was cool until I got busted on a fluke.

Bicycles were very popular in California. Everybody wanted

a fancy Schwinn. Many of us couldn't afford to buy a bike, so we ripped them off from the rich white kids in the suburban communities. It was very easy to do because the rich are sinfully careless. The white kids didn't bother to chain and lock their bikes most of the time.

We stole the bikes, stripped them, filed serial numbers off, and repainted the frames. We rode around showing off for a while, then sold them for whatever we could get.

One afternoon two friends and I had just finished a couple of joints in front of the pool hall when a neighborhood kid rode up on a stripped-down, newly painted bike. We knew it was stolen, but poor people tend to take foolish chances, especially when they're high.

"Hey, kid," I said, "you ever see anyone ride one of those things backwards?"

"No, I ain't," the boy said. "Did you?"

"Young blood," I boasted, "it just happens you're looking at three of the best."

"I'll believe it when I see it," the boy said.

I rolled up my pants, got on the bike, and rode to the end of the block. Then I mounted the bike backwards and continued around the corner. At the next corner I nearly ran into an unmarked patrol car.

One of the officers got out. "What the hell you think you're doing, boy, practicing for the circus? You got papers for this bicycle?"

"It's not my bicycle. I just borrowed it from a kid around the corner," I said.

"I'll bet you just borrowed it," the other officer said, getting out of the car with his hand on his gun butt. "Put your hands behind your head and turn around."

"The serial's been filed off this one, and they didn't do a very good job of it, either," the first officer said.

His partner handcuffed me and shoved me into the backseat. "Call the bike squad and tell them we want a pickup and a check on this bicycle."

The bike squad reported a "tall young colored boy" had strong-armed the bicycle from the son of a rich white doctor in the Berkeley Hills area a week earlier. My admission to having the bike in my possession was an automatic guilty plea. I was convicted of a felony and sentenced to be placed in the custody of the California Youth Authority at Lancaster. I was nineteen years old.

Lancaster, a scattered assortment of military-style barracks and other buildings enclosed by a high, barbed-wire-topped chain-link fence, constituted a desert concentration camp for hundreds of rebellious young people who were fast becoming social outcasts. Everyone at Juvenile Hall in Oakland looked upon Lancaster as a status symbol, the last stop before San Quentin or Folsom.

"It's like going through high school before going on to college," said John Henry, my cell mate at Juvy. John Henry had gone to Lancaster for house burglary at fifteen and now he was going back for robbery one. "Once you graduate from Lancaster, you're ready for the big time," he said. "When I went in, I only resented authority. By the time I got out I hated it with all my heart."

They cuffed and shackled us and loaded us on a bus before daybreak one morning. We arrived at Lancaster shortly before noon. "Damn," I said aloud as we pulled up to the gates, "I didn't know this place had gun towers."

"You better believe it," said John Henry. "With real guns and guards who love to use them."

Stern-looking guards led us to the reception room. Our personal property went into large manila envelopes. Those with money got receipts and were warned not to lose them. We had to strip, run our fingers through our hair, open our mouths and lift our tongues, pass short-arm inspection (pulling back the foreskin), and bend over and spread our cheeks. Then came the delousing spray and the cold shower. The uniforms came in two sizes: too big and too small. Shoes, on the other hand, came in large only. Once you got settled in, however, you could work out a trade with the inmate clerks for cigarettes or other canteen items.

"All right, you guys, listen up," a short, muscular man shouted from a platform before us.

"That's Sergeant Blank," John Henry whispered. "He's bad news—hates blacks and Latinos. I think he even hates himself."

"Some of you already know me," Sergeant Blank continued. "The rest will get to know me before you leave. You are here because you committed a crime and got caught. Our job is to keep you locked up until the Youth Authority orders us to let you go. Here you have no rights, only privileges granted by the director. If you obey the rules and stay out of trouble, you will get all your privileges. If you get out of line, they will be taken away and we will come down on you with the full weight of the California Youth Authority. Do what you are told, when and how you are told to do it. Anything else and you're in deep trouble."

Loaded down with our bedding and extra clothing, we shuffled across the compound to our barracks.

A desk on a raised platform in the middle of the barracks gave the guards a clear view of both its wings, with the twin rows of single bunks and the upright metal lockers that lined both walls. The end of each wing formed an L-shaped space for open toilets and showers. The entire place was spotless.

"This place reminds me of the Army," I said to John Henry.

After lunch we made the beds, arranged the lockers, and met some of the other inmates. A guard took those who had money slips to the canteen to buy padlocks, cigarettes, matches, sweets, and toilet articles. In the evening, John Henry introduced me to some of his friends. Most of them had returned for a second time on parole violations or new charges.

The following morning, Sergeant Blank herded the newcomers together and took us to meet our assigned counselors.

"I'm Mr. Thompson," a thin, pockmarked man said to me. "I'm here to help you with any problems you may encounter during your stay with us. Do you have any questions?"

"As a matter of fact, I do," I said. "How long will I have to stay in this place?"

"Well . . . it depends upon the seriousness of your case as well as your attitude and conduct while you're here. The review board will make a decision when your case comes up."

"When will that take place?"

"I really can't say. Each case is handled individually. Felony cases usually take about a year. Now, let's talk about what you want to do while you're here."

"What choices do I have?" I asked.

"I see you haven't finished high school, so why don't we start there? We have an excellent educational program."

I didn't want to face a classroom again, especially in prison, so I asked what my job choices were. There were only two: the kitchen or the mattress factory. I chose the mattress factory. As far as I was concerned, Mr. Thompson was just another white police official. I didn't trust him—but he seemed more open and honestly concerned about the young bloods in Lancaster.

I expected to see a modern factory filled with up-to-date machinery. Instead, I found everything was done by hand and on antiquated electric sewing machines. Still, the work was clean and I hoped I could learn something to help me after I got out.

Time is a problem for prisoners the world over. Some have no interest in inmate activities. They count every minute, and time hangs over them like a dark fog. This is called hard time. Learning to disconnect from your surroundings and participate in the activities of your choice is part of what's commonly called jailing; those who know how to jail don't do hard time.

The only news about the outside came from visitors. During free time, we could go to the Quonset hut gymnasium and use the weights, boxing ring, or full-length basketball court. There was even a field for tag football and softball. Dominoes were more popular than chess or checkers at Lancaster—inmates usually find dominoes easier to learn and better for gambling.

Most of the young men at Lancaster were from very poor families: They didn't have visitors or get money through the mail. As a result, those who did get money or other gifts faced extortion. And if you didn't know anyone when you walked through the gates, or if you showed any sign of weakness, you were a prime candidate to be gang-raped. Everyone moved around in small groups and carried some kind of homemade shiv for protection.

"The best way to stay out of trouble when you're doing time," John Henry said, "is to remember the four don'ts: Don't lend or borrow, don't gamble, don't mess in other people's business, and don't fool around with anybody else's old lady."

I'd learned those same rules in Fort Knox, Kentucky. I knew that no matter how careful you were, there'd always be some fool who wanted to fuck with you just because he was half crazy or didn't like your looks.

One Sunday, two months after I'd arrived at Lancaster, I received my first visit. Mother and I sat on opposite sides of a long table. We were separated by a double wire-mesh screen that ran the entire length of the table and reached up far overhead.

"How are you?" Mother asked. "Are you getting enough to eat? Are they treating you well?"

"I'm fine," I answered. "They don't feed me the way you did but the food ain't too bad."

"I got a letter from the California Youth," Mother said. "They say I have to pay for your room and board during your time in here."

I jumped up and screamed, "What? They said you had to do what?" The guards started walking toward me.

"Don't worry. I wrote them a long letter telling them exactly what I thought of them. I told them I would be responsible for your room and board when you were back home and not while you are in prison."

Back in the barracks, I learned that some parents had actually let the Youth Authority intimidate them into paying. Mother, however, never heard another word from them.

I managed to avoid trouble for the first six months. Then one day it caught up with me in the mess hall. I had finished eating. I got up, dumped the tray, and started out the door. A stupid-looking runt of a guard stopped me. "Go get that tray and dump it," he ordered, pointing to a tray someone else had left on the table.

"I dumped my tray," I said.

"Don't give me no lip, boy," the guard growled. "Get the tray and dump it."

"It's not my tray," I insisted.

"No, it's not his tray," someone in the line said. "I'll dump it."

"No, you won't," the guard said. "I want him to do it, and right now."

Sergeant Blank suddenly appeared out of nowhere. "What's the problem here?" he demanded.

"This boy refused to dump his tray, Sergeant," the guard said.

"What's your name?"

"William Brent, Sergeant."

"All right, William Brent, you come with me. The rest of you keep moving." I followed the sergeant to the administration building. "Why didn't you dump your tray, William?" Sergeant Blank asked. "You know the rules. Why do you people always have to make trouble?"

"I didn't make the trouble, Sergeant. Everybody in the line saw me dump my tray."

"I know all the people I work with," Sergeant Blank said. "They're good, honest men. Are you calling one of my officers a liar?"

I spent the night in the hole: a dingy five-by-eight cell with a concrete slab for a bed and a foul-smelling toilet at one end. The next day I went before a disciplinary board and received ten days in isolation for insubordination and creating a disturbance in the mess hall.

Prisoners in isolation received only one meal a day: a gelatinous blob of garbage. They called it RD, for restricted diet. The blob, I learned, contained all the leftovers of the day before, plus whatever other junk was added to it, mixed with stock and left to set overnight. I refused to eat for two days. On the third day, a doctor came to examine me. He took my pulse, checked my heart, and advised me to eat the RD because, if I didn't, they would force-feed me and make my life miserable from then on.

I took the doctor's advice and ate part of the RD. The rest I flushed down the toilet. A week later, the guys in the barracks welcomed me back with coffee, cookies, and candy bars.

The months crept by. The mattress factory became boring, so I asked Mr. Thompson to change my work schedule to a half day work, a half day school. The new arrangement worked out well for a while, but I just couldn't adjust and felt a desperate need to get away from those fences and gun towers.

Mr. Thompson turned out to be more sympathetic than I'd expected. He recommended that the review board send me to a Youth Authority forestry camp. Within a week I found myself miles away from the hellhole in the desert and happily situated in the Santa Cruz Mountains—with no fences, no barbed wire, and no gun towers. Instead, we were surrounded by verdant foliage.

The forestry camp at Ben Lomond was a godsend. The camp boasted a less rigid regimen, more affable officials, and good food. Located near the affluent seacoast town of Santa Cruz, Ben Lomond formed part of a network charged with protecting vast areas of trees, shrubbery, and luxurious estates from the ravages of forest and brush fires. The Forestry Department, according to word around camp, paid the prison system two dollars an hour for the work inmates did. Inmates received only fifty-two cents a day.

We were on one of the highest accessible peaks in the area and could actually look down on the clouds and the early-morning fog that hung over the valleys far below. The air was crisp and fresh, and the greenery stretched out as far as the eye could see. The tense atmosphere of Lancaster soon faded from memory. Inmates in Ben Lomond Forestry Camp knew they were only one step from being released, so they acted with more restraint. I paid attention to firefighting classes and threw myself into the work sessions.

One Sunday, a few weeks after I'd arrived at Ben Lomond, Mother and Ella drove down from Oakland on a surprise visit. There were no screens or bars to separate us, no intimidating guards to watch our every move. We embraced openly, spread our food out on a picnic table, and enjoyed a wonderful two-hour visit. I told them about life in camp, about how hard firefighting was, and about the protective measures we had to take so no one would get hurt.

Our main job, I explained, was to make and maintain firebreaks all over the area so that when a fire did occur we had a head start on stopping it. When we weren't working, there were enjoyable activities. We played softball both in camp and in the nearby town of Felton. We went to the movies in town, and we rotated going to the beach on Sundays. On visiting day, parents were permitted to take their sons to town. It was a hundred times better than Lancaster, but still a prison; even though they treated me more humanely, it was a long way from being free.

One morning, while everyone was busy preparing for breakfast, a newcomer to the camp burst through the barracks door babbling with excitement. "I just saw a lountain mion," he yelled. "It's over by the kitchen door. A lountain mion."

When we realized Paul meant he'd seen a mountain lion, we all burst out laughing. Mountain lions and other animals frequently strayed into camp. But none of us feared them as much as we did the diamondback rattlesnakes that thrived in those parts. The rangers told stories about workers who'd been bitten while out on the fire lines.

A feeling of friendship and playfulness pervaded the camp. After all, we were little more than overgrown kids. On occasion, pranksters would put a nonpoisonous snake in someone's bunk just before lights-out. When the unfortunate person climbed in and rubbed up against that cold, squirming snake, the screams could be heard for miles.

At Lancaster there'd been more people, but time had dragged on endlessly. In Ben Lomond we were always busy at something: work, play, movies, the beach, and comfortable extended visits. Six months went by so fast I didn't realize the time had passed.

"You won't be going out with us this afternoon," our crew chief told me after lunch. "The director wants to see you in his office right away."

The director, I thought. Why would he want to see me and why such urgency? I was a little nervous when I walked into his office. He greeted me with a big smile and a handshake, and hit me with the good news right away.

The review board had granted me a parole. The director congratulated me and said I was free to leave as soon as transportation was available. I was so glad I could have started dancing right there in the office. I immediately called Mother. She and Ella picked me up early the next morning. They were just as happy as I was.

Compared to my arrival, the trip down the mountain had more meaning for me. The trees were greener and the air fresher. I felt the unmistakable thrill of freedom in every part of my body.

▼

WEST OAKLAND HADN'T CHANGED AT ALL DURING THE EIGHTeen months I'd been gone. The houses were run-down, the streets were dirty and in need of repair, and the people were still chasing after the pot of gold at the end of some fading rainbow.

A major change had taken place in our family, however: Ella had given birth out of wedlock to a beautiful baby girl she'd named Beverly. She was able to stay in school because Mother helped take care of Bev, her first grandchild.

An old family friend helped me get a job at a lumber mill in Palo Alto, a twenty-minute bus ride from home. I started unloading thick boards from flatbed railroad cars onto large, four-wheeled carts and pushing them to a shed where they were cut into planks on a noisy table saw. Sawdust filled our eyes and noses, stuck to the backs of our necks, and itched worse than a fresh haircut.

I was determined to make this job work out and prove I could make it on the outside. I wanted to get married, settle down and raise a family, do something honest to make Mother and Ella proud of me. I started at a dollar thirty-five an hour and worked a six-day week, with overtime on Saturdays. I visited my old hangouts only to score grass, catch the latest street gossip, or pick up some sharp dress clothes cheap.

"You're doing well," the parole officer said. "Your employer likes your work and you're staying away from the old crowd. Keep it up and you'll be free in no time at all."

The job was demanding, but what bothered me most was the fact that the majority of the workers were poor white southerners and the undercurrent of racial tension kept everyone uptight and nervous. I explained the situation to the parole officer. He wasn't at all pleased with my attitude, and said he would only give me permission to quit the lumberyard when I'd found another job.

Fortunately the postwar building boom was in full swing and I managed to land a job with a highway construction company. The work was easier and the pay better. I was living with Mother, helping with the rent and groceries, stashing a few coins away in the bank, and hoping to buy myself some secondhand wheels. Three months after I changed jobs, the company decided to cut overhead. Some twenty of us, all black, were laid off.

My Lancaster mattress-factory skills were so outdated they were useless outside the prison. I finally wised up and bought my way into a job with another construction company, but, as luck would have it, bad weather set in and I worked only a few weeks.

Like me, Ella's new boyfriend, Charles Bailey, was an unemployed high school dropout. So were Ernest Howard, a quiet, pensive teenage friend I'd met at the pool hall, and George Devereaux, an old school buddy who was thin as a rail and walked with a limp because of a birth defect. We hung out together and looked for work off and on, but spent most of our time on the streets smoking weed, hustling, and talking about making a big sting someday.

The streets were my home-away-from-home, but I also worked my library card overtime. I remember feeling strange inside, as if I were in some sacred place, when I walked through the doors. My reading was disorganized and undirected. I read everything: detective novels, science fiction, Westerns, fairy tales, plays. My favorite authors were Shakespeare and Sir Arthur Conan Doyle. And, although I didn't understand most of the poetry I read, I enjoyed the way it made me feel. Among my favorite poets were Edgar Allan Poe, Kahlil Gibran, Omar Khayyám, and Alfred Noyes.

I had lost interest in looking for work when an old friend offered to get me on at a downtown restaurant busting suds. I had to work like hell and take a lot of bullshit from the cooks, but the job was steady; it helped with the rent and groceries and kept the jive-ass parole officer off my back. I held on, resentfully, for several months. Trying to figure out why I couldn't land a good job, I recalled my poor showing on the Air Force recruitment test. The answer was obvious—I was poorly educated and had no special job skills or training. There were lots of jobs out there, but I didn't know how to do any of them.

I thought about going to night school, but the idea of sitting in a classroom again turned me off. Maybe all I have to do is be a little bit more aggressive, I thought. Hell, I know how to cook. What's to stop me from answering one of those ads for fry cooks I see in the *Oakland Tribune* every day? I decided to give it a go. If it didn't work out, I could always try something else— become an apprentice to an electrician or carpenter or even a mechanic.

I applied at a small restaurant on Broadway near the Tribune Tower. The place had a counter on one side, tables covered with checkered oilcloth on the other, and a pinball machine and an old upright jukebox near the door. One pallid waitress took all the orders and passed them on through an opening in the wall behind the counter. A smell of burnt cooking oil and cigarette smoke hung in the air. The owner, a fat, red-faced dude with a cigar stub stuck in his face, did the cooking and handled the cash register. He hired me on a trial basis at a buck-fifty an hour. I got the impression he would have hired anyone who walked in and asked for the job. Cigar Stub and the overworked waitress helped me get started. In a week I was fielding orders like a pro.

Our customers worked in the area and were always in a hurry. The menu seldom varied: cornflakes with milk, bacon or ham and eggs, French toast, hotcakes or waffles, and toast and coffee were the breakfast items; beef stew, hot soup, and hamburgers with or without cheese were tacked on for lunch.

I kept the job at the restaurant to satisfy the parole officer, but I also started boosting my pay by dealing a few matchboxes and cans. Before long, I was earning more on the street than in the kitchen and enjoying myself a lot more, too. Why wait until you're old and gray to start having fun, I thought, especially when there ain't no guarantee you're going to live to get old.

The more money I hustled, the more I spent or gambled away. I didn't have a cent in the bank and I owed damn near everybody on the streets. One night a friend of mine called Cat (for cat burglar) and I got cleaned out in a dice game in Richmond. We decided to try our luck at housebreaking. Wearing tight-fitting women's gloves, I hot-wired a Chevy—one of the skills I'd picked up in Lancaster—and we drove to a middle-class neighborhood in Berkeley. We spotted a house with open windows upstairs and down, and no lights on. We parked the car a block away, hurried back, masked our faces with handkerchiefs, and climbed through the downstairs window.

Our targets were money and jewelry, usually kept upstairs in the master bedroom. As we carefully inched our way up the stairs, we could hear someone snoring away. The sound got louder as we slipped through the open bedroom door. Our flashlights revealed two figures huddled together in the bed. A pair of dress pants hung from the back of a chair. A dressing table near the open window was loaded with jars, bottles, and fancy wooden boxes. Cat went for the pants, and I for the boxes.

As Cat was fishing the wallet out of the guy's pants, a ring of keys crashed to the floor. Cat sprinted for the door. I dropped the box I was rifling and jumped out the window just as the lights clicked on. I hit the ground running, my friend close behind. We made it to the Chevy, drove off quietly, and ditched it several blocks away. The wallet yielded a hundred and sixty bucks.

I really don't want to be doing this shit, I thought later. I could have broken a leg. The guy in the bedroom could have had a gun and blown me away. The police could have caught us and I'd be on my way to the joint for a lousy eighty bucks. It just ain't worth the risk.

I stayed away from the street crowd for weeks, but no matter how much I resisted, I was drawn back to them. On the streets I knew the ground rules and fit in. I spent more time on the streets than at work or at home because I felt more comfortable there than anywhere else. On the streets I was my own boss. I made more money and lived better with less effort than I possibly could slaving for whitey. In attitude, philosophy, actions, and lifestyle, I had gradually become a street nigger. I was hooked on street life and couldn't seem to do a damn thing about it.

Chuck, George, Ernest, and I were constantly together. One night, after losing heavily in a crap game behind the pool hall, we counted the few dollars left between us and decided the easiest solution to our economic problem was to stick up a liquor store.

"You do the driving," I said to Chuck. "Devereaux, you stand on the corner, and whistle if the cops show up. Ernest, you and I will stroll into the store, ask for a pint of Seagram's, and, if everything looks cool, rip the sucker off. Okay?"

We found a Chevy—one of the easiest cars to hot-wire—drove to a liquor store in a quiet neighborhood on Grove Street near Twenty-second, waited until the last customer left, then ambled through the door.

The proprietor didn't want to cooperate, but my .32 revolver with the extra-long barrel convinced him we meant business. The hit went without a hitch. Ernest and I got back into the car with Chuck, but George had disappeared.

"The nigger must have gotten scared and split," I said.

"Yeah," said Ernest. "Less for him and more for us."

We divided the two hundred dollars we'd stolen, let Chuck off at the pool hall, and got rid of the hot Chevy. One third of two hundred dollars didn't amount to much, so Ernest and I bought a couple cans of Acme beer and decided to go looking for something else to rip off.

Our aimless wandering took us to a side street in downtown Oakland, where we spotted a 1951 four-door Buick parked at the curb. The windows were down and the door on the passenger's side was ajar. We walked over to the car and looked in. It was empty—the keys in the ignition and not a soul in sight. I slipped in behind the wheel and turned on the dashboard lights; the gas gauge registered nearly full.

"Come on," I said to Ernest. "I know a brother in Los Angeles who'll give us a bundle for this baby." Traveling more than three hundred miles over the scenic "Grapevine" highway would have been a pleasure in daylight, but at night—because of the steep grades and hairpin curves, and the many eighteen-wheelers thundering up and down the mountain—the trip was dangerous and exhausting.

We made it to Los Angeles without incident. But while we were driving around looking for the guy who would buy the Buick, we got busted. We were charged with possession of a stolen vehicle and flown right back to Oakland in handcuffs.

The Oakland police rushed us to a small suburban jail and threw us in separate cells in different parts of the building. We weren't allowed to contact a lawyer or even make a phone call. An hour or so later, two detectives who looked like Mutt and Jeff showed up and started grilling me.

Tall, skinny Mutt loosened his tie, pushed his hat back on his head, and stationed himself near the door. He was picking his teeth with a wooden toothpick. "Where did you steal the car?" he squeaked.

"We didn't exactly steal it. We found it parked on the street with the keys in the ignition and the tank full of gas, so we decided to go to L.A."

Jeff had turned a chair around backwards and plopped his short, flabby body down on it. "What time was it?" he growled, wiping sweat from his thick neck with a grimy handkerchief.

"Somewhere around ten o'clock," I answered, "maybe a little later."

"Who was driving?" Mutt asked around his toothpick.

"I was."

"You drove all the way to L.A.? What time did you get there?" demanded Jeff.

"I don't know exactly, but we hadn't been there long before the cops stopped us."

"Okay, you claim the car was parked on the street." Mutt pointed the toothpick at me. "In the middle of the block . . . on the corner . . . where on the street?"

"It was closer to the corner," I answered.

"Did you guys go to a school yard after you took the car?" Jeff asked casually.

"To a school yard? No. We didn't have no reason to go to no school yard. We went straight to L.A."

Jeff stood up and walked around the room, wiping his sweaty neck. "Do you know a George Devereaux and a Charles Bailey?"

"Yeah," I answered, sensing the shit had hit the fan. "I know them. Why?"

"We'll talk again tomorrow," Mutt said. He stuck the toothpick back in his mouth. "And if I were you I'd do some serious thinking about how and when I got the Buick."

Two well-dressed and soft-spoken inspectors from the robbery division took over the questioning. From them I learned that on the night of the robbery my good friend and soul brother George Devereaux had been picked up for indecent exposure. In an effort to stay out of jail, he'd given the cops a complete account of the liquor store robbery.

Acting on George's information, the police had picked Chuck up the same night. They went upside his head a few times and he quickly confirmed what George had already told them. An all-points bulletin went on the air for the immediate arrest of William Brent and Ernest Howard, listed as armed and dangerous.

Several weeks of questioning passed before Ernest and I found out that the owner of the Buick we'd driven to Los Angeles had died of a heart attack the same night his car disappeared. His body was found in a school yard, and we were suspected of having caused his death. The district attorney's office was working overtime to find a way to charge Ernest and me with manslaughter, at least.

We couldn't afford bail, so all four of us spent several months in the county jail awaiting trial. Chuck and I were in the same cell. Finally we all went to court, charged with armed robbery. Mother and Ella didn't bother to come to the trial. They were just fed up with all the shit I'd dumped on them for so many years. Through our assistant public defenders, Ernest and I pleaded not guilty and asked for a jury trial. The public defenders representing George and Chuck had them testify for the state.

The jury, all-white, middle-aged, and hostile-looking, believed George and Chuck and found Ernest and me guilty of first-degree robbery.

George won a "not guilty" decision from the jury and limped away clean. Chuck got off with a county jail sentence and five years' probation for giving state's evidence. Ernest was turned over to the California Youth Authority because he was still underage. A wizened judge, influenced by a police report that classified me as a menace to society, socked it to me with a five-years-to-life sentence in San Quentin State Prison. At twenty-two years old, I had finally made the big time.

"Why did you do such a stupid thing?" Mother asked on her first visit to the county jail after I'd been sentenced.

I'd kicked myself in the ass and asked the same cursed, mind-boggling question hundreds of times. Each time I tried to answer it, other questions cropped up. Why was I born into a dirt-poor and nearly illiterate family? What had caused my father to be so withdrawn and violent? Why had we moved from state to state and always lived in the poorest neighborhoods? How come poor people worked themselves to death and never had anything to show for it? Who could explain to me why the prisons and jails were always full of young black men with the same background and problems I had? Why did I have to obey and respect laws that didn't respect me?

I did what I did because I was tired of begging for work, of working for just enough to make ends meet and being the last one hired and the first one fired. I was tired of watching my mother break her back working for rich white people while all we had were a few ragged-edged U.S. savings bonds, a couple hundred dollars in the bank, and a vermin-infested house we'd be evicted from if we missed one month's rent.

No matter how hard we worked, we still lived from day to day, from hand to mouth. I was truly sorry I had hurt and disappointed my family, but in my own way, I was fighting fire with fire. I felt hopelessly trapped and had to do something to make myself feel I controlled some part of my life.

During the investigation and the trial I kept to myself and picked my friends carefully in the county jail. Jake Jacobs was among the few people I got to know there. He had spent eight years in San Quentin and was still bitter about the whole system and everyone in it. "You did a stretch in Lancaster," Jake commented, "so you know how to mind your own business and stay out of trouble. The only difference in the joint is, some of the crazies up there don't respect nothing but force and violence. So what you got to do is be as crazy as they are or worse. It's the only way you can survive."

"Don't take no shit off of nobody," agreed Big Toby, who had spent two of his six San Quentin years in the hole. "If some motherfucker even looks at you wrong, run upside his head without thinking about it twice. If you let one of 'em push you around, others will do it too, and before you know it, they'll make pussy out of you. The bottom line wherever you are is respect. You got to do the time but it's up to you how you do it."

"Pick your friends wisely," Jake added. "Stay out of debt, and always remember the old rule for doing time: 'Drink lots of water and walk slow.' "

▾

THE SPECIAL PRISON BUS CARRYING US TO SAN QUENTIN FROM Oakland took the ferry to the San Rafael peninsula, then followed a narrow hillside road to a point where I got my first view of what would be home for the next few years. San Quentin abounds with beautiful plants: flowers and well-tended shrub-bery against a background of towering, cold, gray walls.

The bus entered the sally port and parked. The gate slammed shut behind us. Hard-faced guards hustled us into a reception room, removed our shackles, checked our meager belongings, strip-searched and deloused us, supervised our showers, and handed out the institutional issue: blue denim uniforms, black high-top shoes, towels, and toilet articles. From Lancaster to the military to the big house, the process is all the same, I thought. It's all part of a system.

Whistles, kissing sounds, catcalls, and shouts flowed freely from the regular prisoners: "I'll be waiting for you on the main line, sweet thing," or (holding their crotches) "Guess what I've got waiting here for you, baby." Their lifeless laughter followed us all the way to the cell blocks in the reception guidance center.

The dark, musty eight-by-ten double cell that would serve as my home for the next six weeks had a toilet bowl, a washbasin with a narrow shelf above it, and two cots with paper-thin mat-tresses. My cell mate was a small, light-skinned, curly-haired young blood from East Oakland named Elton Smith. We flipped a matchbox for the bottom bunk. I won and took it as a sign of good luck.

We would stay in the guidance center for a minimum of six weeks before the authorities decided what to do with us. First we received intensive physical and psychological checkups from the prison's headshrinker and counselors. Then, according to the whims of our examiners, we were classified and slotted: troublemaker, potential troublemaker, mentally retarded or in-competent, passive, suicidal, sexual deviant, and, above all, black, white, Latino, or other. Mainly on the basis of these so-called professional evaluations, and available space, the prison-ers either went to the main line at San Quentin or were transferred to some other prison.

I'd asked to be assigned to the kitchen because Jake and Big Toby had warned me about the racism at San Quentin and told me the best places to work were in the textile shop (which paid from two to sixteen cents an hour), the laundry, and the kitchen. You could always tell the kitchen workers by their white uniforms. The other inmates wore blue cotton work shirts and blue denim pants and jackets. Some also sported high-crowned short-bill caps made of the same denim.

"Almost every con on the Big Yard wears his uniform and cap starched and ironed and his shoes spit-shined," Jake had said, "even though it's a violation and the bulls can write you up if they want to." He also told me, "Food rations are so damned small, everybody gets hungry before the day is out."

"You never have to worry about being hungry or having canteen once you get set up in the kitchen or the laundry," Big Toby had added, " 'cause you can always wheel and deal."

I had a lot of dead time in the guidance center. There was nothing to do and nowhere to go. My cell mate was all right, but all he talked about was his mother and his dog. Sometimes, late at night, I could hear him crying under his blanket. He'd be somebody's old lady the first night he hit the main line. I spent much of my time feeling sorry for myself and cursing the motherfuckers who had snitched me off and testified against me. I daydreamed of getting even with them when I got out. I'd fry them in oil, cut their hearts out, or gut-shoot them and watch them die slowly while they begged for help.

I was finally assigned to the kitchen crew and moved to the main line. My new bunky was a young brother from Fresno named Ellis, who worked in the mess hall. He had done three years on two consecutive five-to-life sentences for armed robbery, and still hadn't seen the parole board.

My first night on the main line, I saw why Jake and Big Toby had suggested working in the kitchen or the laundry. Five different people came by offering sandwiches or special laundry services in exchange for cigarettes.

"Best not to deal with most of them cats," Ellis said. "They just out to get cigarettes and don't care who they burn in the process. When you need to buy something, let me know. We kitchen and mess hall brothers got our own people, and they won't try to fuck you around."

A block consisted of five tiers with twenty cells to a tier—two hundred constantly hungry men who had to be fed three times a day. The menu was always the same. It looked good on paper, but the food was half-cooked and tasted like it was full of chemicals. Some people said that saltpeter was added to help hold down the inmates' sexual urges. The only choices were take it or leave it.

My job in the kitchen, along with two other blacks—a youngster named Tommy and a brother in his late forties named Shep—was to keep the big aluminum and stainless-steel steam pots shining. My equipment consisted of a wooden stool; two heavy-duty aluminum-handled spatulas with long, thin blades; two wire scrub brushes; a long-handled wire brush; and rolls of steel wool.

The jangle of keys and the clanging of doors began at 5:00 A.M. as the guards came around to wake the kitchen and mess hall crews for breakfast. The rest of the inmates were shocked awake at 6:00 A.M. by the odious clamor of a gong fixed to the wall in the center of each cell block. Once morning chores were over, I went back to my cell to get more sleep or write letters and reread the ones I'd received from Cora and Ella. I also read books I got from the library and listened to the canned music they piped into the cells. Benny Goodman and Stan Kenton were good, but I would have been happier with Count Basie, Wes Montgomery, Billie Holiday, Bird, or Sarah Vaughan.

I often played handball with Tommy and Shep in the small

kitchen yard. (The Chicanos were the undisputed prison hand-ball champions; only a few blacks or whites played well enough to challenge them.) I also sharpened my skill in dominoes during the slack time we had between meals. The hours were long, but the schedule was one day on, one day off, as it was for the cooks. A bonus for the kitchen and mess hall crew was the chance to shower every day—the other main-line inmates showered only once a week.

"The first thing you got to watch for," Shep said, "are finks and bootlickers. They're everywhere, and they'll snitch you off in a minute if they see you taking anything from the kitchen to the cell block."

"You also have to be careful of the shakedowns the guards love to surprise you with when you go back to your cell," Tommy added. "Every time you smuggle something out, you're taking a chance on getting busted and being kicked off the kitchen crew."

Civilian cooks supervised the kitchen. Prison guards and in-mate informers, who were never searched, maintained discipline and controlled the quantity of food pilfered from the kitchen stores. Inmate cooks prepared breakfast, lunch, and dinner for the main-line population.

To become a main-line cook, all you had to do was ask for the job and be approved by the administration. Experience wasn't necessary. As a result, the food served to the general population was poorly prepared. Some of the diet-line cooks—who pre-pared the bland foods for the hospital patients and inmates on special diets—did have experience, either from some other prison or from the outside. But only experienced inmate cooks—usually of Chinese ancestry—cooked for the people on death row. Death-row food was eaten by the civilian staff and kitchen guards as well as the death-row inmates. It was also the preferred food to steal, to buy, and to sell in the cell blocks.

All the cell blocks at San Quentin were segregated. Whites, white-skinned Latinos, and Asians could live together, but blacks—no matter how light-skinned—couldn't share a cell with any of them. Nor could black prisoners work in the electrical, plumbing, or clerical shop or the hospital, much less aspire to become outside trusties (those permitted to work outside the prison buildings).

The inmate kitchen staff was multiracial. The mess halls were segregated: One section of each was set aside for whites, white-skinned Latinos, and Asians. Another, larger section was reserved for blacks and the few white, Latino, or Puerto Rican rebels who refused to sit in the whites-only section.

The administration claimed that every attempt they made to desegregate the mess halls resulted in blacks and whites going for each other's throats. The truth was that prison authorities used segregation to keep blacks and whites from getting their heads together and doing something to improve conditions. Most of the fights between blacks and whites happened because of gambling debts or problems with homosexuals—or because some screwed-up guard provoked them. Out-and-out racial confrontations were the exception, not the rule.

San Quentin had two recreation yards, the upper and the lower. Both were always heavily patrolled by prison guards. After the evening meal, and on weekends and holidays, inmates could go to the lower yard to practice sports or just hang out. I jogged there whenever I had the chance and threw myself into the basketball and softball games, glad for the physical and emotional release. I also cheered the touch football players on from the sidelines and yelled like a wild man at the track-and-field events. Most of the boxing matches I attended were funnier than a Laurel and Hardy movie; some of them, however, were as good as any I'd seen.

The textile industry, laundry, and shops were located on the lower yard, which was also the preferred area for escape attempts.

San Quentin's upper yard, known throughout the California prison system as the Big Yard, was surrounded by high concrete walls, crisscrossed with steel catwalks, and dominated by gun towers. I soon grew to hate the Big Yard as much as I did the pompous guards who strutted back and forth above me with their rifles always at the ready. I felt I was being castrated psychologically, and I often dreamed of jumping up to one of the catwalks, wringing a guard's neck, and using his semiautomatic rifle to shoot my way out.

A heavily guarded double gate in one wall of the yard gave access to the library, classrooms, administration buildings, chapel, and visiting hall. That area was off-limits unless you were accompanied by a guard.

The center of the yard was the hub of most leisure activities. The domino gamblers, chess freaks, and aged checker players sat at large wooden tables off to one side. I stayed away from the domino tables, except to watch, because the dominoes were marked, and gambling partners used intricate hand and face signals, body language, coughs, and grunts to let each other know what they held in their hands. The games were dominated by pros, who paraded around the yard with their handmade boxes of plastic dominoes wrapped in a piece of blanket and tucked under one arm. The pros knew the game inside out. Knifings were common among them because they often got caught cheating or couldn't pay off when they lost.

All the inmates had to line up in formation in the Big Yard before going to their daily routines, returning to their cells, going to the mess halls, or doing anything in groups. I spent much of my idle time there talking to people I knew, waiting to go to the library, and supporting my nicotine habit by selling sandwiches I'd smuggled out of the kitchen.

At the front of the prison was the visiting room, located "between gates"—the gate for the general prison population and the gate leading to the outside world. Sunday was visitors day. Like letters or Christmas packages, visitors had to be approved by the prison authorities. Often parents and other relatives would come a long way for their one-hour visit, only to be told they weren't on the approved list, or the inmate they wanted to see had lost his visiting privileges.

Long wooden tables, arranged in facing pairs, divided the visiting room. The partitions separating the tables permitted you and your visitor to see and talk with each other without being able to touch. Guards were stationed at both ends of the tables, and others prowled the room like lions waiting for a meal. Most people talked very low while visiting, and there was an almost constant whispering sound—shattered only when someone broke down and started crying.

Inmates and visitors were searched before and after their visits. Mother came early the first time, and had to wait for over an hour until they searched her outside the gate, and again before she entered the visiting room. When the loudspeaker blared out, "William Brent, you have a visit," I hotfooted it to the gate, gave my name to the sergeant in charge, and anxiously followed a guard to the visiting-room door.

"How are you? Are they treating you well?" Mother asked, pain showing on her strong, beautiful face. I wanted to touch her, to hug and squeeze her and let her feel how much I loved and missed her. But I had forfeited that right and had no idea when, if ever, I would enjoy it again.

Fighting back tears, Mother asked quietly, "How long do you think you'll have to stay in here?"

With my sentence, I explained, I couldn't expect parole in less than three years. So I'd asked permission to go to one of the minimum security prisons where there were no high walls or gun towers. I told her minimum security was a long shot for me. But since all the maximum security prisons were overcrowded, if I stayed out of trouble for a couple of years, they might give me a break. Mother's face relaxed and she smiled for the first time. We were both happier by the time she left. The possibility, at least, of my going to a minimum security prison gave us something to hope for.

I was no angel in prison, but I did try to avoid unnecessary trouble. Nevertheless, I paid two cartons of cigarettes for a pair of low-top dress shoes from someone leaving on parole, then spent over an hour spit-shining them. I knew I was taking a chance, but I was bored to death and had to do something to shake my feeling of impotence. Next day I got all dressed up in a new, starched blue denim uniform and a high-crowned cap. I stepped into my new low-cuts and headed for the Big Yard. But the same son of a bitch who'd sold me the shoes had snitched me off. The yard sergeant was waiting at the cell-block door, and he pulled me to the curb as soon as I stepped into the yard.

"My, my, my," said the sergeant as he looked me over from head to toe. "You 'bout the sharpest thing I've seen on the yard in months. Who does your laundry?"

"I just send it through regular channels," I said.

"Regular channels, huh, and I'll bet you got those dress shoes through regular channels, too. Right?"

"No. I bought these on the yard, Sergeant."

"Who did you buy them from?"

"I don't know his name."

"No, of course you don't know his name," the sergeant said. "Do you know *your* name?"

"My name is William," I said, "William Lee Brent."

"Well, Mr. Brent," the sergeant said sarcastically, "you come with me. We have to decide what to do with a sharp-looking dude like you."

I waited in the sergeant's office for nearly two hours before a guard took me to the clothing room, had me take off the uniform and new shoes, then sent me back to the Big Yard barefoot and dressed in baggy coveralls. I thought I would surely get a write-up, go to the hole, and get kicked off the kitchen crew, but I never received even a disciplinary hearing. The incident was never mentioned. Shep and I figured the sergeant was saving it to use against me if he ever wanted me to give up somebody in the kitchen or mess hall.

▼

THE OAKLAND DISTRICT ATTORNEY'S OFFICE COULDN'T charge Ernest and me with murder or manslaughter just because we'd been arrested in the dead man's car in Los Angeles. So they finally charged us with felony auto theft instead. After two years of San Quentin and the Big Yard, I went back to court in Alameda County and received another five-to-life sentence for auto theft, "to be served consecutively" to the term I already had for armed robbery. This meant I had to finish one sentence before starting the other, and since the indeterminate sentence did not fix a specific time to be served, there was no way of knowing when one sentence ended and the other began. Catch-22. With no money and no lawyer, I couldn't do a damn thing about it.

I returned to San Quentin more depressed and powerless than ever. If I could have gotten my hands on George Devereaux and Charles Bailey, I'm sure I would have found a way to kill both of them. Two consecutive five-to-life sentences almost made me give up hope of ever getting out of prison or going to a minimum security institution. I kept busy at my job, spent a lot of time with Tommy, Shep, and Ellis on the handball and basketball courts, and got interested in weight lifting and chess.

During this period of my stay in San Quentin, the Black Muslims were gaining considerable notoriety among the prison authorities and popularity among the black inmates. Shep introduced me to a Muslim minister. Many of the things the minister told me matched my own negative feelings about whites at the time.

One of the requirements for becoming a Muslim was to give up pork and cigarettes. I had no intention of doing either. What really turned me off the Muslims, however, was their conviction that white people had been created in Africa thousands of years ago by Yakub, a mad black scientific genius with a deformed head. I attended one meeting on the lower yard and decided I wasn't quite ready for the Black Muslims.

I spent a great deal of time in the small prison library, reading just about anything to keep my mind off the time I had to serve.

With a great deal of help from my friends, a constant flow of letters from my family, and my own determination to keep myself busy mentally and physically, I managed to hang on to what little sanity I had left. Three years later, the parole board ordered my transfer to the minimum security men's prison at Tehachapi, California. My spirits soared: There was still a chance I'd see the light of freedom again. I immediately wrote Mother and told her how happy I was.

▼

THE CALIFORNIA INSTITUTION FOR MEN AT TEHACHAPI crouches in the desert some sixty miles from Bakersfield. Formerly a women's prison, it was converted into a minimum security men's prison after an earthquake damaged several of the buildings. From a distance, it reminded me of Lancaster: the same barren landscape, the same isolation, the same chain-link fencing.

This time we wore no handcuffs or shackles as we quickly filed off the bus. A guard checked names off a list and signed for us. Then we followed him to the director's office.

The director began by reminding us that this minimum security prison ran on the honor system. There were no gun towers and the guards were unarmed. Although some of us were in the high-risk category because of our sentences, everyone would have the chance to prove he could be trusted. But anyone who messed up would be sent right back to maximum security.

We gathered our belongings, clothing, and bedding, and marched slowly to our barracks. Willie Smith, an inmate I'd met in Quentin, and I decided to bunk together. The cream-colored prefab structure reminded me of the barracks at Fort Knox. Large windows provided good lighting and excellent ventilation—two things lacking at San Quentin. Double bunks separated by upright, olive-green metal lockers lined each wall. Each bunk had a wall jack and a set of earphones. The toilets and showers were immaculate. There was a small reading room near the center of the barracks. Tehachapi also had two-story cottages, each with its own dormitory and semiprivate two-man rooms with keyless doors. Every cottage had its own recreation room. Inmates were assigned to the cottages on the basis of seniority and good behavior.

The California Adult Authority's big stick at Tehachapi was the newly introduced group-therapy programs. They weren't mandatory then, but inmates could forget about parole until they signed up.

Because of its smaller, better-motivated population and its minimum security status, Tehachapi offered more realistic vocational training programs, such as welding, auto mechanics, and carpentry. Teachers from the town of Tehachapi came in to give high school classes. The California Board of Education honored the grades. The Tehachapi school system issued diplomas.

The Bakersfield and Tehachapi speakers' clubs sponsored the inmate speakers' club. Regular club meetings were held at the prison, with enthusiastic outside participation. I recognized the importance of improving my speaking abilities and joined up at the first meeting.

I played the hot corner on our softball team and right or center field on the hardball team. The competition between the outside teams and ours was fierce but friendly.

After two months, I sent home for some of my street clothes for evenings and weekends. Mother sent regular care packages. She and Ella made me very happy with several long visits: We could touch, hold hands, and walk around the grounds.

The prison personnel took more interest in my problems. In most cases, they weren't pushy or bossy. They were more sociable and less officious than their counterparts in Lancaster or San Quentin, and went out of their way to be friendly.

I decided to take up auto mechanics. After a year of theory and practice, I could make minor repairs on the institution's vehicles.

Two more years and I got lucky: I was moved into a room in one of the cottages. I also graduated from high school and became president of the speakers' club. Shortly thereafter, I got the best surprise of my life. The parole board met and set my time at fifteen years—eight and a half in prison and six and a half on parole. I had eighteen months left to serve.

On a clear, crisp morning in early March 1962, Mother and Ella came to pick me up. I promised myself I'd die in the gutter before I would ever go back to prison.

3
▼▼▼▼▼▼

BLACK PANTHERS

MY PAROLE OFFI-
cer was an ex-
prison guard I
knew from San Quentin named Saul. He was known throughout the joint as an okay guy, hard but fair. Saul had moved up
through the ranks to land a position with the parole department.
He greeted me with a big friendly smile when I walked into his
office, shook my hand, and got right down to business. He assured me the only thing my new employer cared about was
punctuality and work well done. "I won't hound you or make
any unreasonable demands," he said, "but if you get involved in
any more criminal activities, I can't do a damn thing for you and
I won't even try."

From the parole office I went to the East Oakland wrecking
yard where I had been offered a job as a mechanic's helper. A job
offer was a condition for parole, and, since this was the only one

I'd received, I grabbed it. A large, grease-spattered mongrel growled menacingly as I stepped through the entrance. The place was a mess. Used car parts of all descriptions littered the front of the building.

I saw a bell on the crowded countertop with a sign saying RING FOR SERVICE. I rang it twice and heard a loud clanging in the back of the building. After a short wait, Max, my new, Chinese-American boss, walked in from the rear entrance wiping his hands on a greasy rag. I introduced myself and we shook hands. Max called the dog over and made it shake hands with me too. "Joker here helps to keep away the thieves. He knows you now, so you can move around without worrying about him biting you." Max's words reassured me a little, but I wondered why he had named the dog Joker, and I did worry about being bitten.

I followed Max through the jungle of wrecked and dismembered cars in the narrow, high-fenced yard. Joker followed close behind as we made our way to a small garage at the far end. The place was dimly lit and it reeked of transmission fluid. Partially dismantled transmissions covered the floor and tables. There was a 1956 Chevy sitting on stands in the middle of the garage. Its leaking Powerglide transmission sat beside it on a large hydraulic floor jack.

Max told me I'd be working with automatic transmissions and I shouldn't worry because he would teach me everything I needed to know. I would start at a buck-fifty an hour and lots of overtime. The yard was open from eight to five Monday through Saturday, and I could start the following day.

I came home one evening a week later to find Mother had taken in a boarder. At thirteen, Melba Herring had been lured away from her home in the South by a traveling preacher and had lived on her looks and wits ever since. Now, over forty, she was divorced, with two grown children, and was still a very attractive and sexy lady who loved to have a good time. She and

Mother had been close friends for several years. Before long, Melba and I began sharing the same bedroom.

I worked hard at the wrecking yard, made friends with Joker, stayed out of trouble, and reported to the parole officer on time each month. After we closed down in the evening, Max often shared a bottle of Seagram's in the office with me and a part-time worker who was nicknamed Frog because of his gravelly voice. The work was going well, and Max assured me I could earn a good living repairing automatic transmissions if I stuck with it.

Melba and I had several months of exceptionally good sex, nightclubbing, and wild parties. I remember one party where the host, a friend from San Quentin, sold joints at the door and charged fifty cents a shot for cheap scotch and bourbon. Thinking about the parole officer and going back to prison, I was the first one out the door when the fighting started. After a while Melba and I started fussing and fighting over trifles. The relationship became a drag and we broke it off.

Every evening I'd been noticing a young Latin woman with a pretty oval face, large black eyes, long, wavy black hair, fair skin, a beautiful ass, and good legs pass by the yard. She sure is one fine mama, I thought. I wonder if she lives around here.

One evening, as I left the yard, I saw her walking toward me. I waited until she got close enough, then took a deep breath and stepped out in front of her. She stopped and looked up at me without a sign of fear in her eyes. I introduced myself and said I'd seen her walking by before and wanted to know more about her. Her name was Gloria Harness and she lived a few blocks away. I mentioned a jazz club I knew in Berkeley. Gloria said jazz was her favorite music and she'd love to go hear some with me.

Two months later, on April 21, 1964, Gloria and I were married in the Alameda County Court House. We moved into a neat studio apartment in a quiet working-class area of East Oakland. We were the only black-white couple in the neighborhood.

We ignored the familiar whispers and disapproving stares, made friends with several open-minded neighbors, kept decent hours, and paid the rent on time. We enjoyed each other and wanted to be together in spite of what others thought of us.

Gloria was Portuguese-American. We talked honestly about our past experiences from the first day. Like me, she had spent more time on the streets than at home. It was a miracle that she hadn't served any time.

My family accepted Gloria because I loved her. "I think she's very pretty," Mother said, "and she's got such good manners too. She's so sweet and respectful I don't know what she sees in such a mean good-for-nothing like William. But they do say love is blind."

"She's all right, I guess," Ella said, "but I don't see why the nigger couldn't fall in love with a black woman just as easily. After all, there are more of us in his life than there are white women."

Gloria's secretarial skills kept her busy while I plugged away at the wrecking yard.

In the mid-sixties, the California Parole Board came under pressure to cut its budget, so it granted early release dates to scores of parolees. I was one of the deliriously happy beneficiaries. After Saul handed me the discharge papers, Gloria treated me to a night on the town. We went to some of the popular nightspots, drank and danced till dawn, and had a wonderful time. Neither of us could go to work the next morning.

I'm crazy about good jazz and blues, tunes like Thelonious Monk's " 'Round Midnight" and John Coltrane's "A Love Supreme" that make me feel good inside. Muddy Waters's Chicago blues can make me stop and listen no matter what song he's belting out. I like classical music and some rhythm and blues too, but jazz and good old down-home blues really turn me on. A friend in San Quentin had taught me a few guitar chords. Learning them made me feel good and helped pass the time.

Now, when we were sitting around the house on weekends, I'd get out the old secondhand Gibson and sing a tune made famous by Big Joe Williams and Count Basie's band: "Every Day." My darling wife always wanted to know when I would learn another song. Gloria and I were wrapped up in each other. We laughed a lot when we were together. Neither of us liked going to parties, and the only people we visited were Mother and Ella, or Gloria's younger sister, Nyla, and her Chicano husband, Bobby. I can still see the four of us lighting up a couple of joints and tripping out while the Beatles opened our minds with "Lucy in the Sky with Diamonds." Gloria didn't like to cook, so we ate out a lot. We especially liked Chinese and Mexican restaurants.

The two and a half years I worked at the wrecking yard were the longest period I'd ever held a job on the outside. Max had taught me a lot, and I was making extra money buying wrecks and selling parts on my own. The grease and grime were getting to me, though, and no matter how much I bathed and splashed on cologne, I always smelled like motor oil and transmission fluid. Besides, I figured it would take years to make any real money fucking around with used cars and rebuilt transmissions. So, freed from the restrictions of parole, I quit the wrecking yard and took a job in an electrolytic capacitor factory. This new job was clean, the pay was good, and, if I learned enough about electronics, there were plenty of chances for advancement. I also enrolled in a night school course in basic electronics. I was determined to make something of myself yet.

We were doing very well. Neither of us had any illusions about becoming rich, but our joint bank account grew a little every payday. Gloria's father died suddenly, leaving her a few hundred dollars, and we talked about going into some kind of business. I wound up buying a couple kilos of weed instead, thinking to sell it at a huge profit. We ended up smoking most of it with Nyla and Bobby, and barely broke even.

Gloria also quit her job, but instead of getting another one, she began hanging around with her old street cronies. Many times I came home from work to an empty, unkempt house and a sink full of unwashed dishes. She always claimed she wasn't feeling well or was visiting a sick friend or relative. What really bothered me was when she started running up large clothing bills on our credit account. I didn't try to stop her from seeing her friends, but I did close all our accounts and insisted, since she wasn't working, she help keep the place we lived in clean.

▼

GLORIA AND I TALKED ABOUT POLITICS NOW AND THEN, BUT WE never got involved. "Trusting a politician is like going to bed with a poisonous snake," an uncle once told me. "You know it's going to bite you but you don't know when." Ella was even more cynical. She insisted black politicians were the worst because all they did was imitate white politicians, make empty promises, and live high off the suffering of their people. "Their only real value to the man," she said heatedly, "is they help keep their own people under control by feeding them lies and encouraging them to 'keep the faith.' And the only time the man pays any attention to them is when he needs the black vote or when niggers go crazy and start tearing things apart demanding their so-called rights."

Mother liked the NAACP because she believed it had done wonderful things for black people and it had both colored and white people in it. She also admired the Reverend Martin Luther King, Jr.

I respected the people who participated in King's peaceful sit-ins and marches because of their courage, but I was not attracted to them. And although I sympathized with the "burn baby burn" attitude of the spontaneous and disorganized rioters in Watts and elsewhere, I had no desire to join them. Gloria and I talked about the politics of racism and the lack of both civil and human rights in the United States, but we didn't think the current uproar would lead to anything worthwhile.

One day, I came home as usual, picked up the *Oakland Tribune* and, with a mixture of disbelief and mounting excitement, read the front-page story about a group of some thirty armed blacks calling themselves the Black Panther Party for Self-Defense. Led by their chairman, Bobby Seale, they had invaded the state capitol at Sacramento to protest a proposed gun bill designed to limit a person's right to carry firearms. Only the women members of the group were unarmed. The men carried everything from .38 pistols to shotguns.

This daring, organized action by unknown black rebels in the citadel of white California scared the daylights out of Governor Ronald Reagan—who happened to be in the capitol at the time—and thousands of others across the country, including a lot of blacks. Furthermore, following the Sacramento incident, which took place on May 2, 1967, California police classified the Panthers as armed and dangerous, a threat to authority and power.

The audacity of these young blacks excited me and stirred emotions I thought had died years ago. I was proud that they had armed themselves and faced the enemy on his own ground. I felt cowardly and ashamed because I was just sitting around bitching or pretending indifference about the shit going down in our communities while these young people were making history. I wanted to find out more about their cause. Maybe I could do something to help.

Asking around, I discovered: In late 1966, Black Panther Party founders Huey P. Newton and Bobby Seale had printed up a thousand copies of their ten-point platform and program—a declaration of the group's political beliefs, desires, and intentions—and had taken them into the heart of the black community in Oakland. Fifteen-year-old Bobby (Little Bobby) Hutton, the first foot soldier of the Panther Party, helped with the distribution. They didn't just pass those copies out. Instead, they stopped and discussed each of the ten points with the brothers and sisters on the block, hustlers and thieves, people just out of jail or prison or those who were on their way to one or the other. They explained those ten points to black housewives, high school students playing hooky and hanging out at the pool halls, anyone who showed an interest and wanted to know what the Panthers were all about.

Huey, Bobby, and other members of the Party had stood up to the police with guns in hand on many occasions. Many people said they were just a bunch of crazy niggers looking for trouble by provoking the police. When I joined the Party and began catching up on its history, I thought they were the baddest and smartest brothers I'd ever known. In April 1967, their guns in plain sight, they investigated the murder, by a Contra Costa County deputy sheriff, of Denzil Dowell on a deserted street in Richmond. This investigation led to the creation of the black community news service, *The Black Panther* newspaper—an idea Bobby Seale kicked off with a mimeographed leaflet done by an underground hippie group in San Francisco. *The Black Panther* had an initial circulation and distribution of three thousand copies at ten cents apiece. Also in 1967, the Panthers provided an armed escort from San Francisco International Airport for Malcolm X's widow, Betty Shabazz, and they stood the police down at the office of *Ramparts,* a sympathetic radical magazine that gave honest coverage and support to the Panthers. Its office was one of the stops Sister Shabazz would make during her stay in California during the Malcolm X Memorial Day Conference (held on the anniversary of the month Malcolm was assassinated).

My chance to learn more about the Panthers firsthand came some months later, when the group held its first big rally in the Oakland Auditorium to celebrate Huey Newton's twenty-sixth birthday and to raise support and money for his defense. Huey, the Party's minister of defense, was being held without bond in the county jail on a first-degree murder charge after being seriously wounded in a gun duel in Oakland on October 28, 1967. One policeman died and another was badly wounded in the confrontation. The Panthers insisted the police had shot each other while trying to murder Huey Newton because they hated him for educating black people politically and offering them radical solutions to their problems.

The rally took place on February 17, 1968. This extraordinary event brought together the largest crowd of activist blacks and whites ever assembled in the area. It also brought out a goodly number of curious nonactivists like Gloria and me. There was no happy birthday song, but the building trembled at the thunderous roar rushing from thousands of throats demanding: "Free Huey! Free Huey! Free Huey!"

From the minute we arrived, I was impressed by the no-nonsense way the young Panthers ran the gathering. Uniformed Panthers patrolled the parking lot in groups of two and three. The Panthers guarding the main entrance wore black berets jauntily cocked over one ear. I noticed one of them, a tall, thin youngster with a huge Afro, fussing with the collar of his powder blue shirt. He adjusted his half-length black leather jacket and hastily shined his black wing-tip shoes on the backs of his pant legs. As Gloria and I approached, the guards looked us over carefully. There was no doubt they, rather than the scattering of police, were in complete control of the situation.

The stage was filled with black revolutionary personalities, including H. Rap Brown, James Forman, and Stokely Carmichael of the Student Nonviolent Coordinating Committee

(SNCC). I'd known of these brothers but had never heard any of them speak. The Black Panther Party was represented by chairman Bobby Seale, chief of staff David Hilliard, and minister of information Eldridge Cleaver. (The previous year, while still in prison on a rape charge, Cleaver had smuggled out some of his writings; these became the best-selling book of essays titled *Soul on Ice.*) The newly organized Peace and Freedom Party had also sent some of its leaders to take part in this historic event at the Oakland Auditorium.

Stokely Carmichael spoke about the importance of black power and mentioned some of the countries he had visited on his recent world tour, among them Cuba, Ghana, and Vietnam. Stokely shocked the audience by stating that socialism was not for black people. He thought blacks should first gain their freedom and then decide what type of government suited them best.

Witty and politically caustic Rap Brown reminded us: In U.S. society in general everything white was good and everything black was bad. "White eggs are good," he declared, "and brown ones bad. Santa Claus is a white honky who slides down a black chimney and still comes out white!" The crowd went wild. Rap finished by saying, "You are either free or a slave. There is no such thing as second-class citizenship. Second-class citizenship is like being a little bit pregnant. The only politics relevant to black people today is the politics of revolution."

James Forman insisted blacks could not afford to allow their leaders to be brutally murdered without retaliating. He blew everybody's minds when he suggested that if he himself, as a leader of SNCC, were to be assassinated, blacks should blow up fifteen police stations and kill one southern governor, two mayors, and five hundred policemen. If other, more important black leaders should be murdered, the price was to be tripled. As for Huey, he said, "the sky is the limit."

Panther chairman Bobby Seale stressed the nonracist character of the Black Panther Party. He said the Panthers would work with anyone who was serious about fighting to end racism, social and political injustice, and police brutality. He also spoke of what the Party had done in the black communities since its founding in October 1966, especially monitoring street arrests to advise black people of their basic legal rights and keep the police from abusing their authority. Black people, he said, had the right to govern their own communities. They should also insist on full employment or guaranteed government-supported incomes, decent housing, and quality education for all black and minority children. Bobby Seale was quite clear on coalitions or close associations with the Party: They had to be based on support for the campaign to free Huey Newton.

Eldridge Cleaver emphasized the need for closer cooperation between blacks and whites. At one point he told the audience to repeat the words "Fuck Ronald Reagan" as a sign of opposition to Reagan's governorship. For several thrilling seconds the building reverberated with thousands of voices screaming: "Fuck Ronald Reagan! Fuck Ronald Reagan!" When Eldridge raised his fist in the air and shouted with pride that the street niggers had finally gotten their shit together, he was talking about what Marx had called the lumpenproletariat—the brothers and sisters off the block, the pimps, hustlers, thieves, and robbers—as the principal targets of the Panthers' organizing efforts. This abused, rejected, seemingly worthless mass would soon become the backbone of the Black Panther Party, the foot soldiers who would challenge the black bourgeoisie's hold over black communities throughout the nation. They would constitute both the Party's strength and its greatest weakness, because, as the saying goes, you can't make a house nigger out of a street nigger overnight.

For the first time in my life, I heard black leaders who weren't preaching the gospel or telling me to play it cool and keep the faith. Mixed feelings of pride and guilt flooded over me—pride for having taken part in this historic event and guilt because I had done nothing positive to help my people survive. What I saw and heard convinced me I should join the Black Panther Party. I felt I'd just awakened and could never go to sleep again.

Gloria was pleased I had reacted so positively to the Panthers. Mother and Ella were afraid of my being involved in something so radical and dangerous. After many frustrating phone calls and fruitless trips to Party headquarters, I got David Hilliard's address in West Oakland from someone I'd known in the joint who was now a Panther. He advised me to go early and go alone: "These cats get real nervous around people they don't know."

I found the place without trouble, parked my '56 Olds around the corner, and locked my gun in the glove compartment. As I climbed the short flight of stairs to the porch, I saw a window curtain move slightly. The sound of Aretha Franklin's "Respect" told me I was at the right place. I knocked at the door. The music stopped abruptly. It was so quiet you could hear a rat piss on cotton.

I was about to knock again when the door opened a few inches and a young black brother with an Afro stuck his head out and asked me if I was looking for someone. I gave him my name and said I wanted to see David Hilliard about joining the Panthers. He looked me over carefully, opened the door a bit wider, and invited me in with a wave of his hand. I stepped into a large, sparsely furnished room curtained in semidarkness. The brother closed the door and proceeded to shake me down. I congratulated myself for having left my piece in the car. "Have a seat," the young man said when he finished. "David will see you in a minute."

There were several people in the room, all staring at me as if I were some kind of freak. I guessed the average age to be around twenty-six; this put a good ten years between them and me. I crossed my legs and casually lit a cigarette, forgetting how a lighter always shakes in your hand when you don't want it to.

I was just finishing my smoke when a medium-height young man with a huge Afro, intense dark eyes, and a thick mustache walked into the room. "I'm David Hilliard," he said. "I understand you want to join the Black Panther Party."

"Well . . . yes, I do," I said hesitantly.

"Why?" he asked. "Why do you want to join?"

"Look brother, I'm thirty-seven years old. There wasn't anything like the Panthers going on when I was young, and I've never experienced anything as moving, thought-provoking, and educational as what I heard at Huey's birthday rally. It opened my eyes and made me realize I need to do something to help my people. The Panthers might be my last chance."

I lit up another Pall Mall and adjusted my position on the small hard-backed chair. I hoped no one noticed my shaking hands or the sweat running down from my armpits. I kept telling myself there was no reason to be nervous, but it didn't do any good. A phone rang in the next room. I reached for yet another Pall Mall and noticed the other smokers in the room were burning Kools.

A woman's soft, melodious voice called out, "David, telephone." These youngsters probably all knew each other, I thought. They had likely gone to the same school, played and fought together, and now here comes this old man, a complete stranger, wanting to become part of their thing. Would they accept me? Doubt shadowed my mind.

David finished his phone conversation and returned to the table. He said he had to leave and I should go visit Huey in the county jail. Then he stood up and told one of the other Panthers to fill me in on the details. "Hang around and rap awhile if you like," he called back over his shoulder as he patted his hair with both hands.

A young Panther with Ray Charles sunglasses assured me all I needed now was a gun, a black beret, and a black leather jacket. He gave me a copy of the Black Panther Party Platform and Program and a *Little Red Book* of quotations from Chairman Mao. He also told me to come down to the office early every morning and David would tell me what had to be done.

The meeting was over. I was a member of the Black Panther Party.

I walked—almost floated—back to my car, unlocked the door, slipped in behind the wheel, and leaned over to check the glove compartment. The lock had been forced and my gun was missing. I couldn't help but laugh. Imagine having your gun ripped off during a meeting with the Black Panther Party leadership.

When I told Gloria I had joined the Panthers, she let out a little squeak, jumped up, and threw her arms around my neck and kissed me. I picked her up and carried her to the big comfortable bed in the corner of the living room.

I already had the beret and I knew I could pick up another gun dirt cheap at the pool hall. Sure enough, I bumped into Fast Freddy, the speed freak, as I stepped through the door. We walked to his house a couple blocks away, and for twenty-five bucks I bought a brand-new 9mm Browning he'd recently picked up.

I bought four boxes of cartridges and a little booklet, *The Care and Cleaning of Handguns*, at a suburban gun shop. Then I drove out into the countryside and took a few practice shots.

A feeling of sheer joy and power pulsed through me each time I pulled the trigger and the gun bucked in my hand. It worked perfectly. I picked up a half-length leather jacket on the way home, and later in the evening, while cleaning my new piece, I began memorizing the Panthers' platform and program.

Next morning, my beret cocked jauntily over my right ear, I

walked into Party headquarters on Grove Street and asked for David. My leather jacket still smelled new. David came out of an office at the rear of the building and extended his hand. Then he told me to go to the University of California campus at Berkeley—where Eldridge was scheduled to make a speech—and mix with the crowd. When Eldridge showed up, I was to keep an eye on the gathering and, if anything went wrong, get him out of there as quickly as possible.

My first assignment went off well. Trying to be as cool and inconspicuous as my uniform would allow, I moved silently through the hundreds of people of all ages who had come to hear Eldridge speak. Nothing unusual happened, not even heckling.

From the university, I went to visit Huey P. Newton in the Alameda County jail. Through the thick glass rectangle of the visitor's port, Huey looked younger than I had expected. His face seemed a bit pale and drawn but his eyes were alert and intelligent. I introduced myself and explained why I had come. He flashed a warm, knowing smile and told me the Party needed brothers like me. He then thanked me for coming to visit. Looking at him, I knew I had made the right decision. There were others waiting, so I cut my visit short. We parted with a smile, each of us raised a clenched fist Black Power salute and said, "Power to the People."

Everyone called Bobby Seale Chairman Bob. When I got back to headquarters he and a few others were standing outside talking. Someone introduced me and we shook hands. I liked him immediately and felt good just being around these people. I felt I belonged with them, and I believed in their rhetoric so strongly I was willing to make any sacrifice to further what I felt at the time was our cause.

I also met heavyset, brown-skinned Captain Crutch, who sported processed hair, a thin mustache, and a goatee. He was called Crutch because he walked with a limp. We hit it off right away. Several of us stood around drinking Bitter Dog (white port wine mixed with lemon juice) and rapping about the ten-point program. Spontaneous political rap sessions, I soon learned, took place on a daily basis. You could find small groups of Panthers discussing politics in the office, on the way to a meeting, or just hanging out getting high. Less than a week after I joined the Panthers, I had memorized the entire platform and program.

"That's one hell of a memory you got there, brother Bill," Chairman Bob told me one day after a political education class. Memorizing the ten points was easy because I believed in them. An avid reader, I devoured all the books other members of the Party recommended. From Malcolm X's *By Any Means Necessary* I learned that black people had a right to win their freedom by using whatever means they found appropriate. Earl Ofari's *The Myth of Black Capitalism* convinced me black capitalism didn't really exist in the United States because blacks didn't own the means of production. E. Franklin Frazier's *Black Bourgeoisie* confirmed my suspicions of the existence of a privileged black middle class in America, and Frantz Fanon's *The Wretched of the Earth* gave me insights into the psychological, emotional, and political reasons why oppressed people often turned their rage and violence against themselves, and why armed struggle and revolution were necessary.

All kinds of people hung around the Panther office—members and nonmembers. Whites, especially antiwar and antiracist activists, were constantly coming in to make contributions of money and office supplies, offer their skills and services, and seek more information about the Party or find someone to speak at their homes. Many of them lived in Berkeley and took an active part in progressive political activities in the Bay Area. They and the Panthers got along well.

Blacks who came in had been fucked over by the police, needed a lawyer or bail money, or wanted the Panthers to help them with some domestic problem.

Music also attracted people to the Panther office. One minute James Brown would be blasting and grooving with "I Feel Good" or Bob Dylan would be putting down the white middle class with songs like "Ballad of a Thin Man." Then the Temptations would take over with their popular, upbeat "My Girl," or the Righteous Brothers would be telling it like is, with "You've Lost That Loving Feeling." Ray Charles, Otis Redding, the Supremes—all of them suited our musical tastes.

People were also drawn to the Panthers because, in the beginning, they really tried to live up to their political promises. The Free Breakfast for Children program, for example, allowed the Party to collect food and money from local businessmen and set up breakfast kitchens and dining rooms for kids in local churches. (The donations were all tax-free.) Party members assigned to the program got up at six in the morning to make sure things were neatly and properly prepared when the children arrived at seven or seven-thirty. Community volunteers put in at least two days a week working on this program; some put in much more. The Panthers also initiated a protection service for the elderly black people who were getting ripped off after they cashed their welfare checks.

I'd been a Panther for only a couple of weeks when David sent me to lead a political education class in the Hunter's Point area of North Richmond, some twenty-five miles from Oakland. I was nervous because I didn't know any of the six young brothers and sisters in the small apartment and I had no idea what to talk about. The ten-point program immediately came to mind.

I waited until everyone was seated, then introduced myself and started. "The Black Panther Party Platform and Program is composed of two parts: what we want, and what we believe. The ten points are written so the average person can understand them." I looked around. "Who can tell us about point number seven?"

Several hands shot into the air. I pointed to a petite, neatly dressed young woman with a short natural.

"What we want in point number seven," she said, "is 'an immediate end to police brutality and murder of black people.' What we believe states: 'We believe we can end police brutality in our Black community by organizing Black self-defense groups that are dedicated to defending our Black community from racist police oppression and brutality. The Second Amendment to the Constitution of the United States gives a right to bear arms. We therefore believe all Black people should arm themselves for self-defense.' "

The rest of the class went over without a hitch.

The Party soon began sending me out to speak to middle-class white sympathizers in the area. My Tehachapi speakers' club skills gave me an advantage in explaining what we wanted and what we believed. I also read several newspapers every morning to keep up with current events.

Most of the people I addressed asked sincere and valid questions: What were the Panthers' objectives beyond getting Huey out of jail? Why couldn't whites be members of the Party? How large was the Panther membership? There was always someone who claimed not to be racist, yet couldn't resist asking: "What do you people want?"

The Party's long-range goals, I would tell them, were clearly stated in the platform and program: control of the black communities; a voice in the economic, social, and political decisions that affected us; and the elimination of racism. As to excluding whites from Party membership, Bobby and other leaders had explained: Although the Black Panther Party was not racist, we felt whites could more effectively organize and fight against racism in their own communities than in black neighborhoods. As to the size of the Panther membership, the Party had a pat answer: "Those who know don't tell; those who tell don't know."

In answer to "What do you people want?" I always told them we wanted the same things they did, but without having to fuck over other people or ethnic groups to get them: the right to honorable, rewarding work; a decent place to live; adequate health care and education for all black people; justice in the courts; nonbrutal police who didn't abuse their power; and a government respectful of the rights of all people regardless of race or creed. I was learning fast and doing a good job.

There was an unmistakable aura of secrecy and mystery about the Party—not only for whites but for black people as well. For reasons of security, the Party never let its right hand know what its left hand was doing. Each member had just enough information to be able to do a specific job. A special characteristic of Party members was that they seldom got to an engagement on time. And they were masters at making a lie sound like the truth.

The Party's hierarchical structure, beginning with self-appointed minister of defense Huey P. Newton and Party chairman Bobby Seale, was anything but democratic. Decisions were made by Huey and passed on to David Hilliard, chief of staff, and Chairman Bob. In his book *Seize the Time*, Chairman Bob leaves no doubt about who was calling the shots. "I just had a tendency to follow Huey. I was never ashamed of the fact that I always followed Huey. I just followed him, and tried to understand what he was saying. If I disagreed with him, I tried to disagree properly." Bobby never tried to hide the fact he also had serious drinking problems.

Members of the national central committee had to be approved by Huey. Eldridge Cleaver, minister of information, and his wife, Kathleen, communications secretary, were no exceptions. The same was true of other central committee members.

Stokely Carmichael was first drafted into the Party as a field marshal and then promoted to honorary prime minister. George Mason Murray was a San Francisco State College professor when Party leaders appointed him minister of education. The Reverend Earl Neal, rector of the black Saint Augustine Episcopal Church, let the Panthers use the building to hold meetings. The Party, in general, wasn't into churchgoing, because the members didn't trust preachers. Nevertheless, they held Reverend Neal in high esteem for his work in the community and appointed him their minister of religion. Emory Douglas, Panther artist and minister of culture, added a powerful humorous touch to Party newspapers by portraying the police as comic pig characters who preyed on and terrorized black people.

Melvin Newton, one of Huey's brothers, was the minister of finance. The economic and financial status of the Party was never discussed with the general membership. Money we collected at rallies, speaking engagements, or other events, we turned over to the leadership—mainly David and his staff at Party headquarters. We never knew how the money was used or distributed. I, for one, never asked. On various occasions people I'd meet on the street said they believed the Panther leadership and Huey's family were getting rich by diverting Party funds into their private accounts. There was also talk of a Panther jail and of goon squads who went out to beat up dissenting members or people who didn't turn in the money they got from selling papers or taking up collections at rallies.

I never asked questions, because I knew when poor people and large sums of money came together, weird things started happening. I also realized the Party had to have some way of enforcing discipline. While Huey was in jail, David had to shoulder a lot of responsibility and was under constant pressure to keep things running smoothly. He was also deep into alcohol and weed. The goon squads and jail probably seemed a logical solution to the problem of enforcing discipline on a bunch of unruly street niggers who understood only imposed authority and violence.

So I looked the other way and concentrated on my assignments. I believed I had joined a truly revolutionary organization, one whose leaders, many with deep character defects and police records going back to their teens, were working hard to reorganize America's black communities politically. I didn't know they were also making some serious mistakes in the process.

▼

THE POLICE FOLLOWED US AROUND, STOPPED AND HARASSED US for no other reason than that we were Panthers. Once, two young police officers parked their squad car in front of Panther headquarters and shot the place up with semiautomatic weapons. Fortunately no one was there at the time, but the upstairs neighbors were scared out of their minds. Friends in City Hall had warned us the Oakland police rode around with pictures of known Panthers who were considered dangerous clipped to their sun visors. Furthermore, they were unofficially authorized to blow us away if the right occasion presented itself—a dark, deserted street would do nicely. I knew there were police out there just itching to gun us down.

On top of the constant threat from the police, many of our own people were pimping and exploiting the black communities and hated us because we wanted to eliminate their reactionary hustles.

The Panthers' community relations in general were a mixed bag. Sometimes I would greet a young black on the street with the power sign and a "Right on, brother" only to be rebuffed with: "I ain't your motherfucking brother, nigger." I was always hurt when this happened, but figured those brothers just hadn't been educated politically and the system still had a firm grip on their way of thinking. And in the Berkeley street community, Hell's Angels tried to provoke us and our supporters by walking around with FRY HUEY buttons instead of FREE HUEY.

It is easy enough now to forget, but there were people of all races who admired the Panthers because of their image as bad blacks who walked around with guns and wouldn't take no shit off the police, and not because of their rhetoric or political promises. Unfortunately, these same people were often afraid to let themselves or members of their families get involved with the Panthers, because they had become accustomed to playing it safe and didn't want to get into trouble.

I and everyone else knew from childhood that the black middle class enjoyed every political favor the system offered to blacks who tried to put as much distance as possible between themselves and their less fortunate black brothers and sisters. Middle-class blacks feared that the Panthers' revolutionary approach to politics might cost them their political control of the black communities and their "favored nigger" status with the government. We had no doubt they would turn us over to the police without thinking about it twice.

By this time, however, nothing could stop me from wanting to be a Panther. I devoted all my time to working for the Party, and ate and slept whenever and wherever I could. I saw my wife and family so seldom they thought I was in jail or dead. I knew they worried about me when they heard the wailing of a distant siren or the jangling of the phone late at night, or whenever someone knocked unexpectedly at the door.

The only other black organization that packed any weight in the Bay Area at the time I joined the Panthers was the Nation of

Islam—the Black Muslims. And though many Panthers believed the Muslims were directly responsible for the murder of Malcolm X, the Party's attitude toward them was reserved and nonconfrontational. Several of the Panthers, including Chairman Bob, David, and Eldridge, had admired the Muslims' efforts to introduce pride and self-improvement into the black communities across the country.

One day David sent me to East Oakland to locate a place where we could hold a sizable meeting and set up some kind of security. This was my toughest assignment so far. I talked to people on the streets, visited churches, schools, parks, theaters, and even union halls. Although the Party was known throughout East Oakland, I learned that many of the street brothers and sisters were distrustful of the Panthers because their policy of confronting the police drew too much heat. And, too, the heavy drug users and dealers didn't think the Panthers would help them if they ever got busted.

Finally, a young black city park director with a strong desire to know more about the Panthers and their political activities offered us his small park near East Fourteenth Street. He seemed like a right-on brother to me. I went back and explained the whole thing to David. He took the information and didn't say if there would be a meeting or not.

I never missed a scheduled meeting or PE class. I pitched in wherever I was needed and tried to do my assignments well. One night, only weeks after I had joined the Party, I was called into a meeting with Chairman Bob, David, and several members of the central committee. David told me I was being made a captain and a spokesman for the Black Panther Party. I didn't even know what a captain was supposed to do.

I looked around at the five or six brothers in the office and lit a cigarette to calm down and give myself time to think. I pointed out I'd been in the Party only a few weeks and still had a lot to learn. I was perfectly willing to accept whatever responsibility they gave me, but I wasn't sure I was ready for this. I also reminded them my wife was white, and said I wondered how the younger brothers and sisters would relate to having one of their spokesmen married to a white woman.

Chairman Bob assured me other members of the leadership were also married to whites—David's brother June in particular. He reiterated: The Party was not racist and education was a continuous process. They were all still learning, but things were happening right now and we couldn't wait around. We had to get our training in the field, learn from our mistakes, and move on to another level. Some of us might know a little more than others, but no one knew it all.

Recognizing all the risks, but filled with a sense of pride I'd seldom felt before, I accepted this new responsibility and secretly vowed not to let my brothers and sisters, or more specifically, the Black Panther Party, down. David sent me to speak at middle-class home meetings all over the Bay Area. I also addressed an important Peace and Freedom Party meeting in an Oakland suburb. I assured the gathering of unwavering support from the Panthers as long as we could depend on them to help the Free Huey campaign and continue to organize and fight against racism in their own communities. Sometimes I went to these meetings alone in my '56 Ford Thunderbird (donated to me by a widowed sister who didn't know how to drive and thought the car fitted my personality). When there was a group of us going somewhere, however, we used Captain Crutch's '56 Cadillac or some other Panther car with more seating capacity.

Everyone in the Party knew I carried my gun wherever I went. And, just like the rest of the Party leadership, I drank excessively, smoked weed, and dropped pills on a daily basis. In spite of the Party's rules of conduct about not drinking or using dope while doing Party business, any member who didn't drink or smoke a joint once in a while wasn't completely trusted by the rest of us.

Not everything in my life was as rewarding as my work with the Panthers. Gloria was falling back into her old street life. On several occasions I'd come home to find two or three young black dudes in the apartment, and I knew they weren't there just to listen to the stereo. Arguments followed. She felt that since I spent so much time away from home, she had a right to have a few friends over once in a while. Also, on the advice of an inexperienced doctor, Gloria had an expensive appendix operation that took a large part of our savings. After the operation, it turned out there was nothing wrong with the appendix, after all. Not only was the surgery unnecessary, the stitches wouldn't hold and I had to take her back and forth to the hospital.

To be able to keep up with Panther activities and complete the assignments David gave me, I had quit my job a week after joining the Party. I told David and Chairman Bob I loved working with the Panthers but the unemployment checks my wife and I had been living on were about to run out. I didn't see how I could continue giving all my time to political work and still pay my expenses without some kind of income.

David explained the Panthers were in a life-and-death struggle, and everyone had to make sacrifices. The Party helped some of its members with rent and food but couldn't give salaries. "Revolutionaries have to live off the land and get whatever they need by scratching it out of the terrain, guerrilla-style," he said.

"Yeah, that shouldn't be no problem for an old cooncan skinner like you," Chairman Bob said. "With your street skills and experience, I bet you can hustle rings around all these younger brothers put together."

"Just do your thing," David added. "We'll back you up all the way as long as you're straight with us."

I remembered Eldridge's words at Huey's birthday rally:

"The street niggers [meaning those who lived outside the law] have finally gotten their thing together."

Whenever Chairman Bob, Eldridge, and other top members of the Panther leadership went on speaking engagements they were heavily guarded—even if they sometimes didn't know about it. I took great pride in being part of their security. Sometimes I introduced Chairman Bob before he spoke at a large gathering. I loved to stride to the middle of the stage, adjust the mike, and open up by quoting from the Declaration of Independence: "When in the course of human events, it becomes necessary for one people to dissolve the political bands which have connected them with another. . . ." When I reached "a decent respect to the opinions of mankind requires that they should declare the causes which impel them to the separation," I would introduce Chairman Bob as the Panther representative most qualified to explain the cause of black people.

During the course of my reading, I ran across a book put out by the New York City Fire Department that had a section on explosives. It gave step-by-step instructions for making time bombs and explained the structural weaknesses of various types of building construction. The idea of setting a bomb off in the basement of the county jail to show the authorities we were serious about freeing Huey flashed through my mind. I studied the part about bombs carefully, then went out and bought several cheap alarm clocks and some 1.5-volt flashlight batteries.

The following night a friend from Quentin and I raided a construction site and made off with two cases of dynamite and some blasting caps and fuses. We pulled onto a side road and carefully transferred the explosives to a duffel bag and put it in the trunk. The blasting caps and fuses we kept separate, under the backseat of the car. I don't know what we would have done if the police had stopped us.

At home, Gloria watched anxiously as, unmindful of the other people in the building, I taped two sticks of dynamite, an alarm clock, and four batteries together. I drove to a deserted place I knew of in the Berkeley Hills, set the timer, and placed the device next to a decayed tree trunk a good distance from the car. I smiled with satisfaction when it exploded, sending a cloud of dirt, wood shavings, and smoke into the air. I'm invincible, I said to myself. There ain't nothing the police can do to me I can't do to them.

The next day Captain Crutch and I went to give a political education class to some young members in Richmond. When I reported back to headquarters, I saw Gloria coming out of the building. "What you doing here?" I asked lovingly. "Checking up on me?"

"I just wanted to know when you would be coming home," she said nervously as she walked by me.

David called me into his office and told me he'd heard I'd ripped off some explosives, fuses, and blasting caps. He said any weapons, munitions, or explosives Party members ripped off should be shared with the Party.

I suddenly got this empty, sinking feeling—like when you throw craps on the last five dollars of your rent money, or when you find out your lover can't be trusted. I was sure Gloria had told David about the explosives.

I had intended to tell him in my own time and way, but now the only thing to do was tell the truth.

"It's all yours if you need it," I said.

"We never know when we'll need stuff like that, brother, but it's best to be prepared just in case. Bring it in so we can take a look."

Gloria seemed fidgety and avoided my gaze when I walked into our apartment an hour later. "You got here fast," she said. "I didn't expect you home so soon."

"I'm not staying," I said curtly. "I just came to pick up the stuff in the closet and take it to headquarters."

I took out my duffel bag, threw in a few personal things, and walked to the door.

"What time you coming back?"

"I'm not sure," I said. "I'll call you."

On the way out I stopped at the super's apartment and paid an extra month's rent. Then I drove the explosives to the office. I didn't mention I had kept some for my personal use.

I couldn't forgive Gloria for going behind my back and telling someone else my business. I wondered what else she had run off at the mouth about, and to whom. I was sure I would never feel comfortable around her again; the best thing to do was stay away from her.

Two people knew I had those explosives, but only one knew where I had them stashed. I asked some of the sisters who worked in the office what they knew about Gloria. She had visited the office on several occasions, I learned, each time talking with David or Bobby. "I thought you knew about her always hanging around," one sister said. "Otherwise I would have pulled your coat myself."

Many young girls, black and white, thought their revolutionary duty was to sleep with a Panther. Sleeping around was both accepted and expected. I moved in with a beautiful young white flower child from Texas named Keith. I'd met her through David, and we'd been seeing each other from time to time. Keith's main interests in life were sex and plenty of good weed.

"You're coming to New York with us," David told me one morning in July 1968. "We're going to try to speak before the United Nations. Pack light and be prepared to stay at least a couple of days. We leave tomorrow morning."

David, two other brothers, and I would go ahead to make the necessary arrangements and check on the security. The Oakland airport was noisy and crowded. I didn't like planes but I was excited about going to New York for the first time. When we arrived, some of us stayed at the home of Elizabeth Sutherland, a progressive journalist and organizer who managed to protect and promote us simultaneously.

On our second night in the Big Apple, Bobby spoke at the Fillmore East to a standing-room-only crowd that included the legendary black author and political activist LeRoi Jones, whom I met briefly before Bobby's speech. I recall standing onstage as part of Chairman Bob's security, feeling uncomfortable during the entire speech. I kept glancing from side to side, afraid of missing something. An atmosphere of uneasiness pervaded the theater, and I felt more uptight than I ever had before. I reasoned it was because, to my knowledge, I was the only one there carrying a gun. Later, Bobby went to Harlem to speak. Again I was next to him, and again I got those negative vibes. This time, however, we got word the New York City police were planning to create a disturbance. Remembering Malcolm X had been murdered while making a speech in Harlem's Audubon Ballroom only a few years earlier, we got Bobby out of there in a hurry.

One of the high points of my stay in New York was when James Forman, longtime black activist and a leader of SNCC, invited Chairman Bob and me to his apartment to talk about black politics. Forman asked me to check my gun as soon as we walked in. Since he was a high-ranking official in SNCC and honorary minister of foreign affairs of the Black Panther Party, and besides, I was in his house, I handed the gun over without question. What neither he nor anyone else knew was that the gun was empty and I had another—fully loaded—strapped to the inside of my left leg.

It was no secret Forman supported H. Rap Brown over Stokely Carmichael as head of SNCC. Rumor had it that Stokely wanted to ace Forman, who was older and in bad health at the time, out of SNCC's leadership. An intense rivalry and struggle for control of the organization and its political direction had been going on for some time. In addition, disagreement over Stokely's strong antiwhite position—which was at odds with Huey's view favoring principled coalition with supportive white progressives—was also a factor. What started out as an intelligent merger of SNCC's skills and experiences with the Panthers' street daring, and a shared desire to get the system off our collective backs, had turned into an ugly brew of mutual mistrust and suspicion. Each group felt that the other was trying to take control of and use the other to further its own designs.

Our brief encounter, and especially the questions Forman asked Chairman Bob about Black Panther Party structure, activities, and plans, gave the impression he was afraid of the Party and had no intention of letting us become as powerful in New York as we had become in California. Bobby told Forman that he, Bobby, was only a spokesman for the Panthers and that Forman should direct such questions to Huey and the central committee.

Sitting hunched over with my hand close to my gun leg, I hoped with all my heart that this madness wouldn't end in bloodshed. The tension in the room had become almost unbearable. Finally Forman relaxed, smiled, got up, and gave me back the gun he had taken from me earlier. He assured us that he would continue to support the Panthers and hoped that no hard feelings would result from our meeting. We shook hands all around, and Bobby and I returned to our base of operations at the New York SNCC office.

Bobby's report that Forman had insisted I check my gun and then tried to pump him for information about Party activities didn't go over well with David and Eldridge. They didn't really trust Forman, and they suspected he was planning to weaken the Panthers' influence with other groups and organizations in the New York area.

The following day I was sent to meet with a predominantly white group called the Freedom and Peace Party. My mission was to explain the Panthers would live up to their agreement to support the Peace and Freedom Party, based in Berkeley, and would not back any takeover effort by the newly created Freedom and Peace Party.

The Panthers didn't get to speak before the United Nations, but they did hold a joint press conference with some white New York radicals and got very good coverage. We wanted to get the United Nations to investigate our claim of genocide against black Americans—an idea first proposed by Paul Robeson and William Patterson in 1951—and hold a plebiscite that would give blacks in the United States the right to self-determination.

"We're going back home tomorrow," David said after the press conference. "I'm sending you to D.C. to help Stokely for a few days. Don't worry, he'll explain everything when you get there."

I'd met Stokely in Oakland after I joined the Panthers, and I liked him. I took the air shuttle to Washington the same day. Stokely sent someone to meet me at the airport. I spent a pleasant night at his home talking with him and one of his close friends about the Party and some of the uptight black businessmen in D.C.

The next morning we went to a meeting Stokely had set up with some of those same businessmen. I stood quietly in the background with a practiced frown on my face. To give members of the small audience the impression I was looking directly at each of them individually, I fixed my gaze straight ahead and slightly above the people seated in the last row. Stokely spoke to the businessmen about their responsibilities to the black communities and the need to support black leaders.

Next we visited a white supermarket owner who had unjustly fired some black employees. The owner took one look at us and agreed to rehire them. My Panther uniform and evil look were enough. I didn't have to say a word. I'm sure Stokely took me along to intimidate those people with the image of the big bad Black Panther.

The most important thing I learned from the trip was that the black liberation movement had serious problems of disunity, especially around the Panthers and their policy of coalition with whites. One of the main problems seemed to be that there were too many separate black groups—or gangs—in New York, and most of them were competing with one another for followers and territory to practice their illicit activities. Many were heavily infiltrated by police agents. These people also felt threatened by the Panthers' efforts to change lifestyles and politics in black communities across the nation.

In Bedford-Stuyvesant, I saw so-called black leaders, covered with jewelry and dressed in expensive African gowns, being carried around on litters by their young followers. The Panthers were gaining popularity, but we were as fiercely resented by the street hierarchy in the black communities as we were by the black middle class.

In one New York Panther Party chapter I visited, they knew next to nothing about Huey P. Newton or the Party's platform and program. Moreover, the sisters were dubbed Pantherettes and had to serve the brothers without question. I didn't like what I saw, and I couldn't shake the gut feeling that one day there would be serious trouble for the Panthers in New York.

I returned to Oakland and eagerly fell back into the daily routine of Panther life. I was glad to be back in the Bay Area.

4
▼▼▼▼▼▼

SHOOTOUT

▼▼▼

A T THE UNIVERSITY of California at Berkeley, in the mid-sixties, a loose coalition of student groups gave birth to the Free Speech Movement (FSM). The entire area became the scene of intense political activity. Berkeley was a mecca for young white middle-class dropouts, hippies, flower children, and free-love advocates caught up in the wonders of sex, psychedelic drugs, and music. They were known as the Berkeley street people.

Walking away from Gloria and not looking back wasn't easy. She had become an important part of my life, and even though I knew I could never trust her again, I still loved her. After we separated, I spent a lot of time with the Berkeley street people. At first I was interested only in gaining support for the Panthers and talking about the problems of black people. As time passed, however, I began to understand that the street people, too, wanted the same things: the right to make decisions based on our own understanding of what was important to our lives; the freedom to love and live in peace and happiness; a government that did not prey on our ignorance and prejudices or sacrifice our individual growth and development on the altar of the so-called greater good; a world without fear, hatred, greed, and corruption, where differences could be resolved without resort to violence. We didn't always agree on how to go about getting these things or what we would do once victory had been won. Nor did we know exactly what was meant by victory.

We danced and sang together, comforted each other when we were down, hustled food from the neighborhood markets and restaurants, made love, picked lice off one another, and shared our money, our dope, and our dreams. I listened to their hopes for the future and they listened to mine. We laughed and argued together. Gradually the black revolutionary street nigger from West Oakland and the white middle-class rebels of Berkeley began to understand and accept one another. To many of them, I was an unofficial ambassador from the Panthers they could hang out with at the Cafe Med on Telegraph Avenue or pass the night with—listening to music, getting high, and trying to figure out how to live without money or someone always telling you how to live your life. "We respect your leaders," one of the flower children explained, "but they're so distant, and they preach too much violence. We feel only love and understanding will change the way people relate to each other."

"A beautiful thought," I said, never missing an opportunity to make a speech, "but just listening to the national anthem makes you realize power yields only to greater power. In my opinion, humanity hasn't developed to the point where reason, logic, love, and spiritual harmony can guide our lives. And I'm not sure it ever will."

Not all of my Berkeley street friends believed love alone

would solve their problems. Amos, a lanky, slow-talking ex-marine from Georgia, and member of the New York group Up Against the Wall Motherfuckers, had other ideas. "I think armed violence is a logical part of any serious liberation struggle," he said. "If you want peace, love, and justice you've got to go out there and fight for it." I agreed.

In spite of the Party's policy of cultivating white support against racism and police brutality, some of my fellow Panthers thought I was getting too involved with the Berkeley street people and not spending enough time hanging around Party headquarters the way they did. Nevertheless, I always completed every assignment David gave me, sold more than my share of Panther newspapers, and served as a bodyguard for top Panthers on nearly every occasion they spoke in the Bay Area, especially Eldridge, who spent more time with white Berkeley radicals than any other Panther leader. Besides, even though I didn't check in at headquarters every single day, David knew where I was and what I was doing. What some of the brothers seemed to resent was that I—a newcomer—had been promoted to the rank of captain and was allowed to speak in the name of the Panthers at rallys and in private homes, and even to appear on television. I was being given important assignments over others who had been in the Party much longer. Still, no one ever raised any question about my loyalty or commitment to the organization.

Some days play a major role in the course of our everyday lives. Saturday, November 16, 1968, was one of those decisive days for me. Chairman Bob, Captain Crutch, a brother named Harvey, and I were sitting in Crutch's living room interviewing a blood who claimed he wanted to set up a Panther branch office in Southern California. His responses to Chairman Bob's questions led us to suspect he might be a police agent trying to infiltrate the Party. Harvey went upside the dude's head and wanted to stomp him, but Chairman Bob said no and warned the fool to stay away from Party activities or he'd really get fucked up. The poor stiff stumbled down the steps, made it to the street, and took off like a scared jackrabbit.

We sat around in Crutch's living room for quite some time rapping and drinking Bitter Dog. "I knew there was something funny about the nigger the minute I saw him," Crutch said.

"Yeah," Harvey said scornfully. "He talks and acts too bourgeois to be for real."

"What made him think he could trick us into believing him?" I asked.

"Niggers like him are stupid," Chairman Bob said. "We gonna have to deal with more of his kind as we continue to grow and develop. They are all the same, middle-class bootlicking niggers who can't be trusted."

I don't know what came over me, but in a sentimental gesture of loyalty, I took the 9mm Browning I'd bought from Fast Freddy out of my waistband and held it out, butt first, to Chairman Bob. "This gun will always be at your service and at the service of the Party," I said emotionally.

Chairman Bob failed to grasp the symbolism of the gesture. He took the gun from my hand and accepted it as a personal gift. I had practiced drawing and firing the gun so much I hardly had to aim to hit a target at close range. I felt naked and defenseless without it now, but for the life of me, I couldn't think of an honorable way to ask Chairman Bob to give it back. So I sat there looking like a fool and let him keep it.

After the group split up, I decided to surprise Mother and Ella with a visit. They said I looked unkempt and skinny and warned me again I was headed for serious trouble if I kept hanging around the Panthers. I left around midnight and spent the rest of the night with friends in Berkeley.

The following Monday morning, David Hilliard collared me

Above left: William Lee Brent, five years old, with his sister, Elouise, three years old, in Franklin, Louisiana. (*All photos from author's collection unless otherwise indicated.*) *Above right:* Bill Brent, about seven years old.

Left: Bill Brent about fifteen years old, Oakland, California. *Right:* In the U.S. Army, around 1947.

Above right: Working in the
Ben Lomond Forestry Camp,
Santa Cruz Mountains, 1951.
Above left: Bill Brent in 1955.

Bill Brent with Gloria Harness in 1964.

Above: Bill Brent, Eldridge Cleaver, and Emory Douglas crossing the lower Sproul Plaza of the University of California at Berkeley. Bill Brent is on the left and immediately behind Cleaver. *Below:* Bill Brent (*extreme left*) leading honor guard of Panthers at the funeral of Bobby Hutton, April 1968. Marlon Brando is standing on the right.

Above: Bill Brent speaking at a rally to free Huey P. Newton, Defermery Park, Oakland, California, July 28, 1968. *Below:* Overhead view of the van in which Bill Brent and seven others were riding when a shootout with the San Francisco police occurred, November 19, 1968.

Above: Bill Brent the day before skyjacking TWA Flight 151 to Havana, Cuba, June 1969. *Below:* Bill Brent, speaking before the Union of North American Residents in Cuba at a commemoration of Malcolm X's birth, May 19, 1973, in Havana. Jane McManus is sitting at left.

Top: Singing songs at a May Day presentation to the Venceremos Brigade, April 28, 1974. From left to right: Bill Brent, Anita Suarez, Margery Emerson, Jane McManus. *Above:* With Jane, in a rare moment of relaxation, at Jibacoa Beach near Havana, early 1970s. Pupu, our beloved Volkswagen, can be glimpsed behind us. *Left:* At Jibacoa Beach outside of Havana on the north shore, early 1970s.

Top: Bill Brent (left) and Huey P. Newton at the Riviera Hotel, July 1977, Havana. *Above:* Pupu breaks down in Pinar del Río, late 1970s. *Right:* In Grenada, early 1980s.

REPUBLICA DE CUBA
MINISTERIO DE EDUCACION SUPERIOR

El Rector de la
Universidad de La Habana

en uso de las facultades que le están conferidas,
y a propuesta del Decano de la Facultad,
expide el presente Diploma de
Lic. en Estudios Hispánicos para Extranjeros
a favor de *William Lee Brent*
en atención a que el mismo ha cumplido los requisitos
establecidos para los estudios de la especialidad y
ha realizado los ejercicios correspondientes para
la culminación de los mismos el día diecinueve
de julio de mil novecientos setenta y siete.

En testimonio de la cual, se suscribe en la
Ciudad de La Habana, a los doce días del mes
de noviembre de mil novecientos ochenta y uno

Rector

Referendado:

Secretario General

Registrado al folio **86** número *2325* del libro correspondiente a la Secretaria de este Centro de Educación Superior
Registrado al folio **7 8** número *2/44* del libro correspondiente a la Oficina de Filología

Top: Diploma awarded to Bill Brent upon his graduation from the University of Havana, November 12, 1981. *Above left:* On the terrace of El Arabe, a Middle Eastern restaurant located in Jaruco Park, high in the hills east of Havana, 1982. *Right:* Bill Brent with Steve Wasserman, editorial director of Times Books, Havana, Christmas Day, 1994.

as soon as I walked into Panther headquarters. He criticized me for not checking in more often and not taking my turn at guard duty. I explained no one had mentioned guard duty to me before and promised to report in more often. It just happened I was on tap for that very night, at Party headquarters, from midnight to eight.

David also told me Crutch and I had been chosen to accompany minister of education George Murray on a speaking tour of several universities in the Deep South. We would be leaving the following day. I hung around the office rapping with the brothers for a while, visited a friend in Berkeley who promised to get me a brand-new 9mm Browning the following day, then went home to get some much-needed sleep.

A series of unexpected visitors, including two old Quentin buddies who wanted me to help them sell four kilos of weed, kept me awake until it was time to leave for guard duty. When I got to headquarters I found out I would be nursemaiding two Panthers-in-training, who had duty with me. Our job was simple enough: Make sure no one broke into the office, and check the outside rear of the building every hour. For the fifth straight night I stayed up on dexies and Bitter Dog.

Tuesday morning, just before my eight o'clock relief showed up, David rushed into the office and said he was sending me and Crutch to the Panther newspaper office in San Francisco to bring some brothers back for an important meeting. He didn't say who they were and I didn't ask, but I heard a note of urgency in his voice.

I had planned on going to a friend's house to clean up and sack out for a few hours, but this new assignment eliminated the possibility. I knew the smart thing to do was explain to David I needed some sleep, but I had already been criticized and I didn't want them to think I was shucking and jiving. I had an assignment to complete and I would do it no matter what. Besides, I reminded myself, I got enough pills to stay awake for a week if I have to.

I walked up to the corner liquor store, bought two small cans of lemon juice and a fifth of white port wine. Two brothers and I went into an alley alongside the headquarters building, mixed the Bitter Dog, and finished it off behind a couple of Dexedrines. Then, with Captain Crutch at the wheel of the Panthers' news delivery truck, he and I took off for the newspaper office. The truck was an old white flat-nosed step-up delivery van whose battery worked only every once in a while. It had no radio. On its sides, in large black print, the van had the words THE BLACK PANTHER, and beneath that, BLACK COMMUNITY NEWS SERVICE. Pasted to each side were large posters saying KEEP ELDRIDGE CLEAVER FREE.

Shortly before we reached the San Francisco–Oakland Bay Bridge, Crutch pulled over and stopped. Looking in the side view mirror, I saw a dark green Thunderbird pull up behind us. Captain Crutch leaned over and handed me a 9mm automatic. (Looking back, I can't help but wonder if Providence didn't have a hand in my giving Chairman Bob my gun. If I hadn't had a gun, the shootout would never have happened and my life would not have taken the turn it did.) I checked the clip to make sure it was loaded, then stuck it in my waistband. We got out of the van and walked back to the car to find out what was going on.

Brother Harvey, the driver of the T-Bird, explained: After we'd left headquarters, David remembered he had wanted to send some rifles over. Harvey happened along and David ordered him to catch up with us and have us carry them the rest of the way. In broad daylight, with early-morning traffic whizzing by, Harvey and the brother riding with him quickly loaded six old M-1 carbines into the back of the van. I climbed into the passenger's side, Crutch cranked the van up, and we continued on across the bridge to the newspaper office at 774 Haight Street. To my surprise, Brother Harvey was waiting for us when we got there. I thought it was a little strange but didn't ask about it. Perhaps he'd come over to help out at the office. I left Crutch and Harvey standing near the back of the van talking while I went upstairs to the office. Later, we collected the brothers who had to go back to Oakland, loaded them into the van, and headed for the freeway. Of the eight people in the van, including Crutch and myself, I knew only two others: Raymond Lewis, the Panther paper's editor, and Sam Napier, our distribution manager. Sam sat up front in the cab between me and Crutch. The others were crowded into the back of the truck. Once Crutch put the truck into gear and we got under way, Sam took an envelope from his pocket. "I've got some pills here," he said, "that will knock your dicks in the dirt."

I took one and leaned back against the door waiting for a reaction. It didn't take long. Within minutes, I began to feel the effects of the tension, the pills I'd taken over the past five days, and the lack of sleep. My mind slipped in and out of fantasy, my speech was slurred. One minute I was crystal clear and the next I had no idea where I was. Nevertheless, I was determined to finish this assignment before I caved in.

Crutch pulled into a Shell service station at the intersection of Seventh and Twenty-fifth Streets and asked the attendant, a short, middle-aged black man with a bald spot, for two dollars' worth of Ethyl. Then he jumped out to go to the men's room. I asked the dude pumping gas if he had any change so I could pay my share on the next bottle. He said I could get it from the other attendant at the cash box in the center of the island. Half dazed, I got out of the truck, walked over to the cash box and asked for change for a twenty.

My jacket was open and the handle of Crutch's automatic was sticking out of my waistband. The attendant looked down at the gun, then up at my face. Whatever he saw there made him scoop up all the bills in the cash box and hand them to me. Without thinking, or even glancing at the money, I stuffed them into my jacket pocket, walked back to the truck, and climbed in.

Captain Crutch was waiting behind the wheel. He asked me to pay for the gas. I fished out two one-dollar bills and handed them to the man standing at the pump. We rolled out of the station onto Twenty-fifth Street, heading for the freeway. A short time later, instead of going on to the Bay Bridge and Oakland, Crutch pulled off the James Lick Freeway's Seventh Street exit, near the Hall of Justice and the San Francisco police department.

I felt sleep settling over me. I was dozing off when the van suddenly veered to the curb and came to an abrupt stop. I would later learn that the service station attendant had reported a robbery and described the van. A patrol car had spotted us on Seventh Street as we passed the San Francisco Hall of Justice and had given chase. Crutch jumped out on the driver's side. I shook off the fog of sleep, jumped out on the passenger's side, and instinctively took cover behind a parked car. Sam followed me out and kept on running.

I tried to get my surroundings in focus and figure out what was going on. I could vaguely make out several uniformed police running toward me, guns in hand. This is it, I thought. These motherfuckers are going to gun me down as sure as my name is Bill Brent. Well, I ain't going to make it easy for them. I pointed the automatic in the direction of the nearest policeman and silently repeated what I had learned in target practice in the Army and at National Rifle Association ranges in the Bay Area: Squeeze the trigger, don't pull it. Squeeze, don't pull. The gun bucked in my hand. Once . . . twice.

Someone screamed. I rushed to the opposite side of the car and squeezed off another round. My head was filled with the noise of gunshots. From my new position I could see one policeman lying on the ground near the rear of the van and another one aiming a gun at me from a kneeling position beside a parked police car. I squeezed off two quick shots in his direction before the gun clicked on empty and locked in the open position.

I cursed and ran into a nearby alleyway, only to find it was a cul-de-sac between a Ukrainian Orthodox church and a janitorial supply company on Seventh between Harrison and Folsom Streets. Captain Crutch and Sam were trapped in the same alley. We realized the hopelessness of our situation and, hands above our heads, walked slowly out to a street swarming with police. I still held on to Crutch's empty automatic.

The police grabbed me and threw me facedown onto the ground. A giant in a blue uniform kneeled on my head while someone cuffed my hands behind me. They wrestled me into a police car and sped into the police garage at the Hall of Justice, just across the street from the scene of the shootout. Before I passed out in the back of the patrol car, I noticed a mobile TV crew filming the scene.

Two cops dragged me by my handcuffs across the rough basement floor to the elevator. The pain in my wrists forced me back to consciousness. I could smell my own urine. Caged dogs growled in the background, waiting for the order to attack. The elevator doors opened. A policeman yanked me inside and stood on my neck until we reached the jail floor. I was thrown into a cell with several shadowy figures. While sitting on a cold metal bench, trying to clear the confusion from my brain and the tears from my eyes, I passed out again.

Shackled to a gurney, I woke up to the insistent voice of a doctor in the emergency ward of the county hospital: "What kind of drugs did you take? What was it? We want to help you, but you must tell us what you have taken." I could feel my body convulsing as the muscles reacted to the pills and alcohol as well as to the beating. Doctors in the emergency ward had revived me with smelling salts. One of them kept repeating: "Tell us what you took. We want to help you, but we don't know what you have taken." The doctor drew back quickly as I opened my eyes. I raised my head a few inches off the table and tried to sit up. The police guards, hands on the butts of their holstered guns, moved in closer. I struggled to break free of the unyielding bonds that held me to the table. I tried to yell at them, but the only sound I could make was a muffled groan.

My head fell back on the table. I was barely conscious, but the miracle of survival overwhelmed me. I'm still alive, I remember thinking. I lost the battle but the war goes on. Praise to all the gods! I'm still alive.

▼

TWO POLICE WERE SERIOUSLY WOUNDED IN THE SHOOTOUT: Lieutenant Dermott Creedon was hit in the chest near the heart, and an officer was shot in the left side, just below the rib cage, and in the groin. A police inspector was nicked in one finger.

At the grand jury hearing a week or so later, another officer, John Hanifin, testified under oath that after he and several others subdued and handcuffed me, another shot was fired and a police inspector was nicked in the finger. This same officer also said he'd been shot at and had returned the fire. A criminalist for the City and County of San Francisco testified that in addition to the jacketed bullets fired from the automatic and found at the scene, there were several lead bullets recovered. One found in the cab of the van was definitely fired from Lieutenant Creedon's revolver. Another, found in the van's side panel, came from Officer Hanifin's gun, and the third one matched Inspector O'Mahoney's weapon. The slugs themselves, outside of the ones from the 9mm, were all determined to have come from police guns.

All of the Panthers from the truck were arrested. No other

weapons were found in or near the truck. At first, Crutch and I were charged together, but after all the witnesses had been questioned and their statements signed, the San Francisco grand jury decided I had shot the three police officers and charged me with one count of robbery and three counts of assault with a deadly weapon upon a peace officer. Crutch was released without charges. My bail was set at $62,500 and later reduced to $50,000.

The Panthers had sent a doctor up to see me in the county jail. He reported back that I was in bad shape: My speech was slurred and my conversation incoherent. His professional opinion was I needed immediate psychiatric treatment. At which point, the Party leadership decided I was more of a liability than an asset.

A short time later, Eldridge Cleaver called a press conference to announce my expulsion from the Panthers because I had violated the group's principles of not carrying a gun and not drinking or doing drugs while on assignment. He also said that at the time of the robbery and shooting, I was either loaded on dope, drunk, crazy, or an agent. Cleaver knew that I always carried a gun—that was one of the reasons I accompanied him on speaking engagements and on out-of-town trips. He also knew I used alcohol, grass, and pills the same as he and the others did. But he nonetheless saw fit to denounce me—largely, I believe, because when the shootout occurred, he had only six days to go before his own court appearance, and he and his supporters were desperately trying to work out a deal with Mayor Alioto and the California Parole Board. Condemning me might win him points with the men who were trying to put him away.

Earlier that year, in April, right after the Reverend Martin Luther King, Jr.'s assassination, Eldridge Cleaver had organized a group of like-minded Panthers—including David Hilliard—to go out and find some cops to shoot in revenge for King's murder. A shootout between the Cleaver gang and the Oakland police took place on Twenty-eighth and Union Streets, in a quiet black residential section of West Oakland. Two policemen were wounded. Cleaver and seventeen-year-old Bobby Hutton took refuge in the basement of a house, which the police fired on and teargassed mercilessly. After a half hour, the two besieged Panthers came out of the basement with their hands in the air. Eldridge was stark naked. What really happened then may never be known: One version is that Hutton stumbled on his way to the patrol car and the police opened fire on him. The official version is that Hutton tried to make a break for it and was gunned down. Whatever happened, I, and many other people, hold Eldridge Cleaver directly responsible for Little Bobby Hutton's death because he organized the confrontation with police on Twenty-eighth Street for no other reason than impatience with Huey's refusal to endorse reckless attacks on the police in response to the assassination of Martin Luther King, Jr.

Nevertheless, I, along with thousands of loyal Party supporters, had immediately rallied to the defense of the accused Panthers. Now, when I needed support, the Party turned against me. David, Bobby, and the others followed the line Cleaver had taken at the news conference, because it fit in with both the doctor's report and the information the lawyer brought back from the brothers in the county jail. They decided to expel me from the Party. In a press release in early January 1969, Hilliard stated that "Panthers don't go around pulling any shit like that. . . . We think that Bill Brent was obviously insane at that time. Whatever Eldridge said is consistent with our present position." They made it clear I was on my own; they would not raise money for my bail or give me any legal assistance. This decision betrayed the Party's principle that everyone should be considered innocent until proven guilty, as well as the precedent the Party had set in defending Cleaver and the other Panther leaders busted in the shootout with Oakland police nine months earlier.

The Panther Party's position toward me gave people the idea I was not only guilty of the police allegations but was also a police agent. This made it easier for them to cut me loose and more difficult for me to raise funds or rally support for my defense. The Black Panthers had become a vital part of my life. I loved the organization, and I was torn to pieces emotionally and psychologically by their treachery.

I knew I was in big-time trouble when I woke up in the emergency ward at the county hospital. But the real seriousness of my situation didn't hit me until my arraignment. I'd been identified as the person who'd robbed a Shell service station in broad daylight, in a white delivery truck easily identified blocks away—and who'd done it in the most casual manner imaginable. I had shot two policemen who were now close to death. (Fortunately, they would recover completely from their wounds.) I had no money, and the Black Panther leadership had expelled me from the Party's ranks and forbidden the membership to have anything to do with me. I knew I had been wronged. As I told the *Berkeley Barb* at the time, "I am not a police agent. I have never been a police agent and I never intend to become one. A lot of people thought Fidel Castro was irresponsible. A lot of people thought Che Guevara was totally irresponsible. I am what I am."

There were eight people working in the Shell station at the time, but, under oath, only one of them said there had been a robbery; the other seven hadn't seen or heard anything out of the ordinary. Regardless of whether the service station got ripped off or whether the attendant who claimed to have been robbed had simply panicked when he saw the gun handle sticking out of my waistband, the shootout did happen and policemen were shot.

On the one hand, I wished the whole thing had never happened so I could just keep on talking about black liberation and playing at being a revolutionary. On the other hand, I was so damned proud of myself, I thought I would burst. On a street in San Francisco on November 19, 1968, thirty-eight years and nine days from the day I took my first breath in a field worker's house in Franklin, Louisiana, I was reborn. I had taken control of my own destiny and done what other people only talked or dreamed about doing. From the moment I'd squeezed the trigger, life for me would never be the same. I considered the police enemy soldiers wounded in battle. They were the bad guys. I was the good guy. And yet, I wasn't as tough as I thought. I didn't want them to die, because I would then be charged with murder. More important, it would be very hard to live with the death of two fellow human beings on my conscience.

The Panthers were struggling to change their political image. I was to be sacrificed in their fight to survive as part of the very system they had condemned as the irrevocable enemy of all black and oppressed people.

After preaching to people about their right to bear arms in self-defense, the Panther leadership announced that its members were strictly forbidden to carry loaded weapons. The position that had catapulted them into national prominence in Sacramento had suddenly been scrapped. True, they had every right to survive, but to me and scores of disappointed Party members and supporters, there was no possible justification for abandoning their warriors in the field.

Many members resigned and said openly the Black Panther Party had gone bad: It now represented only the selfish ambitions of leaders who had gradually been corrupted by too much popularity. My position was, whatever problems existed between the Party and other groups should be resolved without blacks gunning each other down in the streets. Deep inside, however, I had the sickening feeling the Party, lacking a strong, competent leadership, was doing as much to destroy itself as its enemies were.

Huey Newton built the Black Panther Party on courage and daring, and opened a political Pandora's box. Neither Huey nor anyone else could possibly control the results from a jail cell. Eldridge Cleaver spent more time feeding his ego and playing big shot than trying to become an effective black leader. Bobby Seale had the special magic peculiar to talented, charismatic spokesmen. Unfortunately, both he and David Hilliard were followers, not leaders; neither of them could provide the experienced leadership needed to save the Party from its enemies or from itself.

The Berkeley street people and other progressives refused to believe the charge that I was an agent. Whether or not I had robbed a gas station was less important to them than making sure I didn't get crucified by the Party or by the system. At certain historic moments, large sectors of a given society condone and encourage rebellion. This was the case with the Berkeley street people and others who actively fought against the political system in the sixties. Many of them had grown to hate the status quo so much they were happy someone they knew and trusted had survived a shootout with the police. One thing everyone was sure of, though, was that if I had shot those cops, it was because I truly believed my life was in danger.

Although I had not put my life or freedom on the line for any of the Berkeley street people—by speaking out in their defense publicly or bodyguarding them—as I had gladly done for the Black Panthers, we had developed a relationship based on mutual respect and understanding. The Berkeley street people came to my aid when I needed help most.

While the Black Panther Party was doing its best to discredit me politically, a very special woman I'll call Martha and two of my closest friends in Berkeley, Kathy and Gary G., helped set up a defense fund, got an attorney named Frank Brand to represent me, and raised the $50,000 needed to get me out on bail.

Martha met me at the county jail. She saw I was a wreck and on the verge of losing it altogether. My thoughts were jumbled and confused, up one minute and down the next. I was extremely paranoid—sure that either the Panthers or the police were waiting to gun me down. My only thought was to get another gun and start blowing motherfuckers away. Martha took me into her home and into her heart. She, more than anyone else, nursed and loved me back to sanity. She and her husband, Daryl, were ardent supporters of the Panthers and their political ideas.

Martha talked to me and made me talk to her. We made love, and the heat of our passion burned through my fears and suspicions. She kept me away from guns and out of trouble with the Panthers and the police. She negotiated with the lawyer and helped organize the group of middle-class radicals who insisted if the Panthers had proof I was an agent, they should make it public.

Mother and Ella were outraged at the things the Panthers said about me in their press conference and the way they were treating me in general. Ella reminded me how she and Mother had instinctively known the Panthers were no good and had often warned me about getting involved with them. There was precious little my family could do to help me financially, but, as always, they made sure I had all their love and moral support.

I recommended continued community support for the Panthers. "It's obvious the Party is being set up by the police and the FBI," I told anyone who would listen. "They want you and everyone else to withdraw support so they can more easily eliminate the Panthers." As if I didn't have enough trouble on my hands, several ex-Panthers who had been expelled from the

Party or who had quit because of political differences, tried to get me to join them in denouncing the Black Panther Party's leadership. These disgruntled people, some of whom felt that the Party increasingly failed to practice what it preached and would later come to be considered part of the Cleaver faction, thought I would feel the same way.

This was a time of intensifying struggle over the direction of the black liberation movement. Some groups, like Ron Karenga's Los Angeles–based US organization, emphasized "cultural nationalism" rather than political revolution. Huey Newton had long felt that the cultural nationalists' excessive emphasis on the roots and virtues of black culture obscured the essential fact that blacks formed an oppressed colony in the midst of white America. He frequently cited Frantz Fanon's point that black culture bore the marks of that oppression and that the black man could wrest his manhood from white society only through revolutionary political struggle—not through posturing, dress, or reviving African cultural roots. This was a war not only of words but of real violence as well. In early 1969, two outstanding Panthers in Los Angeles—Alprentice "Bunchy" Carter and John Huggins—were gunned down by members of Karenga's gang. Other Panthers, including Sam Napier, would later be tortured and murdered. Against the backdrop of a government-orchestrated siege of the Party, notably the FBI's counterintelligence program, designed to sow discord and suspicion among the Panther leadership, these bitter battles between brothers who should have been united in common cause were tearing the Party apart. I refused to have anything to do with such people. And so I became another of their enemies—and a potential target for their impotent rage.

Martha and others from the defense fund visited Panther headquarters and talked with David and Chairman Bob. (By that time, Eldridge had fled the country to avoid facing charges stemming from the April 1968 shootout with the Oakland police, and was supposedly living in Cuba.) Finally, five months after the incident, the leadership agreed to meet with me to discuss the problem. They held the meeting at Panther headquarters and I had to go unarmed and alone. I was filled with misgivings. When I got there, David's brother June met me out front with a scowl on his face and a gun bulging under his black leather jacket.

I knew most of the five or six people in the room, Bobby, David, Elton "Big Man" Howard, and June, but I couldn't shake a feeling of foreboding that engulfed me as soon as I walked through the door. Bobby was the only one who tried to put me at ease. I had hoped the meeting would result in my reinstatement as a member in good standing of the Black Panther Party, and the restoration of my right to speak publicly as a Panther in order to raise funds for the Party as well as my own defense. But David made it clear that I was still expelled and could not represent or associate with the Panthers in any way. I asked Bobby if he really believed that I was an agent. The important thing, he replied, was that I had violated Party discipline in such a way that I could no longer be effective as a member. He did agree, however, to publish a statement that I was not an agent and was not working against the best interests of the people. On April 20, 1969, *The Black Panther* published a statement saying that the Party had made a mistake in accusing me of being an agent and that the misunderstanding between us had been cleared up.

This took a lot of pressure off me. My family, especially my young nieces and nephews, took special interest in making me feel happy and comfortable whenever we were together. With their encouragement and support at home and with Martha's constant care and nurturing, I began to feel like a human being again instead of a hunted animal. My body filled out and I learned to smile again.

Time, however, was running out. I had to start thinking of my upcoming trial. The defense fund wasn't bringing in anything, and with my police record added to the existing political atmosphere, I knew the authorities would throw the book at me if I was dumb enough to go to court. I had to make a decision about what to do—and move on it. While trying to make up my mind whether to take my chances in court or catch the first thing smoking and lose myself in the Louisiana bayou, I remembered something that had happened a few days after I'd been released on bail. A young white friend whom I hadn't seen in months walked up to me on the street. He looked into my eyes, smiled, and, without saying a word, handed me five twenty-dollar bills and a paperback book with the title *Spanish Made Simple*, then turned and walked quickly away. I realized he'd been thinking about Cuba, not Mexico.

And why not go to Cuba? The Panthers were known and respected there. The Cuban media had given the Party lots of publicity through interviews with several top Panther leaders, including Huey. Shortly after I joined the Panthers I'd heard that revolutionaries who needed political asylum could get it in Cuba with no problem. I considered myself a revolutionary and I certainly needed asylum.

Martha agreed going to Cuba was a logical revolutionary response to an extremely difficult predicament. The matter was finally settled: I'd go to Cuba and take my chances with its socialist government. My immediate problem was how I would get there. I'd never had a passport and I certainly couldn't apply for one now. I thought about going to Canada or Mexico and trying to work my way to Cuba from there, but I dropped the idea because I didn't know anyone in either country and had little money to move around on. As we talked about writing a letter to the Cuban embassy in Mexico or maybe going directly there, a fantastic idea began circling around in my mind: An airplane, hijack an airplane. Of course. It was clearly the fastest and simplest way. Other people had done it. Twenty-seven other people had pulled it off that year alone, and it was only mid-June. Why couldn't I?

How to do it was the big question. What equipment would I need—a gun, a bomb? Should I try it alone or get someone to go along in case things went wrong? I figured a bomb was too problematical; it could go off accidentally. I had to be in control of the situation, and a gun was the only logical choice. I always worked better alone, and the fewer people who knew about my plan, the better my chances of pulling it off.

What bothered me most was what I would do if something went wrong on the plane. Could I really bring down a planeload of innocent people in cold blood? What if there were children on the plane? I knew desperate situations called for desperate measures, but was this the right move to make? I decided I could either give up and let my enemies have their way with me or do as the true gambler does: Call and bet all.

5

SKYJACK

MARTHA AND
Daryl were sure
I was making a
bad joke when I brought up the idea of skyjacking a plane to
Cuba alone. One man couldn't possibly pull it off, they argued.
Too many things could go wrong. More important was the fact
there would be many innocent lives involved.

I insisted one well-dressed black man would be less likely to
draw suspicion than two or three; besides, at this point I didn't
know who I could trust. For months I'd been living with the
pain of rejection by my former comrades. The fear of being
gunned down in the streets by a vengeful cop was with me constantly. If I were fool enough to go to court at this point, the
only certainty was that I'd be spending the rest of my natural life
in the darkest corner of some maximum security prison or nut-
house. For me the risks were well worth taking.

I knew nothing about Cuba or what living under a socialist government would be like, but I did know U.S. laws had no force in Cuba. I would be free to start a new life: to live and work with revolutionary, socialist-minded people who wouldn't hold my past or my race against me. I wasn't sure I could pull it off, but I sure as hell wanted to try. The more I talked, the more I realized I was trying to convince myself just as hard as I was trying to sway my friends. Finally, they acceded to my reasoning and we began to plan how I would go about ripping off my transportation to freedom.

At first, we were uptight and serious about how to go about it—who would do what and when. Once we got into it, however, it was almost like playing a game. We were like children plotting against the meanies. We decided I should dress conservatively and look like a seasoned traveler: gray suit and hat, white shirt, dark tie, and black shoes. I should pack light, carry a small, well-used travel bag I could shove under the seat, and a new paperback book. Martha knew my size and would get my clothes at JC Penney. Fearful the police might be keeping a close eye on my movements, Daryl picked up a one-way economy-class ticket to New York in the name of Charles Davis. He would also drive me to the Oakland airport. We were pressed for time because I was due to appear in court two days later.

Since the distance from Oakland to Havana is somewhat shorter than that from Oakland to New York City, we figured a nonstop flight from Oakland to New York would certainly have enough fuel on board to get me to Cuba. Everything hinged on my getting a gun before departure time. I hit the streets that same night, confident that I'd pick up a piece without trouble. My mission turned out to be more difficult than I'd expected. I couldn't go to any of my old Panther buddies because they were all on my shit list. My contacts in the movement thought I might be planning another shootout and didn't want to get involved. I wound up paying a weed dealer fifty bucks for an old, beat-up .38 I wouldn't have given a dime for before the shootout. He threw in two joints as a special favor.

Once I had the gun in hand, a feeling of relief and well-being flooded over me. I was determined to see this thing through regardless of the consequences. I knew I could count on Martha and Daryl, and some inner sense told me I'd make it to Cuba without trouble. I spent my last night in America on Martha and Daryl's sofa and slept better than I had in weeks.

On June 17, 1969, I woke up to fresh, clear air, the sound of birds chirping in the nearby trees, and the aroma of fresh-made coffee, bacon, eggs, and toast coming from the kitchen. On my way upstairs to shower, I could hear a smooth popular instrumental coming from the kitchen radio. What were Mother, Ella, and my nieces and nephews doing now? Would I ever see any one of them again after today? I'd wanted to take them into my confidence, but thought it best not to involve them. They'd find out about it soon enough, no matter how things went.

I dressed carefully: white tab-collared shirt, black tie, steel gray business suit, gray snap-brim Stetson, black wing-tip Florsheims, and a pair of dark glasses. The image staring back at me from the full-length mirror looked more like a hip Baptist minister than a fugitive ex–Black Panther. I stuck the empty gun in my waistband and buttoned the suit coat. I was glad to see there wasn't a noticeable bulge.

Breakfast was tense and sad, filled with small talk and forced smiles. No one wanted to talk about what I was about to attempt. Finally it was time to leave for the airport. We could no longer avoid the seriousness of the moment.

The plane would come from San Francisco and start taking on its Oakland passengers at 10:00 A.M. We figured by getting there an hour early I wouldn't have to hang around the waiting room long enough to start getting nervous. I loaded the .38 and stuck it back in my waistband. Martha was on the verge of tears as we hugged and kissed good-bye. Daryl had put my valise in the trunk of his Chevrolet the night before. He and I walked casually out to the car and climbed in. We drove slowly down the tree-lined street, and headed for the airport and my date with destiny.

We were so deep in our own thoughts as we drove along, neither of us spoke. I wondered what the other skyjackers had felt on the day they made their move. Were they nervous, or as calm and self-assured as I felt. With Daryl in the car, what would I do if the police stopped us? If things went according to plan, would everyone guess he and Martha had helped me? Would the police start hassling them and their children? What about Kathy and Gary G. and the other people from my defense fund, especially those who had put up the bail money? How would they react? Despite my outward calm, two questions kept nagging at my mind: Would I really jack the plane or chicken out at the last minute? And what would I do if things didn't work out the way I wanted?

Daryl let me off at the airport parking lot at 8:45. There was nothing to say, because we'd already gone over everything several times at breakfast. We shook hands, and he wished me good luck.

I checked that I had my gun, got a firm grip on my beat-up travel bag, and hotfooted it up to the main terminal building to confirm my reservation. We were right on time. The plane would be loading in less than an hour. The lobby was alive with activity. I'd been in this airport before on Panther business and had welcomed the curious, sometimes fearful stares of the onlookers. Now I didn't want to be noticed, and I was concerned about possibly running into someone who knew me.

I looked around cautiously before going into one of the

shops, where I bought a pack of Pall Malls, a Snickers bar, and a paperback copy of *The Black Panthers,* by Gene Marine, a sympathetic account of the Party that had just been published. I took a seat well away from the main entrance, loosened my tie, pushed my hat back, and began eating my candy bar and reading about the people who had helped change my life forever. I also kept a wary eye on anyone who came near me.

At 10:15 the boarding call for TWA flight 154 to New York came over the PA system. I closed my book and made sure the gun was secure and out of sight. Then, boarding pass in one hand and valise in the other, I took my place near the front of the line. There were no metal detectors. So far so good, I thought after the gate attendant checked my pass and motioned me on board. I followed a gangly teenager up the ramp and into the economy-class section and took a seat next to a middle-aged couple who didn't pay the least attention to me. I stowed my valise, got comfortable, and continued reading. Shortly after takeoff, I had a strong desire to get a last look at Oakland and the Bay Area. But because of the couple next to me I couldn't look out the window.

I found out later that there were seventy-six passengers on the Boeing 707 I diverted to Havana. They were a little noisy, but orderly and courteous. The woman seated next to me got up to powder her nose and apologized profusely when she accidentally stepped on my foot. Thinking back, I don't remember having seen one black face in economy class.

A stewardess began serving brunch an hour after we took off. I glanced at my watch. Almost noon. I didn't know it at the time, but we were passing over a remote section of Nevada known as Wilson Creek when I made my move. The blond, bespectacled young woman looked up with a beautiful smile on her face as I stepped through the curtains separating economy class from first class. I slipped the gun from my waistband and held it loosely at my side. Her eyes widened in surprise and fear.

"Tell the captain we are going to Havana," I said quietly.

She tore her eyes from the gun, picked up the intercom microphone, and said, "There's a man here who says we are going to Havana. He's very insistent and he also has a gun."

"Tell him we don't have enough fuel to go to Havana," the pilot's strong, calm southern drawl came back. "We'll have to go on to New York."

I gripped the stewardess's arm firmly, guided her to the pilot's cabin, and had her knock on the door. None of the other passengers seemed to be paying attention to us. After she knocked a second time, the door to the cabin opened and we stepped inside.

I quickly closed the door behind us, released my grip on the stewardess's arm, and glanced out the cockpit window: nothing but billowy white clouds and here and there a patch of blue sky. I sat down in a crew seat between the window and the cabin door. The three men in the cockpit turned halfway around in their seats to get a better look at me.

The stewardess couldn't take her eyes off the gun. I ordered her out of the cabin, locked the door, pulled the hammer back, and pointed the .38 in the direction of the pilot, copilot, and flight engineer. "We're going to Havana," I said firmly, "and I know you gentlemen will get us there without any trouble."

The three men at the control panel glanced nervously from the gun to my face, then turned back to the controls. A few seconds later, the pilot's comforting drawl filled the plane's PA system. "Good morning, ladies and gentlemen. This is Captain Behnke. We have had a change of plans. We are going to Havana. We will stop in Havana for refueling before continuing. If there are further changes of flight plan, we will let you know." Behnke switched off the mike, and I breathed easier. My baptism of fire was over. The plane's crew had decided to cooperate, and the passengers would have something to talk about over dinner for a long time.

The stewardess brought me two miniature bottles of scotch, a Coke, and a ham and cheese sandwich. I didn't touch any of it for fear it might be drugged.

I had never been in the cockpit of a plane before, and as I sat there looking at the fascinating array of dials, gauges, and lights and listening to the beeps from the control panel, I began to get a little paranoid: What if the pilot goes to Miami instead of Havana? I won't know the difference from the air and by the time we land it will be too late to do anything except curse myself for having played the fool. Still, I couldn't turn back; I'd just have to deal with things as they came up. I tightened my grip on the .38 and promised if anything went wrong, the pilot would be the first to go.

My thoughts turned to my family. What would Mother and Ella think when they found out I had skyjacked a plane to Cuba? Mother would surely get out the family Bible and say a prayer for her misguided son. She'd keep herself busy to take her mind off the trouble.

Ella would probably say, "I knew the nigger was going to do something dumb. Why in hell did he go to Cuba? He can't speak Spanish—he ain't even learned to speak English yet." She'd fuss and fume but deep inside she'd say: Go for it, little brother.

I also thought of Martha and Daryl. How would they react if things went badly and innocent lives were lost? And what if I did make it to Cuba? Would they feel proud and happy for me?

I was suddenly jerked back to the present as the pilot said, "I've got to make contact with Cuba and get permission to enter their airspace."

Gun at the ready, I asked, "How long before we get there?"

"We should be entering Cuban airspace any minute now. They probably already have us on radar and a MiG or two waiting up ahead to look us over. I'll have to explain it's an emergency hijack situation so they'll let us land in Havana. They're pretty touchy about U.S. planes in their territory."

"Do whatever you have to, Captain. Just make sure we get there in one piece."

The pilot switched on the plane's transmitter, adjusted the frequency, and began: *"This is TWA flight 154 from California to New York calling Havana. We have an emergency. Repeat. We have an emergency. Do you read me, Havana? Over."* He then switched to RECEIVE, waited a few seconds, made another frequency adjustment, and repeated the call.

Everyone in the cockpit waited tensely for Havana to answer. Suddenly the radio erupted in sound and a voice speaking in English with a heavy Spanish accent filled the cabin: *"Flight 154 California to New York. You are about to enter Cuban airspace. What emergency do you have? Repeat. What emergency do you have? Over."*

The four of us in the cabin relaxed. The pilot, smiling now, flipped the switch to TRANSMIT: *"Flight 154 to Havana. We have a man with a gun on board who wants to go to Havana. Repeat. Man with gun on board who wants to go to Havana. Request permission to land. Over."*

As he finished speaking the clouds opened up. Two Cuban warplanes, dipping their wings from side to side, streaked past us and disappeared in the distance. I no longer doubted we were truly approaching Cuba. The radio came to life again. The voice on the other end asked about our fuel situation and put us in a holding pattern. Within minutes we received landing instructions.

The pilot and copilot busied themselves at the controls. I was tempted, but resisted the urge to open the little bottles of scotch. Be cool, brother, I said to myself. This shit ain't over yet. The stewardess, bringing sandwiches and refreshments, knocked at the door.

I tightened my grip on the gun and ordered her away, with a warning not to return until we landed in Havana. Following the Havana flight controller's instructions, the plane descended through the clouds. The waters of the Caribbean spread out to the horizon. The jagged landmass of Cuba rushed across the sea to meet us.

Soon the plane was making the wide circle that led to the landing strips at José Martí International Airport in Havana. A light rain was falling, but we touched down without trouble and began taxiing toward the control tower. Flight 154 came to a stop. The pilot switched off the engines and sat back in his seat. "Everybody stay exactly where you are," I ordered. "Don't turn around, and be careful what you do with your hands."

On the ground, my advantage was gone; I'd begun to get nervous. My hands were sweating and the .38 felt like it weighed a ton. I have to be more alert now than ever, I thought. I wanted to look out the window, but thought it best not to take my eyes off the cockpit crew. Tension gripped the cabin as we waited for the Cubans to make the next move.

A voice from the radio broke the silence: *"Flight 154. One of our immigration officers is coming aboard. Please open the port when he arrives. Over."*

In spite of my misgivings about the crew, I rushed over to the window and glanced out. A motor-driven boarding ramp escorted by a jeep filled with armed, uniformed men sped toward us. The boarding ramp banged against the door and the soldiers spilled from the jeep to take up positions around the plane. The pilot opened the port. A minute passed. Two. Three. I was really getting edgy by the time the stewardess's voice reached me through the cabin door. "There's a Cuban officer out here. He wants the man with the gun to come out and place himself in Cuban custody. He promises nothing will happen to him."

Well, I thought, this is it. I can't back out now. I glanced at the pilot and crewmen. They hadn't moved from their seats. Good, I thought, and opened the door. I took a quick look down the passageway and stepped out of the pilot's cabin, holding the gun tucked close to my right thigh. As I entered the main cabin, the passengers stretched their necks, and some even stood up to get a better look. My mind, however, was on the Cuban military officer who stepped forward and extended his hand, palm up. "I'm Lieutenant Galves of the Cuban immigration service. Give me the gun."

Damn, I thought, this peashooter won't do much good in a firefight against the modern automatic shit I saw them haul up here. But to just hand over my piece . . .

The lieutenant read my mind. "It's okay," he said. "You're under our protection now. No one will harm you. Give me the gun."

I hesitated, then flipped the .38 around and passed it to the lieutenant butt first. He examined it briefly and motioned me to lead the way down the boarding-ramp stairs.

On the ground, the soldiers quickly loaded me into the jeep, and we sped across the field to the terminal. There, Lieutenant Galves began his interrogation.

"What is your name?"

"William Lee Brent."

"Are you Cuban?"

"No, I'm not. I'm Afro-American."

"Why did you come to our country?"

I lit up a cigarette and took a long drag to give myself time to think. "I came because the police in my country want to kill me and because I want to learn socialism."

"Who sent you here?"

"Nobody sent me. I came on my own."

"Do you belong to any political organizations?"

"Yes. I was a member of the Black Panther Party."

"You mean you are no longer a member?"

"I was expelled before I left the States."

"Did they send you here?"

"Hey, you don't listen very well, Lieutenant. I told you I came here on my own. No one sent me. I'm not here representing anyone or anything except myself."

I could tell the lieutenant wasn't satisfied with my answers.

He stared at me for a while, then closed the notebook he'd been writing in and stood up. "Someone will talk with you again very soon," he said dryly. "There are many things we need to know about you. My advice to you is to tell the truth and avoid problems later on. In the meantime, if you need something, ask for it."

"How can I ask for anything? I don't speak Spanish and I don't suppose everyone here speaks English as well as you do."

"Don't worry. The guards will understand. Just remember you are not in the United States now and everything is different here. Don't be in a hurry, because everything takes time and we have to check up on everything you tell us. Okay?"

▼

TWO SOLDIERS CAME INTO THE ROOM AND MOTIONED FOR ME TO follow them. A variety of military vehicles, trucks, and buses were scattered around the parking lot outside. Everything except the military stuff looked old and worn, but my attention focused on several well-kept American cars from the forties and fifties. The soldiers took me to a closed jeep. I saw my beat-up travel bag waiting for me in the backseat. Darkness settled in before we reached our destination: high concrete walls, then an inner courtyard.

There's something about prisons—a certain smell, a tense quiet—that sets them apart from any other place on earth. I knew we were on prison grounds as soon as I stepped from the jeep. One of the soldiers took my bag, and the three of us walked toward a door at the side of the building. An armed guard snapped to attention at our approach. Oh shit, I thought, out of the frying pan and into the fire. Ain't this a bitch.

The soldiers led me into the building and down a long hallway to the booking room. They had me take off my hat, coat, tie, belt, shoes, and socks; then they carefully searched every piece. They made me stretch out my arms and open my legs, and they patted me down. I had to sign an official-looking paper that was in Spanish. They kept everything except my shoes, the half-empty pack of cigarettes, and a matchbook. Then they guided me down a semidark hallway with thick wooden doors on each side. Our footsteps were the only sounds I heard, but the stink of urine was thick in the air. In all the years I'd spent in prison in the States, I'd never experienced anything like this. As we headed farther down the hall, I couldn't help but wonder whether the doors we passed led to jail cells or torture chambers.

At the end of the corridor a soldier opened one of the doors and motioned me inside. I shrugged my shoulders and slowly stepped into the cell. Was it possible my coming to Cuba instead of standing trial had been a mistake?

The door slammed shut behind me, and the guard stood outside watching through a small opening. As cells go, this one was rather large, about eight by ten, with a comfortable-looking double bed and a nightstand and reading lamp. I tested the mattress with the tips of my fingers. It was lumpy and hard as a rock and had a damp, moldy smell to it.

On the opposite side of the cell, just below the ceiling, a louvered opening admitted some air but completely blocked any view of the outside. The shower, just to the right of the door, was a rusty piece of piping. The toilet below it, a small hole in the floor, stank terribly no matter how long I let the water run. I kicked off my shoes, and lay back across the bed. "Damn," I said aloud, "if it wasn't for bad luck I wouldn't have no luck at all."

I had no way of knowing what had happened to Captain Behnke or his passengers and crew. Nor did I have any idea what was going on back home. Had I been identified as the hijacker? Had the police hassled Martha and Daryl, or Mother and Ella? What, if anything, were the Panthers saying about me? It wasn't until much later, through letters and a wealth of news clippings Martha sent me, that I learned the plane's crew and passengers had been treated well, and that the plane had been allowed to take off for Miami, to refuel and continue on to New York, where it arrived safely at 11:30 P.M. Among the clippings was an article by Stew Albert in the June 27 *Berkeley Barb* entitled A LITTLE BIT ABOUT BRENT.

> Bill Brent organized the world's longest skyjack to Cuba. He did it by himself, a lone wolf. This is the way he had always lived—the way he joined the Black Panthers and the way he was expelled. Very few really know Bill Brent but there are a lot of brothers on Telegraph Ave. and around Berkeley who loved him and who jumped for happiness when TV told them he was in Havana. . . .

I had been hoping to become part of the beauty of the Cuban revolution, but being taken directly from the airport to a jail cell put grave doubts in my mind the Cubans would allow me to stay in their country instead of sending me straight back to take my chances in a U.S. courtroom.

Tension and fatigue gave way to sleep, opening the door to nightmares: I saw myself running down a long, dimly lit alley. Faceless shadow-people leaned out of holes in the walls yelling and pointing toward the sky. I tried to stop, to raise my head and look up, but my legs kept moving and my head wouldn't turn. Suddenly the din became the wail of sirens and the pointing fingers began shooting at me. I grabbed at one of the fingers; it came off in my hand. My screams drowned out the sirens, and I woke up soaked with sweat, wondering where the hell I was.

6

▼▼▼▼▼▼

HAVANA

▼▼▼

MY ARRIVAL IN Cuba had been spectacular enough, but the reception I received left a hell of a lot to be desired. Straight from the airport to a foul-smelling jail cell, no food that day, and only a hunk of bread with cold coffee and milk the next morning. I felt hungry enough to eat a raw elephant by the time the guards brought my noon meal: a tin pan of watery soup with some floating plantain and spaghetti, and a hunk of bread. Well, at least it was warm and a lot better than Alameda county jail oatmeal mush or Lancaster's restricted diet. Besides, I chose to come here, so I had to go along with the new order of things or go back where I came from. When the guard came for the pan, I went into sign language again, making motions of writing, with the hope of getting paper and pencil. The guard nodded, took the pan and the spoon, and left without a word.

I lit up another of my new cigarettes, careful not to draw too much smoke into my already scorched lungs. I wished they had let me keep my watch, but, what the hell, I'd just have to keep track of the time the same way prisoners did all over the world, by movement within the jail itself. First they gave me breakfast, so I guessed it was early morning. I had lunch sometime after noon. The next meal should be around five-thirty or six. This would mark day two in Cuba.

The evening meal came right on time—fried fish, white rice, boiled plantains, and bread. The guard also brought a ruled notebook and a brightly colored "friendship" pencil made in China. I took my time eating, savoring every morsel in the pan. I saved part of the bread—this old county jail habit came in handy now.

Being in prison was degrading even in my own country, but at least there I knew the rules. The people spoke the same language, and though the food was bad it was familiar. As an uninvited guest in prison in a foreign country, you don't know what to expect, and if you don't know the language you can't ask questions or understand what your jailers are talking about. You're always uptight because you're a complete outsider. You feel stupid and alone, and sometimes afraid.

I dreaded another nightmare like the one I'd suffered the first night. So I tried to stay awake as long as possible. I wrote several letters, took cold showers, and fought off sleep until my eyes closed of their own accord. This time I saw myself hurrying along a dark street crowded with faceless people. I knew I had to make the nearest bus stop as quickly as possible. Looking back over my shoulder every few steps, I rushed along a busy street not knowing where I was going or what to expect. Suddenly the crowds disappeared and I was surrounded by screaming police cars. Uniformed men ran toward me pointing their guns. I snatched at the automatic in my waistband but it stuck to my skin. I turned to run but some force glued me to the spot. Again I woke up soaked in sweat, a scream locked in my throat. Thus began my third day in Cuba.

Soon after breakfast, two guards came to the cell, escorted me to a bare, stifling little interrogation room, and locked me in alone. Hours later, a lieutenant came in and sat down at the other side of the small wooden table.

"I'm Lieutenant Morales," he said in English. "I have to ask you some questions."

"Yeah, sure," I replied. "I've got a few questions to ask you, too."

"Yes, I'm sure you have. But let's stick with my questions first. Then we'll get to yours, okay? We need your full cooperation so my superiors can decide what to do with you. Are you well? Do you need any medication? Would you like to see a doctor?"

"I'm fine. I need something to read and something to put in the toilet so it won't stink so badly."

"Uh-huh. Have you thought of anything you want to tell us you didn't tell the other lieutenant at the airport?"

"I answered all of his questions, but if you have more, I'll be glad to answer those too."

"Well, we want to know your real reason for coming to our country. You said the police wanted to kill you. Why? Are you a criminal?"

"No, I'm not a criminal. I was a member of a black political organization fighting against police brutality and racism in our communities. We also fought for the right to have a voice in the government's political decisions affecting us as a people."

"We want to know everything about you: what political groups you belonged to, who you worked with, what your activities were, what contacts you have here in Cuba. And, above all, we want names, addresses, and dates."

"I have no contacts in Cuba, Lieutenant. And I've already told you people what organization I belonged to, but there are some things I can't talk about without jeopardizing other people. I'm perfectly willing to tell you anything you want to know about myself, but I can't implicate others."

"You mean you don't know anyone in Cuba?"

"I said I don't have any contacts in Cuba. There may be someone here I know, but I am not aware of it."

"Listen, we are asking you to cooperate with us. Make things easy for everyone. Nothing you say here will ever be revealed to anyone."

"Look, Lieutenant, let me ask you something, okay? You personally fought against Batista, right?"

"Of course."

"If you had been forced to flee to another country and had gotten arrested, would you have given the police the names of your comrades?"

"The situation is not the same."

"I know it isn't, but the question is still valid. I am not your enemy, nor am I an agent of any government or organization. I came here asking for asylum because I believe in revolution, not because I want to do you any harm."

"You don't understand. The revolution has many enemies. We must be very careful about who we allow to stay in our country."

"Yes, of course. But from the way you're talking, I get the impression you people think I'm lying to you."

"You didn't tell us the truth."

"What didn't I tell you the truth about?"

"You didn't tell us about the robbery or the three policemen you shot."

"Look, I answered the other lieutenant's questions honestly. He didn't ask me about a robbery or about shooting the police.

But just for the record, I didn't rob anybody, and I shot the police in self-defense."

"What kind of gun did you use?"

"An Astro 9mm automatic."

"Where did you get the gun?"

"It wasn't my gun; it belonged to a friend."

"Who was with you at the time of the shooting?"

"Hey, hey, wait a minute, Lieutenant. The police in my country had declared all-out war on the political group I belonged to. We were fighting against our government the same way you people fought against Batista's. Obviously I made mistakes, but I never did anything against the Cuban revolution."

"Why do you want to stay in our country?"

"Because I want to help Cuba, and I also want to learn about socialism."

"Why didn't you go to some other country?"

"What other country you got in mind, Lieutenant, the Soviet Union? China? Vietnam? Korea? Hell, I'm going to have enough trouble learning Spanish."

"What about Africa? Why didn't you go to an African country?"

"I thought about it, Lieutenant, but Cuba is a lot closer and I was in a hurry."

"What will you do here if you are allowed to stay?"

"Well, first I'll get a job, then I'll go to school and learn Spanish, and then I want to learn about Marxism and Leninism. Or maybe I can do them all at the same time. What do you think, Lieutenant?"

"What kind of work can you do? Do you have a trade or a profession?"

"I'm pretty good with automatic transmissions, and I can handle a pick and shovel with the best of them."

"When you go back to your cell, I want you to think what

you would do with someone who came to your country asking for political asylum but who wouldn't cooperate with you. Think about telling us the truth. We will talk again soon."

"Wait, wait. How long will I have to stay in this jail?"

"You are being held for investigation. It shouldn't take very long."

"I also have some letters I want to send to my family. How do I get them out? And what about a commissary? I need cigarettes, toothpaste, a toothbrush, stamps, and maybe some chocolate or something to hold off the hunger."

"We don't have a commissary here. The guards will take care of your needs. Give your letters to the guards and, if you have a message for me, put my name on it, and they will get it to me."

"Great, but since I can't speak Spanish, would you write your name on a piece of paper so I know how to spell it correctly?"

The lieutenant hurriedly scribbled *Tte. Morales* on a scrap of paper and shoved it at me. "Remember, you are not in the United States now. We have a different system here and we expect everyone to cooperate with us. I will send you something to read, but we don't have very much in English."

"Oh, I'll read whatever I can get. One other thing, Lieutenant. Do you think I can make a phone call to the States? I mean, I'll pay for it."

"Who do you want to call?"

"My family. I want to let them know I'm okay."

The lieutenant handed me a sheet of paper and a friendship pencil. "Write down the names, addresses, and phone numbers of the people you want to call."

I wrote my mother's name, address, and phone number and handed the paper back to him.

"Is this the only person you want to call?"

"Yes, my mother."

Morales stared at me for a second, then handed me a stack of writing paper. "Take this to your cell and write down everything about the robbery and the shooting. We also want to know who helped you come to Cuba and how many people you know here. And remember, it is always better to tell the truth."

Back in the cell, I gave a lot of thought to what the lieutenant had said. One thing was certain: Unless I found out what they were worried about and straightened it out, I could forget about political asylum in Cuba. The following day they moved me into a smaller cell with a steel bunk chained to the wall and a musty, paper-thin mattress. The hole in the floor stank even worse than the first one. They also took away my street clothes. The coveralls they gave me reeked of sweat and pinched my balls.

I could tell my new cell was on a different side of the building because of the sun's heat coming from the wall. And now I could hear other prisoners on the tier, or whatever the fuck they called it in Spanish.

"Please," someone yelled in broken English a short distance away, "bring me someone to love. I need to feel a long, thick dick inside of me. I want someone to make love to my sweet, tight asshole. Please help me."

Someone else began singing to the tune of "Bésame Mucho": "*Bésame. Bésame el culo, coño tu madre, hijo de puta y maricón.*" Keys rattled in a lock down the hallway, a door creaked open, and Bésame Mucho shut up as if his throat had been slit. The place was in complete silence for the rest of the day.

This is it, I said to myself. The main line. Time to settle down and get ready to jail. These people ain't thinking about cutting me loose until I come up with some answers they can accept. I started writing my report on the shootout and my expulsion from the Panther Party. I was sure the Cubans kept up-to-date with what was happening in the States and had read everything the U.S. press had written about me. But if they wanted me to write a firsthand report on it, I'd do it. I started with the morning of the shootout—being very careful not to throw in any names not already published—and ended with the skyjacking. It took me four days because the only way I could sharpen the damned pencil was by rubbing it on the cement floor. I wanted to have the report ready when the lieutenant came again.

I also started doing sit-ups, leg raises, military push-ups, one-legged squats, and shadowboxing. After I'd showered, I would stretch out on the bunk and start going through the multiplication tables. Someone in Quentin had once told me that if a person could do the multiplication tables from 1 × 1 to 100 × 100 he was considered a genius. I could handle the even numbers well enough, but I was a long ways from becoming a genius. Nevertheless, it was a good mental exercise. I tried to organize my in-cell activities before breakfast and before I turned in for the night.

With all my heart, I wanted to believe the good things I'd heard about the Cuban revolution and its leaders. I tried to assure myself every day that the Cubans would give me political asylum and help me learn better ways of dealing with problems and relating to other people. Sometimes, though, I'd get so lonesome for my family and friends, and so depressed about being forcibly isolated from the rest of the world, I'd lose my cool and start thinking one government was pretty much the same as another. What really interested any government was getting rich and hanging on to power. A nobody like me didn't matter much to any of them. After all, what did I have to offer to help them solve their problems? Chances were they'd send my jive-ass right back to the States, and no one would blame them. By my count, a week passed. The promised reading material never showed up, nor did Lieutenant Tell the Truth.

I spent the following week doing my exercises, quietly singing all the songs I could remember, and trying to recall the words to Poe's "The Raven," Wilde's "The Ballad of Reading Gaol," or Alfred Noyes's "The Highwayman." I had lots of time to pray—and to curse the Panthers, the Cubans, the Devil, God, and everyone else who crossed my mind.

Another week passed before the guards came and took me to the same bleak little interrogation room. I sat there planning what I would say to the lieutenant. Better not to get angry, I thought. Smile. Pretend everything is just fine and I'm glad to see him. Turn over what I've written about the shootout, and don't let him know how anxious I am to get out of this place. After what must have been at least two hours, I was about to start yelling and banging on the door when the guards returned to take me back to the cell.

Well, I thought, looks like the head games have really started. I think there is a lot of truth in the theory that an outstanding characteristic of humans is their ability to adapt to impossible situations. I was gradually getting used to the stench of the cell, the mosquitoes, the loneliness, and the constant hunger. Two more weeks of waiting and hoping dragged by. No reading materials and no lieutenant. Finally, the guards came and took me for a ten-minute walk in a walled courtyard. The fresh air was so exhilarating I felt light-headed. Hey, maybe they'll do this every day, I thought.

The long, boring days in isolation without word from the lieutenant turned into months. Patience and anticipation gave way to frustration and disappointment. The guards took me to the barbershop once a month. They brought my food and a weekly change of clothing with their usual silent indifference. Finally, they brought me some Chinese political pamphlets printed on onionskin paper and written in Spanish. I couldn't understand a word, but the paper was real nice. They also brought me copies of some of Fidel Castro's speeches. On several occasions, they made me face the wall in the corridor while they shook me down and searched the cell. They weren't really looking for anything, just fucking with me.

According to my jailhouse calculations, November 10, my birthday, slowly rolled around. This is one hell of a way to celebrate the day I was born, I thought to myself. I'd spent a couple of birthdays in the county jail and Lancaster, eight more in San Quentin and Tehachapi, but none of them made me feel as helpless and alone as I felt in this Cuban isolation cell.

"Son of a bitch," I said aloud, "I haven't heard from anyone back home since I got here. I can't talk to anyone, make a phone call, listen to a radio, comb my hair, or brush my teeth. Damn! I'm not even sure what day it is or how long I've been in this chickenshit jail. They may never cut me loose unless I find out what's bugging them." I knew it didn't matter what I said or wrote. My jailers had decided to put the pressure on and I would just have to stand up under it.

No matter how I tried to keep my mind off the time, the days kept getting longer, and my patience and hopes in the Cuban revolution, and socialism, shorter. My thoughts wandered back to Aunt Bey's mouth-watering gumbo, the blackberry and apple pies I'd loved when I was a child, and those delicious pots of okra with fresh shrimp and tomato sauce Mother used to cook up. I fought the temptation to send for the lieutenant and invent something to get me out of this hole. I knew if I started lying now, I'd be forced to continue lying about everything. From then on, nothing I said would be believed. The next time the guard came to check up on me, I gave him the stuff I had written about the shootout and the hijacking, with the lieutenant's name on it. The next move was up to them.

The nightmares took over again: I was in a semidark room on the top floor of some kind of warehouse. I could hear voices in the distance but couldn't make out what they were saying. I knew I shouldn't be there and silently tried to sneak out. I couldn't find a door, so I made my way to a small, partially open window, got down on all fours, and began squirming through headfirst. Halfway through, I got stuck. The voices were getting louder. I tried to break the glass but my arms wouldn't work and I couldn't turn around. Suddenly a door opened and I could hear footsteps running toward me. I made a last effort to wrench myself free. The window broke and I was falling into darkness, a scream trapped in my throat.

I was grateful to the guards who woke me with breakfast. Later they took me to the interrogation room. Looking stern, the lieutenant sat tapping his ballpoint on the table. He motioned me to a seat, cleared his throat loudly, and said, "We read the report you sent me. Did you put everything in it?"

"Yes, I did. Why do you ask?"

"Because we don't think you are telling the truth."

I fought down the anger building up in me, and the urge to tell this revolutionary policeman he was acting like a real pig. Instead, as calmly as I could, I asked, "*What* don't you think I'm telling the truth about, Lieutenant?"

"We don't think you are telling the truth about the robbery and the shootout. And we don't understand why you refuse to give us the names of the people you know here in Cuba."

"Look, Lieutenant, I've told you I was at war with my government. Whatever I did in the States has nothing to do with Cuba. I can't make you believe I don't know anyone here, any more than I can force you to give me political asylum. If you decide to send me back, you'll be handing me over to the very people who want to destroy your revolution. I am not your enemy. Nor have I ever done anything against Cuba or its people. I don't want to go back, but neither do I want to be locked up and isolated in your jail without knowing whether I will get asylum or not."

"Your case is very difficult. It is being analyzed, but these things take time. It would be wise for you to cooperate with us more and tell the truth about why you came to Cuba and who you know here. If you think of anything else you'd like to tell us, send me a note with one of the guards."

What am I going to do? I asked myself as the guards took me back to my cell. A feeling of complete helplessness came over me. I remembered something by A. E. Housman I'd read years before, and it seemed to fit my situation perfectly:

> *And how am I to face the odds*
> *Of man's bedevilment and God's?*
> *I, a stranger and afraid*
> *In a world I never made.*

▼

I STOPPED KEEPING TRACK OF THE DAYS AND WEEKS. EACH PASS-ing day in that lonesome, tomb-like cell, without word from the outside or any way of knowing what the Cubans' next move would be, made me feel more like a reactionary than a revolu-tionary. I realized the government had more important things to attend to than my particular case, but I was so wrapped up in self-pity I could only relate to my own misery. I felt there was more than disbelief underlying the way I was being treated, and I began distrusting the Cubans. I was sure they were planning to send me back to the States and would use my so-called lack of cooperation as an excuse. If they really wanted to find out whether I knew anyone in Cuba, I thought, all they had to do was cut me loose and follow me.

Normally the cell block was exceptionally quiet: no whistling or loud singing such as Bésame Mucho had done. The guards were especially quick to clamp down on inmates yelling from one cell to another. Occasionally, however, a desperate prisoner would yell out his name and ask if anyone there knew him, or a man would flip out and start screaming and kicking on the cell door, begging to be allowed to talk with someone. I felt like doing the same thing more than once, but fought off the urge.

While I was struggling with the fear I might not get asylum after all, my jailers moved the game to a higher level. I had just finished my morning shower when the cell door flew open and Hey You ordered me out. I thought we were going for a walk in the courtyard. Instead, guards hustled me to the opposite side of the building and into a six- to eight-man cell where there were two other people dressed in prison garb: a Puerto Rican named Louie Freeze, and an American who called himself Lester.

I was completely taken by surprise. I became suspicious as soon as I saw the two new elements the Cubans had introduced into the head game they were playing with me. This could mean they recognized the injustice of keeping me in complete isolation, or it could be a change in tactics calculated to get me talking in the hope I would say something they could use to justify expelling me from Cuba. Whatever it was, I was grateful to have cell mates even if they were working for the police.

Louie Freeze was an emaciated Puerto Rican patriot with a serious drug problem. He claimed to have escaped from a holding cell in Amarillo, Texas, and jacked a private plane to Cuba. Lester, a big man with close-cropped blond hair, intense blue eyes, and a nervous smile, had *pig* written all over him. He didn't say how he'd wound up in an immigration jail, and I wasn't interested enough to ask. Although this cell, like the others I'd been in, had a thick door with a peephole, its location on the opposite side of the building, and its size and cleanliness, gave me the impression this section wasn't normally used to house prisoners but was more likely a dormitory for the guards. The thought only made me more suspicious of my cell mates.

Time went by much faster with someone to talk to and more

room to move around in. The only disadvantage to this new cell was that we had to knock on the door for a guard to take us down the hall to shower, drink water, or use the toilet. Sometimes it took the guards a long time to respond, and then they usually acted as if they were doing us a great favor. Gradually my nightmares diminished and gave way to dreams of my childhood and family.

I remember one dream in particular: A little boy and girl were sitting on the back stoop of a small wood-framed house eating apples. The boy was older than the girl, and she kept giving him bites of her apple. They were laughing. I couldn't make out their faces, but I knew it was Ella and me when we were still in Beaumont.

Lester didn't talk much, and when he did it was only to brag about his alleged Mafia connections in Chicago. On the other hand, Louie Freeze never shut up. He always had a new joke to tell and gladly described what life was like in Havana. He also began teaching me some words in Spanish: *comida* (food), *hambre* (hunger), *baño* (toilet), *agua* (water), *cigarros* (cigarettes), *papel* (paper).

The guards frequently took Lester and Louie out of the cell for hours at a time. Probably making out their reports, I figured. One morning, Louie and I woke up to find Lester gone. Neither of us had heard him leave. Maybe he had been reassigned.

Louie Freeze finally ran out of jokes and the wasted, frustrating days crawled by. I didn't know if anyone in the States knew or cared whether I was alive or dead. I was determined, however, not to let my jailers get the best of me. Lieutenant Morales didn't call me and I didn't call him. The motherfucker put me here, I reasoned. He sure as hell knows where to find me.

I figured their next move would be to isolate me again, then put me in with some screwed-up black dude to give me a taste of how rough it can get when you don't "cooperate."

One morning, while we waited for breakfast, I broke into an old prison blues song I had learned as a child:

Well it's so many mornings got to wake up soon,
I got to eat my breakfast by the light of the moon,
by the light of the moon, by the light of the moon.
Policeman arrest me I'm not guilty of the crime,
but I'm going to prison for a very long time,
for a very long time, for a very long time.
You know I'll be in prison so doggone long,
make me wish I was a baby in my mother's arm.

"Where you learn all those songs?" Louie Freeze asked.

"On the streets, my man, on the streets. I ain't the smartest or the baddest, but I am a sure-enough, hope-to-die, honest-to-goodness for-real street nigger. Everything I know, good and bad, I learned on the street or in the slam."

"Yeah, we got a lot in common. I grew up on the streets too. I've seen and done just about everything. My greatest dream is to see Puerto Rico free and respected the way Cuba is. I'd gladly give my life for that. Nothing else means a damn thing to me."

"I know how you feel, Louie, but there ain't much either one of us can do for our people from a jail cell."

Every day I practiced the Spanish words Louie was teaching me, but I just couldn't wrap my tongue around them well enough to make them come out right. We made a checkerboard from the cover of a notebook and tore off squares of paper for the pieces. I held my own in the regular checker games, but Louie was the master at "giveaway."

What must have been another month crept slowly by. What are Martha and Daryl and my other friends in Berkeley thinking after not having heard from me for such a long time? I wondered. They probably figure I've forgotten all about them, that

I'm lying around under shady palm trees on some beautiful beach, drinking rum and living it up.

Louie never talked about Puerto Rican women, but he always bragged about how fine and sexy Cuban women were. I thought back to the happy nights Gloria and I had spent listening to jazz at the Three Colors in Berkeley, and the time, shortly before I joined the Panthers, we went to see Sly and the Family Stone in San Francisco—they were just getting popular about then, and I thought they were great. I worried about Mother and Ella, and about Ella's children. I imagined the police hassling them day and night because of me. I wished I could be with them again, but I didn't hold much hope I ever would.

Louie Freeze and I were playing ticktacktoe when the door opened and the guards ordered me out of the cell. A few minutes later, I was sitting before Lieutenant Morales.

"Did you think of anything else you didn't tell us before?"

"There's nothing else to tell, Lieutenant."

"And you insist you came here on your own and you have no contacts in Cuba?"

"I am a revolutionary. My life was in danger. I came here looking for political asylum. No one sent me, and I have no contacts of any kind in Cuba."

"Look, when someone travels to another country, he usually knows someone who lives there. There is nothing wrong with knowing people here, but we don't understand why you won't tell us who they are. Maybe they could tell us something to help us make a decision in your case."

"Lieutenant, I know you don't believe me. But I didn't come here to meet with anyone. If I do know anyone living here, I'm not aware of it. The simple truth is I came alone and, sink or swim, I'm on my own."

After the interview, the guards escorted me back to a dark,

smelly isolation cell. Uh-oh, I thought, I didn't say the right thing again. Things could get a little rough from here on.

A couple of weeks later my keepers made their next move in the sadistic head game they were playing with me. They came for me right after breakfast and unceremoniously put me in an even worse-smelling cell with three young black Americans who introduced themselves as Bullet, Razor, and Moman. Bullet, the obvious shack bully of the group, was short and muscular, with a perpetual scowl. "We're from Cleveland," he said gruffly. "We were on the streets until a month ago. They brought us back because we left the farm without permission."

"I'm Bill. Were you brothers on a Cuban farm?"

"A dairy farm," the brother called Razor said disgustedly. "We told them we wanted to work and they sent us to a lousy, stinking dairy farm stuck out in the middle of nowhere." Razor was a tall, gaunt, light-skinned man with gray eyes. As he spoke, he absentmindedly stroked an ugly scar running the length of his left cheek.

"You mean you worked with cows? Like cowboys?" I asked.

"Yeah," Bullet replied, "like cowboys. But we didn't have no pistols, boots, or horses. At first we thought it would be fun, but after a couple of weeks we were ready to come back to jail."

Moman, a thin, dark-skinned man who reminded me of one of my uncles, was the eldest and the most laid-back of the three.

"Hey," he complained loudly, "we had to get up at the crack of dawn and work until the foreman gave us permission to quit. Our main job was cleaning the cattle stalls. Man, you wouldn't believe how much poop cows can produce in a day."

"You woke up smelling cow shit," Razor added, "and you went to sleep with the stench of it in your nose and in your clothes. If the mosquitoes didn't finish you off at night, the flies ate your ass up during the day."

"The food was pretty good," Bullet admitted, "and they got some fine women out there, but they wouldn't give us no action. We lived in run-down barracks and there wasn't a damn thing to do except work."

"Yeah, and the more you did," Moman said, "the more they expected you to do. We talked it over and decided to hitchhike our way back to civilization. They must have put out an alarm for us, 'cause as soon as we got to Havana they picked us up and brought us back here."

"What will they do with you now?" I asked.

"They might send us back to the States," Bullet said bitterly, "but at this point I don't give a fuck. I sure as hell ain't going back to no stinking farm no matter what they do."

The days passed slowly. We four black outcasts talked about whatever came to our minds. I told them about the skyjacking and my reasons for coming to Cuba. The three bloods asked endless questions about the Panthers.

"What do you cats do with all the money you take in from them white folks who think you niggers really gonna make a revolution over there?" Bullet asked.

"The money is used to buy groceries and medicine, and get bail and lawyers for people who are broke when they get busted," I explained.

"We heard you cats were rolling in money, jacking up people in the communities, riding around in big cars and living like kings," Moman said. "Is there any truth to all those stories?"

"The Party isn't perfect," I said. "There probably were some rip-offs, but most of us lived the same way our neighbors did."

"Hey, brother," Razor said earnestly, "we know there are some good people in the Panthers, but there's also a lot of bull-shit going on and everybody knows it."

"Yeah," said Bullet. "One of the things I've never been able to understand is what really happened in the shootout where the seventeen-year-old brother got killed and Cleaver came out buck naked with his hands in the air. I mean . . . what the fuck was going on?"

"The cops did most of the shooting, brother," I said. "What can I tell you except it was just another Panther fuckup? The whole thing never made any sense, and I think most people would rather just forget it ever happened."

I wondered how and why these bloods had come to Cuba, but I figured if they wanted me to know, they would tell me in due time. I also wondered why the Cubans had put me in with these three. Maybe they thought I would talk more freely with them than I had with Lester and Louie. Or that they would change my mind about wanting to stay in Cuba. The horror story about the dairy farm wasn't very encouraging, but at least they'd been on the outside. The three went to sick call nearly every day. They usually came back with bottles of codeine-based cough syrup and enough tranquilizers to keep them spaced-out and passive. Time crept by just as slowly as before, and I wanted more than ever to be out on the streets. Since my last cell change, the guards hadn't bothered to take me for an outside walk.

One day I woke up with a terrible toothache. In the infirmary a dentist examined my teeth roughly, gave me some aspirin and a packet of tetracycline, and sent me on my way. When we reached the cell block, much to my surprise and joy, the guards ushered me into an empty two-man cell.

Here we go with the head games again, I thought, and stretched out on the bottom bunk. What I didn't know at the time was that my toothache had saved me from a major fuck-up—and a possible ass-whipping by my jailers. The day before, on May 10, 1970, almost eleven months from the day I stepped off the Boeing 707 at the José Martí Airport, while my cell mates and I had been complaining about our lack of communication with the outside world, Cubans of the counterrevolutionary group Alpha 66, based in the United States, had attacked and sunk two of the revolution's unarmed fishing boats and kidnapped the crews.

The following day, thousands of indignant Cubans packed the streets around the former U.S. embassy to denounce the aggression and demand that the U.S. government take full responsibility for the action. Bullet, Razor, and Moman chose that same day to stage their own protest against being in jail. Kicking on their cell door, trying to tear their bunks from the walls, and screaming racism and injustice, they demanded to be allowed to communicate with their families in the States. They also demanded that the Cuban government release them immediately and give them jobs in the city instead of the countryside.

The guards managed to transfer Moman and Razor to separate cells by promising to reexamine their cases. Bullet, a piece of angle iron from one of the bunks clutched in his hand, refused to cooperate. The guards rushed the cell, subdued Bullet, and wrestled him, screaming and kicking all the way, into a strip cell.

Eleven more months crept by before I found out what had happened: Moman and Razor had been sent back to the States at their own request. Bullet remained in jail. Months later he was seen on the streets of Havana spaced-out on some prescription drug and telling everybody he would rather be in jail in the United States than spend one more day in Cuba. Eventually he got his wish. I've always wondered what would have happened if my toothache had come a day later.

7

HIJACK HOUSE

I FINISHED MY REGULAR morning workout, in spite of the stifling heat in the airless cell, then stretched out on the bunk and started going through the multiplication tables again. Sensing movement outside the cell door, I sat up. I'd heard no heavy footsteps, no jangling keys, only a whisper of activity. In the immigration jail, the guards walked quietly in rubber-soled boots and seldom carried more than one key at a time.

The peephole cover silently slid open a fraction. Someone was checking out the cell. A key turned in the lock. The door swung open and a young prison guard ordered me out. "*Ven. Ven,*" he said. "*Ven.*"

Wonder what they've got in store for me today? I asked myself. Probably more of the same stupid questions: "Why did you come to our country? Who sent you here? Are you working for your government?" Or maybe they'll take me for a walk in the yard. I quickened my pace at the thought. I loved to see the tops of the friendly trees waving at me above the concrete walls.

Hope of an outing vanished as the procession braked to a stop at the barbershop. The sad-eyed inmate barber was much older than I. His thin, stringy black hair was combed to the side to hide his bald spot. He looked as if he hadn't smiled in years. I wondered what he had done to wind up in jail. After he cut my hair, he gave me a shave and a liberal dusting with talcum powder. The guards put me in an interrogation room and locked the door.

The process was always the same: Sit down on one of the straight-backed chairs at the rickety wooden table and wait— sometimes for hours. I searched my mind but couldn't remember how much time I'd wasted in these airless little rooms. This time I got lucky. After fifteen minutes, a Cuban officer with whom I'd talked before hurried into the room carrying a fistful of papers.

"Good-looking haircut," he said. "Did you do it yourself?"

"It would look much better if I had," I retorted. "What brings you here this time? More questions, or have you people decided to let me out of this place?"

"Why yes, how did you guess? We are going to let you out. You've sponged off us long enough. Now you're going out on your own."

The Cubans had lied to me so many times since my arrival— promising me reading material, leading me to believe they would allow me to make a phone call home, telling me this investigation wouldn't take long—I didn't know whether to believe him or not.

"Hey," I said at length, "sounds great, if you're not still playing games with me."

"No, I'm not joking. I have the papers right here. You will soon be a free man. I told you not to worry, didn't I? You have to learn to be patient, relax, and take it easy."

We stood up and shook hands. The lieutenant walked to the door, turned, and looked back at me with a smile. "You are going to live in a house with other Americans. I'm sure you'll like it there."

I was sure this was just another one of their cruel little games, but my heart beat a little faster in spite of myself. Minutes later, the guards took me to the property room to identify my belongings. Someone had switched suit coats with me. I decided not to make a big thing of it.

Back in the cell, I remembered having gone through the same process about a month before. I'd even been allowed to wear my street clothes back to the cell. Then, after I waited up all night, a grinning guard told me someone had made a little mistake. I felt like shit for weeks. A key rattling in the lock snapped me back to the present. Once again the guards led me to the property room. "Change your clothes," an officer barked. "You're leaving."

I hurriedly changed into my street clothes and prayed I would finally get a taste of the freedom I had come for. I finished dressing, and the officer gave me my personal belongings: the house keys I had absently brought with me, my watch, wallet, and cigarette lighter. I flicked the lighter several times; it still worked. I grabbed the valise and followed the officer to an office where several guards sat pecking away at antique typewriters.

"Sit down and wait," the officer growled, and left the room.

I checked my wallet while I waited. Except for an expired driver's license, a few scraps of paper with phone numbers, and a couple of beat-up photos of my family, it was empty. The ninety dollars I'd brought with me were gone. Just as I started to light up a cigarette, the officer and two guards came over.

"Go with these men," the officer ordered. "They will take you to your house."

I snatched up my bag and hurried along a narrow hallway after the guards. Hey, I thought, they're walking in front of me for a change. This must be the real thing. We entered a walled court-yard, climbed into a jeep, and rushed headlong out of the gates onto the busy city streets. I'd held my breath until we were out-side. Now I gave a long sigh of relief and leaned back in the seat. Waves of happiness flooded over me. A big white sun filled the sky, and a light ocean breeze did nothing to dispel the early-morning heat. It was late April 1971, twenty-two months since I'd come to revolutionary Cuba seeking refuge. I felt like crying and laughing at the same time.

The jeep wended its way among military vehicles, U.S. cars from the forties and fifties, horse-drawn carts, and throngs of pedestrians. Many of the houses and buildings we passed showed signs of neglect, but they didn't look any worse than those in my old run-down neighborhood in West Oakland. Brightly colored signs and posters hung on lampposts, tele-phone poles, and trees. Bright banners fluttered above narrow, well-swept streets. The entire view had a festive air about it.

The scenery gradually changed as we sped through a residen-tial section with wide, tree-lined streets and modern houses. This section, I learned later, had once been an exclusive middle-class suburb called Siboney. The houses reminded me of the fancy suburban homes around San Francisco and the Berkeley Hills. The jeep slowed suddenly and pulled into the rear drive-way of a handsome two-story mansion.

A uniformed man walked out to the jeep and began talking to the guards in rapid Spanish. I suspected they were talking about me and wished I could understand their conversation. Finally the man opened the door of the jeep and ordered me out. "*Ven. Ven.* Hey you, come here."

I jumped out of the jeep and began to follow him. He stopped me with a raised hand and then pointed back toward the jeep. "*La maleta.*"

I just stood there trying to guess what he wanted me to do.

He saw my confusion, and with a smile he reached into the jeep and pulled out my valise. Aha, I thought, *la maleta.* Another word to add to my vocabulary.

I took my bag and followed the man through a small, neat kitchen into a spacious dining room. Large windows looked out on an oval pool. The man called out: "Edna."

Almost as if she'd been waiting in the wings for a curtain call, a beautiful young woman of Chinese descent stepped into the room. She wore blue jeans, a short-sleeved white blouse open at the neck, and black sandals. The man spoke quietly to her for a moment, then left the room. She glided over to me and held out her hand.

"Hi, I'm Edna," she said. "The guy in the uniform is Manuel. He's the person in charge here. He wants me to show you to your room so you can get settled in before lunch."

I knew she wasn't Cuban as soon as she started talking. I hadn't been close to a woman for nearly two years, and her perfume, the touch of her hand, her smile set me on fire. Blood raced through my veins; I felt giddy, almost high.

"Yeah," I blurted out, "I'm Bill. You're not Cuban, are you?"

"No, I'm not. I'm from San Francisco," she said. "Come on, I'll show you where you'll be staying."

My head was spinning. This is impossible, I thought. I woke up in a foul-smelling dungeon and now here I am in this fancy bourgeois crib with a fine Chinese sister from San Francisco showing me my room. There's got to be something wrong somewhere.

Edna's sweet, melodic voice snatched me back to reality. "Most of the others are out right now, but I think Diana and Pat are in their rooms."

I followed her up a short flight of stairs and down a wide hallway.

"This is where the men sleep," she said. "My room is just

down the hall, first door on the left. Pat's is right next to mine, and Diana's is back there through the door behind you."

Imagine. After so much time in jail alone, I'm suddenly going to be surrounded by beautiful women. If I'm dreaming, I sure hope I don't wake up anytime soon.

"You must be tired and hungry," Edna said sympathetically as she reached out and gently touched my arm. "Why don't you pick out a bunk, rest up awhile, and come down to lunch when you're ready. Okay?"

Smiling, she squeezed my arm softly; then she turned and walked down the stairs. I watched her all the way down, wanting to call her back, talk with her, touch her, and have her touch me. I could still feel the warmth of her hand on my arm.

Pulling myself together, I entered the men's dorm, clicked on the lights, and looked around. Not bad, I thought. Not much privacy but a hell of a lot better than what I've had to put up with for nearly two years.

I examined the military-style double-deck bunks and checked to see how much space there was in the upright steel lockers. Then I walked into the large, clean bathroom and was surprised by real toilets, sparkling porcelain washstands, shower stalls, and wall mirrors.

I threw open the windows and stood looking out at the street below and listening to all the sounds. Swift-flying birds added color and music to the scene, children laughed and played in the distance, and a far-off dog barked incessantly. It felt wonderful just to be able to look out of a window again.

As I turned to go downstairs I was transfixed by the sight of a pretty young black woman poised in the doorway. A huge, well-combed Afro framed her girlish face like a halo. A cigarette dangled from the corner of her full lips. She wore no brassiere and her breasts strained against her thin white blouse. A form-fitting black miniskirt caressed her ample thighs like the eager hands of a lover. Smooth, perfect legs and highly polished low-heeled pumps completed the picture. I stepped forward and introduced myself.

"I'm Diana," she said, gripping my hand firmly. "Edna told me about you. Where you from, Bill?"

"California. Oakland, California," I said, still holding on to her hand. "Have you been here very long, Diana?"

"Too long. This place sucks. It's so damned boring I could scream. It's the same old thing, day in day out: Sit around drinking rum, go to the beach or take in a movie in Havana, and back to this damned house again. I mean . . . there just ain't nothing to do. It's a fucking drag."

Diana paused a moment to gauge my reaction, then went on in the same vein. "I also have a baby, and he's driving me up the wall. But maybe it's just me—the others don't seem to mind. Come on, let's go downstairs before they start to think I'm trying to make out with you or something."

Several people lounged around the living room waiting for the call to lunch. Diana introduced me. I was sure most of them didn't use their right names. An athletic dark-skinned brother stuck out his hand and said, "Hey, brother, glad to meet you. I'm James."

A muscular young Latino dude sauntered over. James introduced him as Geo.

"Hi, glad to meet you, man," Geo said with a big, gold-toothed smile.

To my great delight, Diana and Edna led me to a table near the window, where we had a view of the tropical shrubbery. Geo and James joined us, and a short time later Pat and her husband, Benny, came in. Pat was an exceptionally pretty young woman with short blond hair and big blue eyes. Benny was thin and had a short Afro and sharp, penetrating eyes. He and Pat looked good together.

Now she is one fine young white woman, I thought to myself and started on my lunch: watery fish soup, boiled pinto beans, white rice, bread, and cold water—pretty much the same fare they served in jail, but here, in the company of other Americans, I didn't resent it as much.

After we finished eating, Manuel surprised me with clean sheets, a pillow and pillowcase, a thin cotton blanket, a large, soft bath towel, a mosquito net, nice minty toothpaste, and soap. The sweet-smelling bath soap made me think of the times Gloria and I had showered together before making love. Manuel threw in a week's ration of cigarettes and matches, as well as my monthly dole of forty pesos from Immigration.

"The Cuban peso is good only in Cuba," Geo explained, "but it's divided in the same way as the dollar: A centavo equals one cent; a hundred centavos equal one peso."

Geo and James knew about my case from old newspapers that occasional visitors had brought from the States. They felt the Panthers had fucked me over. According to their account, Eldridge Cleaver had come to Cuba from Canada by boat. The Cubans took him in, gave him a house and a car, and let him shop in special stores. He had access to the best restaurants, bars, and nightclubs in Havana. His house was always filled with young Cubans who admired him as a high official of the Black Panther Party. He got away with a lot of things here for a while, but when he started organizing a Panther chapter in Havana, the shit hit the fan. What saved his ass were his strong movement connections and his supporters in the States. They made arrangements for him to go to Algeria. There he was welcomed as a great black American revolutionary and given diplomatic status. He also organized the international branch of the Black Panther Party.

Geo and James were surprised I'd spent so much time in jail for investigation. "Don't nobody do time for just coming to

Cuba," James said. "Somebody out there got a hard-on for you, my man."

I would soon find out how right their observations were, but at the moment I was too damned glad to be on the streets to think about unpleasant things. We talked a long time. James had been a member of the Panther Party in New Jersey. He didn't say how or why he'd come to Cuba, and I thought it best to just accept what he was willing to tell me. Geo was Salvadoran, and a member of Los Siete de la Raza, a group of seven Latin brothers charged with shooting a policeman in San Francisco in 1968. He said he'd come to Cuba clandestinely, hoping to make contact with Salvadoran rebels here and be sent to El Salvador to fight for his people. We learned a little about each other and became friends in the process.

After we'd talked awhile, Geo suggested we go into Havana so I could see what it was like. I was dying to check the city out, but since I'd just gotten out and didn't know the rules, I was hesitant to just up and go on my own. James assured me this was like a halfway house. Manuel and a couple of others who worked with him kept things in order and controlled the supplies. We were free to come and go as we pleased, as long as we stayed out of trouble. However, the doors were locked at eight o'clock, and anyone who got back late had to climb the fence and come in through the terrace.

I filled my lungs with clean, fresh air and hurried toward the bus stop with Geo and James. The tropical sun warmed my body and a cool breeze caressed my face. I felt free for the first time since I'd arrived in Cuba.

A bus came almost immediately. We rode a few minutes and got off across from a small park that had a rollercoaster and Ferris wheel and several other rickety-looking rides.

"That's Coney Island," James said. "It's not very big but the children love it. You can hardly get in the place at night."

"Yeah, and if you go through the cement archway down there," Geo added, "you come to the beach. And man, do they have some fine little mommas down there on the weekends."

"Truer words were never spoken," James chipped in. "We got to take you down there sometime so you can see just how fine Cuban women can be." We sprinted for our next bus, got on, and made our way to the back. Within minutes we were at Central Park in Old Havana. The street scene resembled downtown San Francisco during lunch hour. To be among people again felt good.

"You see the large building over there?" said James, pointing to a replica of the U.S. Capitol. "It was turned into the Academy of Sciences and the Museum of Natural Sciences after 1959. This is mostly a business district. You have to go farther in to see some of the really beautiful old colonial buildings."

Geo enthusiastically suggested we stop off at a little bar he knew and celebrate my release with a few shots of Cuban rum. James and I were in complete agreement.

The most popular rum on the streets was something called *aguardiente*; unaged and untamed, it was the cheapest, most powerful rum in Cuba. We stopped at a crowded little sidewalk bar where the bartender, a friend of Geo's, gave us three doubles right away. Geo raised his glass.

"Here's to the revolution," he bellowed.

"To the revolution," James echoed.

I didn't know what revolution they had in mind, but one seemed as good as another at the time. "Right on," I said as I raised the glass to my lips and took a big hit. I finished slowly, savoring every swallow.

Geo had brought an empty bottle wrapped in an old newspaper. He set it on the bar and ordered the bartender to *llénamela* (fill it up for him). There was a severe bottle shortage in Havana and most of the rum was sold by the shot. You could buy anything from a quarter to a full bottle, but only a shot glass at a time. Naturally it cost more, but you didn't have to hang around funky little bars all night to do your drinking.

Small groups of uniformed students maneuvered their way through the street crowd. My attention fixed on the sleek new Alfa Romeos zipping in and out of the slower traffic. Their powerful engines roared out in protest at the narrow, confining streets of Old Havana.

"How come I see so many new Alfa Romeos on the street?"

"Well now, brother Bill," Geo said slowly, "you just came up with a question lots of people have asked, but they ain't got no answer yet. It seems the Cubans and the Italians made a deal to break the U.S. blockade. Nobody knows what kind of deal, but all of a sudden these new Alfas started showing up on the streets."

"Yeah," James said knowingly. "All the ministers got one. There are lots of things going on here nobody seems to understand except the people at the top. We all look the other way and say it ain't none of our business, but everybody wonders what's going down."

We arrived back at the house just in time for pan-fried fish, white rice, boiled plantains, and chocolate pudding. After dinner, we took our bottle to the living room, where I met some of the others: Ali, Antar, Fela, Macheo, and Yusef, young black militants who had jacked a plane and come to Cuba in hopes of going on to Africa; and Rick and Ronny, black teenagers who talked mostly to each other and had the habit of writing their names on the wall beside their beds in their own blood. Being young and having to live with so many dangerous characters, these two were most likely acting crazy and pretending to be bad so no one would notice how afraid and vulnerable they really were. As we said in the Army and in San Quentin, they were selling woof tickets.

Many of the brothers in the house didn't want to stay in Cuba and had asked immigration officials to help them get to an African country. The Cubans had promised to see what they could do, but so far nothing had happened. The general feeling among these brothers was the immigration officials weren't going to do anything for them because they didn't consider them real revolutionaries.

In talking with people at the house, I learned we weren't the only Americans living in Cuba, and this wasn't the only place the Cubans had set aside for legal and illegal immigrants. "As soon as we got here," Geo said, "some of us asked the Cubans to train us in guerrilla warfare and help sneak us back into our respective countries. The people in charge of us flatly refused. They said the Cuban government didn't believe in exporting revolution."

Cubans, I learned, were divided into three main groups: *blancos, mestizos,* and *negros.* The classifications were made mainly according to skin coloring and hair texture. *Negros,* in general, had the same basic social, economic, and cultural status in Cuba as blacks had in the United States. Most of the American blacks living at Hijack House strongly believed racism was alive and well in Cuba. "They only got one token black leader who fought with Fidel in the mountains," Diana pointed out, "and you can count the blacks in important leadership positions on one hand and still have some fingers left over."

In 1971, black Americans sporting Afros were an oddity on the streets of Havana. With rare exceptions, Cuban men were clean shaven and wore their hair close-cropped. Except in the case of a few top Cuban leaders, beards and long hair did not fit in with Cuban custom. Women office workers were not allowed to wear pants. Men were fined for walking around the streets shirtless or baring their chests in public. A couple years after my release, Yusef and his date went to a concert at Cuba's prestigious Amadeo Roldán Theater. The place was stifling hot, so Yusef took off his shirt. He had words with an uptight usher. Then the police came and ordered Yusef outside, where they began manhandling and insulting him. When Yusef fought back, he was arrested. He ended up sentenced to two years in prison because he took his shirt off in a public place.

Few Cubans spoke English, and a number of the brothers in the house refused to learn Spanish. They regarded Spanish as just another colonial slave language that would make it easier for the Cubans to brainwash them. Their attitude was, they weren't trying to dictate policy to the Cubans, but they weren't going to let themselves be recolonized either. I thought Spanish was a beautiful language and I was eager to learn to communicate in it. I also thought the idea that you'd be recolonized because you learned a new language was taking things to extremes.

Antar headed up a weekly political education class that emphasized Mao's *Little Red Book* and readings from Frantz Fanon, Che Guevara, and Malcolm X and other writers on black pride and racism in the United States. In the weeks that followed, I would attend a few classes and get the definite impression these brothers' heads were still in the States, and they were more into black nationalism than anything else. Cuba, on the other hand, represented socialism. The concept was beyond our understanding at the time because we had nothing to compare it with.

My only experience with Cuba and its revolution was from behind bars. For now, it was best to listen and learn. I had a million questions, and as the conversation stretched on into the night, I wasn't sure what to think. Naturally, I'd felt hurt and confused when the Cubans took me straight to jail. Although I hadn't expected a hero's welcome, I certainly hadn't anticipated nearly two years behind bars. Nevertheless, I knew I had to be here or go back home and face the music. I felt the best way to find out what the Cuban revolution was really all about was by taking an active part in what was going on around me. I truly didn't want to go back. But could I make it in revolutionary Cuba?

The group, that first evening, had drifted out onto the terrace. My mind was filled with questions as the conversation ended and the others went upstairs. I took a turn around the yard to clear my head. Then I went up to shower and turn in for my first free night in Cuba.

▼

I GOT UP EARLY NEXT MORNING, WASHED AND DRESSED QUIETLY, then went downstairs and persuaded the cook to let me out the back door for an early-morning run.

I didn't know what to make of last night's conversation on the terrace. Most of the others didn't want to stay in Cuba. But could I just ignore their criticisms? After all, we learn from experiences—our own as well as those of others—don't we? Besides, I felt a kinship with these people. They'd suffered the same misfortunes and deceptions I had. And, like me, they now had to survive in a country with a different set of political game rules to play by. I wondered: Was there something really wrong, or were they just bad-mouthing the revolution because it wouldn't cater to their demands?

I thought about the time I'd spent in a Cuban prison without the comfort of mail or visitors. I wondered if, after I'd been on the streets for a while, my attitude would be as negative as some of the others'—or maybe even worse.

By the time I'd finished my run, people were up and moving about. After a quick shower and change of clothes, I went to breakfast with James, Geo, and Edna. Edna had been at Hijack House more than a year. She'd come with a boyfriend who had jacked a plane without telling her he was going to do it. She'd broken off with the boyfriend, but didn't go back for fear of being sent to prison.

Edna interpreted for the others whenever Geo wasn't around. When I found out she also gave Spanish lessons, I pleaded with her to take me on as a student. My sincerity persuaded her, and we started right after breakfast.

Edna began by explaining the simple tenses of the verbs *ser* and *estar* (to be). "These verb forms tell you who and what you are as well as where and how you are. In English we say: 'I am Edna. I am in Cuba.' In Spanish we say: '*Soy* Edna. *Estoy en Cuba.*'"

I obediently repeated the phrases and copied them in a notebook. My accent was terrible, but the major problem was that I didn't know English grammar very well, and this made learning a foreign language much more difficult. I was determined to learn, though. I spent the next hour memorizing the conjugations of *ser* and *estar* in the present tense.

Diana came in while Edna and I were huddled over the textbook. "Brother Bill," she said coyly, "there's a white girl waiting for you across the street. She says you're old friends."

I hurried to the front of the house, threw open the door, and stepped out into the driveway. A jeep with a tall young white dude behind the wheel stood waiting across the street. Standing next to it was Virginia Miller, a friend I'd met shortly after joining the Black Panther Party. Virginia, an outspoken supporter of Huey Newton, was highly trusted by the Panther leadership. She was the last person I'd expected to see in Cuba.

I hurried over to the jeep and we fell into each other's arms. Both of us were on the verge of tears. She took my hand, led me to the jeep, and introduced me to the driver, Bob, who lived and worked in Havana. I hesitated when Virginia told me to get into the jeep, but she assured me everything had been cleared with immigration officials. She would explain everything once we got to her hotel. I climbed in eagerly and settled back. This is going to take one hell of a lot of explaining, I thought as the jeep sped off toward town.

Bob dropped us off at the Hotel Riviera and apologized for having to rush off. Virginia stopped at the desk for her key. We took the elevator up to her floor and walked down the cool, carpeted hall to an air-conditioned room. "Make yourself at home," she said.

I knew I would never get over the hurt of being abandoned by the Party leadership as well as some of my most trusted friends. Still, I was overjoyed to see Virginia. I could understand that she and some of the others had run for cover when I first got busted, just in case I started cooperating with the cops; but I didn't understand why they'd treated me as if I had the plague after I got out on bail. Or why Virginia had suddenly turned up on my doorstep only a day after the Cubans had let me out of jail.

Unless, of course, she had something to do with getting me released. If this were true, it could mean only one thing: She was acting on behalf of Huey Newton and the Black Panther Party. My big question was: Why now? What had happened in the past twenty-one months to make the Party prefer to have me free on the streets of Cuba rather than cooling my heels in the slam and reflecting on my errors? I chose a chair facing the door and sat down.

Virginia pulled the other chair over and sat down facing me. "How are you?" she asked in a voice filled with concern. "Everyone was so worried about you."

Right, I thought. They were so fucking worried it took damn near two years for someone to come down here to see about me. But I kept my cool. I smiled and said, "I'm just fine, sister, especially now that I can talk to someone I know and get some news from back home."

Virginia assured me they had tried to find out about me, but the Cubans hadn't even been willing to admit I was here, much less give out any information about me. I asked her what had been going on with the Party and with the movement in general since I'd left. She smiled understandingly and began to fill me in.

Huey had been released from prison in August 1970. He came back to a Black Panther Party plagued with internal strife and individual power struggles. The black movement and the white Left were becoming more fractionalized by the day.

Huey immediately began a vast reorganization of the Party, with special emphasis on survival programs such as the Black Panther school, the free health clinic, food giveaways, and sickle-cell anemia testing. This new emphasis added fuel to the factional fires and led to the expulsion of key Party members and the closing of chapters across the country. Finally Huey gained the upper hand—but not before he and Eldridge had a slugfest by long-distance telephone. Eldridge, then in Algeria as head of the international section of the Black Panther Party, disagreed with Huey and wanted to run things his own way from abroad. Eldridge taped this bitter long-distance argument and altered it in his own favor. He then called a press conference and accused Huey of threatening his life. Later, he sent the doctored tapes back to the States to be sold throughout the movement for a hundred dollars apiece.

Earlier, Eldridge had apparently badmouthed me to the Cubans and convinced them I was an agent. He'd gone to Algeria by the time I arrived but the damage had already been done. To me, this was the principal reason the Cubans had kept insisting I was lying to them and had kept me locked up for so long. Virginia wanted to make sure I understood that Eldridge, not Huey, was to blame.

When Huey found out what had happened, he asked Virginia to come down and straighten things out with the Cubans and get me on the streets. Geo and James had been right: Someone had been poisoning the Cubans' minds against me.

"I never blamed Huey for what David and Bobby and the others did, sister," I said. "After all, he didn't accuse me of being an agent and expel me from the organization. I've always known Eldridge was responsible for that."

Virginia assured me no one believed I was really an agent, but there was no convincing explanation for the alleged gas station stickup and resulting shootout. The whole thing was so scary and unreal, nobody knew what to do or what to believe. And, too, David Hilliard had immediately issued an order stating that anyone caught associating with me would automatically be expelled from the Party. With Huey's freedom still on the line, no one was willing to take a chance. The Panthers, a group I had given my life to, had been in a state of shock. Nothing was more important than to free Huey. No one had run out on me. Chance and circumstance had simply left me holding the bag.

For the hundredth time, I cursed myself for having played into the hands of those jealous brothers within the Party who had wanted to slow my rise. I was more angry with myself than with the Party. Having grown up on the streets, I knew cooncan better than most and I shouldn't have been so careless.

I pushed myself up out of the chair, walked over to the window, and stood looking out at the seemingly endless expanse of water separating me from my family, from my struggle, and from the rest of the world.

I knew Virginia was only doing her duty: defending Huey Newton and the Party. To ask her to do otherwise would be like asking a fish to give up swimming. She's waiting for me to say something she can take back to the others, I thought, so they can feel a little less guilty about leaving me stranded down here.

People have called me crazy all my life, I said. Part of my birthright was my well-known refusal to take shit from anyone, to allow anyone to fuck me over. No one could pin an agent jacket on me, because I'm not built that way. David and Bobby were running scared and some of their supporters convinced them they could take the heat off themselves by sacrificing a few ordinary soldiers. That approach might work on a chessboard, but for the Panthers it added up to political suicide. I wasn't the only one they had fucked over, and once they started turning against their own members—no matter what the reasons were—they went back to being just another street gang without the trust and respect of their members or their communities.

The room was so quiet we could hear people walking by in the thickly carpeted hallway. On the street below us, someone was trying to prove he had the loudest car horn in Havana.

The simple truth is, starting with Huey himself, we had all fucked up. But somehow only the troops were left out there to be crucified.

Virginia was sympathetic, and she was confident everything would work out well for me now that I was out of jail. We stood in the center of the room holding hands, trying to avoid each other's eyes. The memory of a special night together in the basement of a Berkeley collective a few years earlier triggered my desire. I wanted her in the worst way, but I also remembered an occasion when she had stopped me cold with the words "You think about sex too much."

I promised to write letters and bring them to the hotel for her to take back. She told me exactly how to get to the bus stop from the hotel. We hugged and kissed. Reluctantly, I turned away.

The talk with Virginia had at least given me some information to go on. I felt much better. True, she colored everything in Huey's favor, but I suspected that much of what she'd said was true. Now, at least, I had a better idea of why the Cubans had kept me locked up so long. Eldridge, the son of a bitch, I wished him a long and prosperous life.

The conversation had both angered and sobered me. It brought home the fact that by shooting those policemen, and then skyjacking that airliner, I had fucked up way beyond the "I'm sorry" point. It also made me realize exile was only part of the price I would have to pay.

"Well, well, look who's back," Diana said, greeting me at the door. "I didn't think Snow White would cut you loose for at least a couple of days. What happened? She forget to bring her pills or something?"

"Pills ain't got nothing to do with it," I replied dryly. "She's one of my sisters in struggle. Our relationship is political, not sexual."

"What! And you just getting out of jail? Come on, brother, we both know the political shit don't mean nothing when it comes time to get some."

"Oh, Diana," Edna said with a smile, "not everyone has sex on the brain like you do."

"Yeah, I know," Diana shot back. "Ain't it a damn shame?"

I wasn't in the mood for games, so I left them and went up to the dorm. I did fifty military push-ups and fifty sit-ups, then stripped and took a long, cold shower. With a towel around my waist, I sat down to write the letters I wanted to send back with Virginia.

The first letter was for Mother and Ella. I knew they didn't want to hear anything political, so I kept it simple and personal.

April 1971, Havana, Cuba

Dear family,

I'm writing you from a special halfway house in Havana. I arrived in Cuba on June 17, 1969, and was immediately thrown in jail, where I remained until a few days ago. The Cubans have treated me decently (they didn't beat me or torture me), and now I'm living in a nice house with other

Americans. Since I don't speak Spanish yet, it's a big help because I now have someone to talk with.

I've written to you often from jail, but the authorities wouldn't let me send or receive any mail. I'm sure this letter will get to you because it is being taken back by a friend.

I love all of you and I miss you terribly. Take good care of each other. I'll write as often as possible. Lots of hugs and kisses for all of you.

Bill

I dropped the letters off at Virginia's hotel the next day.

I gradually settled into the routine of the house, mostly just hanging out and listening to people complain about one thing or another. I figured it must be costing the Cubans a small fortune to take care of us. I didn't see how they could afford it, since none of us was working.

Many of the hijackers felt our being here was all political propaganda: Having a bunch of Third World freedom fighters, especially those who hijacked airplanes to escape from the United States, made the Cuban government look good. The longer we stayed here, the more political mileage Cuba got out of us.

Certain hijackers also believed that every U.S. plane landing on Cuban soil had to pay the Cuban government several thousand dollars and also buy whatever fuel might be needed for the flight back home. "There ain't no love involved here," one angry resident told me. "They're getting a lot more out of this than we are."

Maybe the Cubans are using us as political pawns to make themselves look good internationally, I thought. But, like it or not, I'm here, and personally I am bored to death just sitting around doing nothing. I didn't feel I was better or more politically aware than anyone else, but I couldn't stand being idle all the time. I needed to get myself a job.

One evening, I was sitting with James on the terrace. "Hey,

brother," I said, "how can you people stand hanging out and doing nothing all day without cracking up? Can't something be
done about getting some kind of work? Isn't there someone we
can talk to about this?"

"Yes, we can talk to Manuel. But he'll just say there aren't any
jobs for us right now."

Geo came out and joined the conversation. He agreed with
James, but added, "I heard ICAP—the People's Friendship In-
stitute—is organizing a brigade to cut sugarcane. Maybe we can
get in on it."

A short while later, Edna and Diana came out to join us.

"Aha," Diana said triumphantly, "so this is where you dudes
been hiding out. What you got in them cups?"

"Something to make you feel good and help you forget about
your troubles," I replied, offering her my half-filled cup of rum.
"Here, have some." Diana took the cup and almost drained it.

"Not bad," she said, and wiped her mouth with the back of
her hand. "I hope there's more."

"There is always more for you, sister," I said, refilling the cup
and then passing the bottle to Geo. "Don't worry about it."

"Tomorrow," Geo said casually, "we are going to ask Manuel
for a letter authorizing us to cut sugarcane with the Nuestra
América Brigade."

For a moment there was absolute silence on the semidark terrace; even the mosquitoes stopped buzzing. "Cut sugarcane,"
Diana repeated. "Why in the world would you want to do
that?"

"Because we're tired of just sitting around all day," I said.
"This is supposed to be a working-class society and I think I
should be working."

"Well, you people can do whatever you want to, but I've got
a baby to look after. And even if I didn't, I ain't thinking about
cutting no sugarcane for nobody."

8
▼▼▼▼▼▼

HIGH TOP, LOW STUBBLE

GEO, JAMES, AND I had just finished breakfast when a jeep pulled into the back driveway. Our bags were already packed and waiting near the door. The driver, a tall, athletic mulatto with a big smile, strode into the dining room and asked for each of us by name. After a round of hot black Cuban coffee, we piled into the jeep and took off for the cane fields.

While the three of us made bets on who would stay in the harvest longest and who would cut the most cane, the jeep sped east along the busy seaside highway, turned south at Santa Cruz del Norte, and headed up into the lush green hills.

Several kilometers later we rounded a curve and got our first look at the rural town of Aguacate, where our driver parked in the shade of some trees. Everyone got out to stretch and get some refreshments. It didn't take long for us to find a coffee bar.

The line moved fast. The hot, sugary coffee quickly restored our spirits.

Campesinos, military personnel, and farm equipment operators crowded the street near the coffee bar. One group of workers wore sleeve guards and chaps and carried sheathed machetes.

"Hey," I asked Geo, "is this the way these people always dress?"

"The professional cane cutters do," he explained. "The chaps and sleeve guards protect them while they work. Some of them cut several hundred *arrobas* of cane a day." (One *arroba* equals twenty-five pounds.) Aha, I thought, just like Three-Bale Shorty and Two-Ton Willie. I wondered if they got paid any better than those brothers did.

Impatient to start cutting cane, we piled back into the jeep and continued on to the campsite some nineteen kilometers away. ICAP and the state-owned sugar mill had set up camp for the workers in a village called La Granja Cervantes.

The village had a scattering of brightly painted houses, surrounded by flowering fields of ripening sugarcane. This area was the center of activities during the harvest. The camp director, Rafael, met us at the supply room. He issued our bedding, work clothes, shoes, gloves, cigarettes, matches, insect repellent, and mosquito nets.

"You can take your choice between a regular machete and a *mocha*," Rafael told us. (A *mocha* is a heavier machete with a short, wide blade.) We chose the *mochas* and then searched around in a pile of straw hats for ones we liked. James's huge Afro made it difficult for him to find a fit.

The men's barracks was a long, low structure with hinged, wood-framed windows. A long, rusty metal trough, nailed to the outside wall for washing up and doing laundry, looked as if it might give way at any moment. Inside, twin rows of double-deck bunks made of two-by-fours and burlap sacking ran the length of the building on both sides. The floors were made of rough, uneven planks. The barracks, lit by naked 50-watt bulbs that dangled from the tin roof, was dark and depressing. It reeked of ash, dampness, sweat, and burnt sugarcane. I wondered about the last people who had lived here: Were they Cubans or foreigners?

Geo, James, and I staked claims to bunks at the far end of the barracks. We threw open the windows, made up our bunks, and went outside to get a better look at the camp. Nico, one of the ICAP people assigned to work with us in the fields, offered to give us a guided tour.

A three-strand barbed-wire fence surrounded the barracks-style buildings in the compound as well as the barren spaces between them. Someone had haphazardly whitewashed everything except the well-fed tomcat grooming himself near the kitchen.

Nico showed us the open-air showers at the rear of the barracks. I reached out to close a leaking faucet. A small green frog leaped from the wall onto my outstretched hand, then zigzagged its way out the door. This is going to be one hell of a trip, I thought.

"The water gets pretty cold this time of year," our guide said, "but then there's nothing better than a cold shower to perk you up after a hard day's work." From the showers we went to the dining room, kitchen-supply room, and administration building.

"We built all of this ourselves," Nico said proudly. "Now, over here," he continued, pointing to a smaller building in front of us, "is the women's barracks. Next to it is the recreation hall."

Because the camp housed volunteers from overseas, it had become a focal point for the local residents. Many of the volunteers were embassy personnel from one country or another. Others lived in Cuba or had come to visit and decided to try their hand at cutting sugarcane for a few days.

Loud Cuban dance music blasted from the camp's PA system at all hours of the day and night. The campesinos living nearby never complained, because the camp provided music for the entire area. The music was good but too loud. I dubbed it people's music and learned to live with it.

The camp was small but well maintained. The food was always well prepared, and no one ever left the table hungry. Everyone said the cane cutters ate better than any other workers in Cuba.

The camp director made sure all of us had enough Havana Club rum to melt away the tensions we'd brought from the city. By bedtime we felt completely relaxed and ready to face the hardships awaiting us in the cane fields.

The merciless PA system shocked us awake at dawn with taunting Latin rhythms. We dressed hurriedly and went to the mess hall for bread and supersweet coffee with milk. After breakfast, the director gave us an animated pep talk. Then he ordered us to climb aboard the waiting canvas-covered military trucks, which immediately took us off to the cane fields to make our contribution to the revolution.

Ravelo, a tall, rawboned campesino in his late fifties, had cut cane most of his life. ICAP had selected him to teach the new volunteers the correct way to work in sugarcane. Ravelo called our small group over and began explaining the basics of cane cutting: "First," he said, picking up a machete and holding it so we could all see his hands, "you must learn how to hold a machete. Wrap your fingers around the handle, in the same way you might make a fist, and relax your wrist. Right-handed cutters should place their right foot slightly forward and to the right of the stalk to be cut. The right knee bends a little and the left leg is stretched back out of reach of the hungry machete. From this position, take the stalks of cane in your free hand, lean forward, and bring the machete around in a downward arc. This motion cuts the stalks low to the ground without letting the blade bite into the earth."

Ravelo held us entranced as he went through all the motions: waving the machete around above his head, gathering several stalks of cane in his arm, and, in one deft stroke, cutting through them at their base. Then he threw the stalks onto the ground behind him, to his right.

"After you cut the stalks," he said, "toss them behind you with the tops facing outward and move up to the next cut. When you finish a row, turn around, backtrack, and cut the tops off of the cane where it lies. This will dull your machete a bit, but you will have time to sharpen it later. When you finish, pick another row and start all over again. Remember, be careful at all times because carelessness causes accidents, and we don't want anyone to get hurt out here."

Ravelo and the ICAP people coached us individually until we began to get the basic idea and rhythm of cane cutting. We then went into the field, picked out a row of cane, and started cutting. By midday, sweat ran from our bodies in rivulets. We gasped for breath like long-distance runners, and we ached all over.

All the cane in this area was cut by hand, using one of two systems: the green-cane system—cut the cane just as you found it in the fields: leaves, grasses, and all—or the burnt-cane system—select a field the night before cutting, then do a controlled burning to get rid of the leaves and grasses and make cutting a hell of a lot easier. Naturally the volunteers used the burnt-cane system.

Cutting burnt cane, however, left our entire bodies covered with a fine black ash and gave the sensation of being covered with fire ants. The more you rubbed or scratched, the more it itched. By the end of the day, I had learned the basics of sugarcane cutting. Amazingly, Geo, James, and I managed to finish several rows on our own. Nothing could have made us feel better than Ravelo's praise for having done so well on our first day in the field.

Wearing big grins on our soot-blackened faces, we swaggered around bragging about who had cut the most cane. Pride pushed our chests out even farther when we learned that some of the other volunteers had quit without finishing a single row.

"You did a good job today," one of the women said as we climbed onto the trucks. "If you keep at it, you will soon become good *macheteros*."

"Yes, it's true," another woman added. "You all did very well, but you are going to suffer for it tomorrow."

I was already suffering. I couldn't straighten my back, and every muscle in my body ached. I looked back over my shoulder as the truck pulled onto the bumpy dirt road. The fields appeared as untouched as when I'd first seen them. Son of a bitch, I said to myself, we haven't even made a dent in this mother!

Back in camp, we scrubbed down vigorously with strong laundry soap and rinsed off with lots of cold water. The icy spray stung like tiny needles and rejuvenated our tired bodies.

Rafael waited for us in the mess hall with shiny metal cups and several bottles of Havana Club. "*¡Viva la Revolucíon!*" someone shouted. "*¡Viva la Revolucíon!*" we chorused, lifting our cups into the air. A warm feeling surged through me. This sure as hell beats sitting around Hijack House doing nothing, I thought.

We all congratulated ourselves on how well we had done our first day in the cane fields. I couldn't remember having felt as tired in my life. My right hand was so sore and swollen I couldn't close it. The blisters I'd noticed at lunchtime had broken open while I was washing my shorts in the shower. Now they were bleeding. My mutilated hands felt like they belonged to someone else.

After a delicious dinner of fried chicken with thick, creamy gravy, white rice and beans, fried bananas, and cold beer, with rich custard pudding for dessert, I felt ready to tackle the cane again. Instead, we all headed for the rec hall. Some folks wanted to dance to the almost irresistible Latin American rhythms blasting from the PA system. Others preferred to try their luck at chess or dominoes. Still others, like me, wanted only to sit around and talk and enjoy the rum and the warm feeling of friendliness characteristic of the campsite.

An hour passed. I filled my cup with Havana Club, excused myself, and went to my barracks. I set the cup of rum on the floor beside my bunk, took off my shoes, and wiggled in under the mosquito net. I had intended to rest and think for a while before getting undressed for bed, but sleep overcame me before my head hit the pillow.

The next morning the dreaded PA system jarred me awake with the blaring upbeat sound of a popular Cuban dance tune. Pain raced through my entire body as I fumbled my way through the mosquito netting and finally got out of the bunk. My hand ached worse than ever when I tried to move my fingers.

I had to use both hands to lift the cup of rum from the floor to my lips. It burned all the way down my throat, but it helped relieve the pain. Geo and James, mumbling to themselves, finished the cup off. Then, painfully forcing our joints to move and our hands to open and close, we did our regular morning exercises.

At breakfast Rafael suggested we go into town to see a doctor. Free dental and medical attention were always available. We refused his offer but accepted some first aid treatment from another camp official, who warned us our hands would get a lot worse if we returned to the fields without medical attention. We thanked him, gathered our equipment, and boarded the trucks with the other volunteers.

Ravelo wasn't the least bit surprised by the condition of our hands. "That's normal," he said, "especially when you use those cloth gloves with rough, uneven seams inside. What you have to do is turn the gloves inside out. They won't chafe your hands then. Also, remember to keep your wrists loose and hold the *mocha* handle firmly without squeezing it. Set a pace for yourself, one you know you can handle, and stick with it. Concentrate on how much cane you're going to cut instead of thinking about your hands. In a few days you won't even remember the pain."

"What about the blisters?" I asked.

"I'll tell you a little secret," Ravelo said with a mischievous smile. "To toughen up their hands, the professionals usually piss on them while they are cutting in the fields."

All the newcomers had some kind of problem: blisters, sore muscles, body aches, headaches. You name it and one of us was suffering from it. Some people had such severe asthma they simply couldn't continue working.

Not getting the expected sympathy from Ravelo, and skeptical about his remedy, I nevertheless strode into the field and pissed on my hands. After turning my stiff, soot-caked gloves inside out, I forced my hands into them. Then, trying hard to ignore the soreness, I grabbed two stalks of sugarcane and brought my *mocha* around in an arc that sent waves of pain up my arm as the blade sliced through the succulent stalks.

Fuck you, motherfuckers, I screamed silently as I cut a narrow swath through the impassive wall of cane before me. Fuck you. My gloves grew wet and slippery from the early-morning dew, but I kept at it. One row down, two, three . . . I lost count. I stopped only to drink water and to apply Ravelo's remedy to my hands. Within an hour I had forgotten about the pain. Nothing mattered now except my *mocha* and the unending rows of sugarcane.

On the way back to camp for lunch, I carefully peeled the glove off my cutting hand. To my amazement, the blisters had stopped bleeding and the swelling had gone down. I could move my fingers without pain. When we reached camp, a friendly Dominican woman named Toni took one look at my hands and led me to the infirmary.

Nothing seemed to get her down. She was an experienced cane cutter who could hold her own with anyone in camp. Shaking her head in disapproval and speaking in rapid Spanish, she made me wince as she jabbed iodine at the ugly, raw blisters in my hand.

I couldn't understand her words but I got the definite impression she was scolding me. When she pointed at the side of my head and made the classic "tsk, tsk, tsk" sound, I was sure she was questioning my intelligence. After lunch, everyone found a nice shady spot and stretched out to rest up before the four-hour afternoon shift.

A regular workday for the volunteers was from nine to ten hours. Anyone who didn't feel up to it could take a day off and go into town. Once we had finished making hogs of ourselves in the mess hall, we had several choices of things to do: hang out in the rec hall, make the nineteen-kilometer trip to Aguacate and take in a movie, or visit with either the villagers or the permanent cane cutters. Nights were usually pleasant, with clear, star-studded tropical skies and a soft evening breeze. Most of the time people broke off into small groups to just sit and talk.

The majority of the volunteers came from Latin American countries. They were at odds with their respective governments and, sooner or later, the conversation always turned to politics. No one ever had a good word for the government of the United States—nor a bad one for Cuba. Most people revered Fidel Castro as a modern-day Simón Bolívar. At the same time, they considered the U.S. government to be the natural enemy of all of Latin America.

The Latin American women in camp were open and friendly from the start. They liked to tease James and me about our bad Spanish. Margarita, an outspoken, dark-haired beauty from Central America, took a special interest in *los negros americanos*.

"You are so very big and strong," she said, squeezing my biceps admiringly. "However, you will never learn to speak Spanish well until you are holding a beautiful Latin American woman in those arms."

"And she will not only teach you about nouns, pronouns, and adjectives," said Beatriz, a small, attractive brunette from El Salvador, "she will also show you how to conjugate more than Spanish verbs."

Their friendly, contagious laughter flowed through the campsite like a fresh breeze. It mixed freely with the braying of a lonely mule on the distant slopes and with the incessant buzzing of the camp's mercilessly bloodthirsty mosquitoes.

One night, Margarita leaned over and whispered something to Geo. He turned to me and said: "She wants to know why you came to Cuba."

"Tell her I had to leave my country because the government is very racist. They treat black people worse than animals."

"Did you fight with the police?" someone asked from the background.

"Yes I did," I answered matter-of-factly. "They tried to kill me and I fought them."

"I knew it," Margarita said excitedly. "I can tell by your eyes and mouth. You are the kind who would fight the police."

"Racism is terrible," Beatriz said. "My friends criticize me because I go out with black men. I just tell them to mind their own business."

"I'm glad I am not a racist," Margarita said. "I don't want to have a baby by a black man but I like to go out with them. They are so big and strong and loving."

"How can you say you're not racist?" I asked. "You admit you wouldn't have a baby with a black man."

"Of course not," Margarita replied emphatically. "I'm not racist because my grandfather and some of my other relatives are black. But my duty, I was taught, is to improve the race. I can't do that by having black babies."

"I learned the same thing," Toni said. "Nevertheless, my daughter is black and I love her more than anything in the world. I think when the baby comes, you love it no matter what color the father's skin happened to be."

I realized this internalized form of racism had a lot to do with why white men didn't want their women going out with black men. They didn't care so much about the women; they just didn't want a lot of little half-white babies running around.

Within a week, my hands had healed and toughened. I also learned a great deal more about cutting sugarcane and making love to Latin American women. Neither was easy. Margarita had taken over Edna's task of teaching me to speak Spanish. First she taught me the most popular Cuban cuss words: *puta, maricón, hijo de puta, come mierda.* . . . I also picked up a few words and phrases in the village, around camp, and in the fields. Everyone wanted to help me learn Spanish. No one, however, could do anything about my harsh, unmistakable American accent.

Not only was Ravelo a champion cane cutter, he was also manager of the general store. On several occasions, he invited Geo, James, and me to help out. Filling bags with beans, rice, and noodles gave us a welcome respite from the cane fields and the sameness of camp routine.

Friday evening, during our second week in camp, James and I were in the barracks getting ready for dinner. An excited Geo ran in with weekend passes for the three of us. "We have to be back in time to go to work on Monday," he cautioned. We rushed to the mess hall, wolfed down our food, and talked Rafael out of two bottles of Havana Club. We caught a ride to Aguacate, found a bus, and were in Havana in no time at all.

Edna saw James and me coming from an upstairs window. "They're back, everybody. They're back," she yelled, and ran to meet us at the front door.

Diana and Pat came down too. "Oh my," Pat exclaimed, "they look so strong and healthy. Maybe we all should go cut sugarcane."

I'd become accustomed to the strong Cuban cigarettes Populares in jail, and by now was doing nearly a pack a day. I lit up, looked Pat over, and confirmed my original thought: She was one fine young white woman. It felt good to be speaking English again after having heard mostly Spanish for so long. As we headed for the living room, Manuel stepped into the hallway, buttoning his shirt and grinning from ear to ear. "They told me you were coming in today," he said. "Congratulations, you did very well."

He couldn't have a drink with us to celebrate, but he happily supplied the cups from the kitchen. The first bottle was about half gone when I got up, took Diana's hand, and led her toward the stairs. "Let's go up to your room and listen to some music," I suggested. I had made my move. A smiling Diana let me lead the way. James and Edna sat quietly, looking after us.

Diana and I had almost finished breakfast the next morning when James and Edna walked into the dining room arm in arm. "Listen up, everybody," Diana said, "I have a plan how we can spend the day together. First we get the housework out of the way. Then we take in a movie in Havana, get something to eat, hang out on the Malecón, then come home and make love." No one objected.

The house was beginning to come alive. James and I decided to go and hang out in La Lisa for a while. "Let's walk," I suggested when we reached the bus stop. The shade trees along this street reminded me of a very special part of Berkeley, California.

In the early seventies La Lisa had a reputation as a rough neighborhood. Its sole claim to fame was the well-equipped Frank País Orthopedic Hospital, where people from all over the island came to be treated by its specialists.

Instead of being intimidated by the neighborhood's bad reputation, James and I felt right at home there. We walked around, had a few drinks, and flirted with some of the women we passed in the streets.

Sunday night came and it was time to head back to camp. Geo, newspaper-wrapped bottle in hand, met us at the bus terminal. When we arrived in Aguacate, a friendly motorist gave us a lift into camp. We got back in time to join in on the music and dancing. Knowing how hard it would be to get up the next morning, I slipped off and went to bed.

In the following weeks, I became a steady, reliable *machetero* in both green and burnt cane. At first I had fought the stalks of sugarcane head-on. Now, the more cane I cut, the more difficult it became for me to go on. Without knowing it, I had entered into warfare with myself. It took great effort to continue getting up at dawn every morning, and it required an iron will to put on my cold, sooty work clothes, pick up my *mocha,* and go out to do battle with those silent unending rows of sugarcane.

I knew I could leave anytime I wanted to without being criticized, and this fact made it harder to do so. The problem was with me, not the people around me. I had promised myself to stay until the sugarcane harvest was over. I would keep my promise, no matter what.

As the harvest neared its end, some of the professionals appeared to be having the same problem. Occasionally, one of them would stop in the middle of the field and lift his voice in a soulful cry: *"Ayúdame, Fidel"* (Help me, Fidel), before bending to the task again.

I didn't call on Fidel (I didn't know him well enough). As a child, however, I had learned a little jingle from an uncle who always talked about cutting sugarcane in Louisiana: "High top low stubble, work real hard and stay out of trouble." I used this jingle whenever I got really tired and started to slow down, or when I truly felt like quitting. It worked wonders for me.

James, however, wasn't so lucky. Two weeks from victory and glory, he cut his left foot and had to be sent back to Havana. He came back during the last week of cutting, but Rafael wouldn't let him work because of his injury. All the other volunteers finished without any trouble. The day cutting was officially over, ICAP threw a big farewell party and invited some of the local residents. Rum, beer, and food were plentiful. Singing and dancing spilled over into the dawn.

Topping and felling trees and fighting fires in Ben Lomond, working in lumber mills and light industry, farm labor—I had done them all. But for sheer hard, backbreaking work, none compared with cutting sugarcane in Cuba. I'd been on the verge of turning in my *mocha* many times, but now the harvest was over and I had made it through with flying colors. I was just over forty. I smoked and drank too much, but overall I was in great physical and emotional shape. I was pulling my own weight in Cuba and felt damned good about it.

My last memory of the campsite is of looking back to watch Ravelo and the ICAP people standing in the road waving their hats in the air until they disappeared in the distance. I no longer doubted I could make it in revolutionary Cuba.

▼

REUNITED ONCE AGAIN, DIANA AND I COULDN'T GET ENOUGH of each other. We spent hours experimenting with new positions to make love in, and trying to make it last as long as possible. The novelty, however, soon wore off and we began to argue and get on one another's nerves.

Geo had moved in with his steady in Havana. James and Edna were as inseparable as newlyweds on their honeymoon. Gradually we all fell back into the old pattern of hanging out and living off the monthly dole from Immigration. Meanwhile, Cuba's antivagrancy laws compelled able-bodied Cubans to either work or study. Many, with the express approval of their employers, worked during the day and studied at night. As guests of the government, hijackers and others who had been granted temporary political asylum received basic necessities free of charge, and we weren't required to do anything except stay out of trouble.

I believed that since none of us was accustomed to working a regular shift plus four or more hours of voluntary work six days a week, and another four to six hours on Sundays, as the Cubans did, the government preferred not to include us in a regular work plan. We were foreigners and our ideas about revolution were vague, naive, and romantic. Nor was it at all certain how long any of us would remain in Cuba. Nevertheless, it seemed peculiar to me that, if any of us really wanted to work in this working-class society, we had to be sponsored by Immigration or some government-approved organization.

Most of the hijackers took the privileged treatment we received for granted. The Cuban people, on the other hand, had to live out of two ration books: one for basic monthly food supplies, and a second for limited amounts of finished industrial products such as clothing, shoes, toilet articles, bedding, and household goods issued on a yearly basis according to availability. In the early seventies you didn't need a ration book to get bread, eggs, fish, butter, milk, vegetables, industrial alcohol, and kerosene. The ration books for other goods were numbered in groups. Group A, for example, covered from 1 to 1000; group B from 1001 to 1999. Holders of books in each group could buy once a month. If the product being sold ran out before your turn came up, as frequently happened, you were just out of luck until your group came up again.

Each page of the ration books for industrial goods had numbered boxes that allowed you to buy one of two choices: a blouse or a skirt, for example; a toothbrush or a comb; a dress shirt or a pair of slacks. A popular Cuban joke of the time reflected the situation perfectly: Sherlock Holmes and Dr. Watson are strolling through Havana one evening when they notice a man walking ahead of them pull out a handkerchief and blow his nose.

"That chap doesn't have on any underwear," Holmes whispers to Watson.

"What a remarkable deduction, Holmes," Watson replies. "But how can you possibly know just by looking at the fellow?"

"Elementary, my dear Watson. If he'd bought underwear, he wouldn't have a handkerchief."

Cubans in general are clotheshorses. They love to dress up and look good. The clothing issued by the state, however, was mediocre in quality, workmanship, and style. For women, the lack of bras and sanitary napkins was a real hardship. Cuban pesos were plentiful because everyone worked and there was nothing to buy. This led to black marketing.

We hijackers had it made, but some of us didn't have sense enough to appreciate the fact. Idleness, boredom, and dissatisfaction tend to generate other negative tendencies. Particularly hard-to-get consumer goods that brought top prices on the streets of Havana began to disappear from our rooms. Bed-clothes, towels, swim trunks, jeans, T-shirts, and toilet articles were priority items because the Cubans would pay almost any price for them.

We began making sure all our belongings were kept under lock and key. Everyone was suspect. The residents of the house became hard to live with. "I think I know what the problem is," I said to James one morning. "Motherfuckers just sitting around all day doing nothing are bound to find something dumb to get involved in. Manuel, or whoever is in charge around here, has to quit jiving and get me a steady job."

Others in the house also tired of hanging out all day and began looking for work on their own. Knowing it would be next to impossible to get a job without a sponsor, Geo, James, and I decided to go through official channels. Manuel listened sympathetically. "I'll talk to the lieutenant in the morning," he promised. "It might take a couple of days, but I'm sure he'll come up with something."

A week or so later, Manuel brought us some good news: "You are going to start doing voluntary construction work at Plan Porcino." The Plan (Cuban Spanish for collective farm), some twenty kilometers from the city on the outskirts of Bauta, was a large hog farm converted into one of the most important food projects in Havana. It already supplied the city with a large percentage of its pork, and its goal was to provide the entire province with the preferred Cuban meat within a couple of years.

We would work six days a week—usually ten hours a day—and do voluntary work on Sundays if we really wanted to exercise our revolutionary zeal. A truck would pick us up early the following morning. From then on, we were on our own. I asked Geo what *porcino* meant. He said a literal translation was young pig. Damn, I thought, I'm going from fighting two-legged pigs in Stateside cities to building pens for four-legged ones in the Cuban countryside. I immediately dubbed the place Plan Pig.

During the conversation with Manuel, we learned that two other black Americans, Chaka and Masai, would be going to the Plan with us. These two brothers and their families lived in the Riviera Hotel and had the habit of strutting around the city in flowing African robes claiming to be Nigerians. They also boasted of being experienced electrical engineers educated in the States.

We could smell the hogs and hear them squealing before we turned off the highway onto the dirt road leading to the work site. Plan Pig was a sprawling complex of small Cuban shacks called *bohíos,* fenced-in pigs, construction equipment, and warehouses and sundry other buildings. Trucks of all kinds were unloading workers and rushing off to fetch more. There were people everywhere, and their movements were punctuated by a wide variety of noises.

The chief engineer at Plan Pig was a prerevolutionary graduate from a prestigious university in the States. He interviewed each of us personally. Geo, James, and I claimed no special skills and were quickly assigned to general construction work. Jesús, the foreman, gave us a pick and two shovels, then led us to a shallow trench to help several Cubans who were digging away as if they expected to find gold any minute.

Chaka and Masai, brand-new engineering books in hand, were sent to the engineer's office to take a test on blueprint reading. A couple hours later I rose up from the trench to stretch and wipe the sweat from my brow. Chaka and Masai were sprinting to catch a local bus for La Lisa. At lunchtime, Geo found out they knew nothing about engineering and didn't know which end was up on a blueprint.

Chaka and Masai later defended themselves by telling anyone

who would listen that the engineer was racist and hadn't given them enough time with the blueprints. They also stated loud and clear they hadn't come to Cuba to work no ignorant sticks for nobody. Months later, they and their families left Cuba without a word, supposedly for Africa.

I felt right at home in Plan Pig. The people we worked with went out of their way to be friendly once they found out we were Americans. Besides, this was the kind of work I knew best: digging ditches, carting cement, unloading trucks of sand and gravel or prefabricated construction blocks. All major work centers had a kitchen and a workers' cafeteria, where you paid next to nothing for a good hot lunch. The food at Plan Pig was plentiful and well prepared. To get to work on our own, we got up at five o'clock, climbed the fence, and caught a bus to La Lisa. After coffee with milk and bread at a roadside café, we hitched a ride on one of the many trucks going to the Plan.

Working a pick and shovel under the merciless sun was hard, but I was happy. I felt I was doing something worthwhile and, in a small way, contributing to the revolution. I certainly didn't feel as useless as I'd felt loafing at Hijack House all day.

Several others from the house had also found work, and the overall relations there improved dramatically. One Saturday evening, about two months after we'd started working at Plan Pig, James and I came home to find Manuel waiting at the door. He took us to his office, where another of the many lieutenants told us we had done so well in the cane fields and at Plan Pig that Immigration had decided to give us a chance at a full-time job for regular wages at a soap factory. The factory, Sabates, produced bath and laundry soap, detergent, perfume, talcum powder, and, to my surprise, margarine. We would work six days a week, nine hours a day, for ninety pesos a month. Everyone worked overtime, but was only paid for eight hours. The extra time was what I called obligatory voluntary work: if you didn't do it, you were put on the shit list and considered uncooperative or problematical. Union membership and all-night guard duty once a month were mandatory. Coffee, low-priced snacks, and hot lunches were always available. Workers who faithfully filled their monthly quotas and put in a reasonable amount of voluntary work received additional perks of free soap, margarine, and coupons to buy extra shoes or clothing. An added bonus for me was that, at long last, I would get to study Spanish in a school.

The factory was located in the Cerro district of Havana, a fifteen-minute bus ride from Hijack House. For security reasons, an immigration officer would have to take us there on Monday morning and introduce us to the director. Otherwise we'd never get in. James and I were overjoyed. At long last we were going to get our wish: a steady job working the same as the Cubans and officially studying Spanish. We rushed off to find Diana and Edna and tell them the good news.

Edna congratulated each of us with a big kiss on the cheek. Diana shrugged her shoulders and said dryly, "You guys sound as if you plan to stay down here forever."

James and I exchanged surprised glances.

"Look, sister," I said gently, "in spite of the fact I just spent nearly two years in jail under investigation, this is part of the reason I came down here: to get a new start, build a new life for myself, and learn new ways of coping with everyday problems. People I didn't even know lost a lot of bail money, and others whom I love very much risked everything they own to help me get this chance at a new life. I'm not about to let them down."

"Oh, Bill," Diana said, "I understand how you feel, but you guys come on so strong. I mean, first the sugar harvest, then you worked your asses off on the pig farm, and now this soap factory and language school thing. How come you two have to be so different? What are you trying to prove?"

She was on the verge of tears. I pulled her to my chest in a loving embrace. Her outburst surprised and stung me, but I was glad she had expressed her true feelings. I couldn't help but wonder how many others in the house felt the same way but just hadn't said so.

I apologized for having come off so holier-than-thou. The only way I could be sure this was what I really wanted, I explained, was by putting everything I had into it. Diana said she understood but she wasn't going to spend the rest of her life in Cuba working for next to nothing and doing without just because someone said it was the revolutionary thing to do. She wasn't happy in Cuba and didn't think she ever would be.

Edna summarized what both of them had been feeling by saying the big things didn't matter as much as the little ones. For example, if you needed soap or toilet paper or almost anything else, you couldn't just go and buy it; you had to wait until someone decided whether or not you should have it. You couldn't solve the simplest problem on your own, because everything had to go through channels. "We're just not accustomed to living like this," she said.

Once you got involved in a permanent work situation here, Diana pointed out, it took an act of Congress to get you out of it. You couldn't quit or change jobs on your own. Everything had to be approved, and if the authorities said no, you couldn't do a damned thing about it. There was no input from the bottom, they complained. Everything came from the top down. The government told you what to do and you did it or else.

Although what they were saying was a fact of life in Cuba, I realized the revolution had the only game in town. Like it or not, you played by their rules or you walked away. I wasn't ready to drop out yet.

James also wanted to be in Cuba. Unlike Diana and Edna, he had some heavy charges waiting for him back home and would have to face them broke and alone if he went back. Looking back on it, this determination to make a new life in Cuba and not put the government down without giving it a try was really what drew James and me together and made us friends, more than having both been members of the Black Panther Party.

"We all came here for different reasons," I said, "and we'll just have to live with the consequences. I hope our differences won't do bad things to our friendship."

"If you think you can get rid of me simply by being disagreeable," Diana said with a smile as she led me toward her room, "you're in for a big surprise."

The soap factory, a former Procter & Gamble enterprise with chain-link fencing and guard shacks, was situated in a residential-industrial zone. Its imposing twin brick chimneys profaned the blue sky with endless spirals of thick black smoke. James and I waited nervously while Carlos, our security person assigned by Immigration, shoved a bunch of official papers under the guard's nose and addressed him in rapid Spanish. The pudgy, silver-haired guard glanced at the papers, looked us over suspiciously, then spoke into a phone. He glanced at the papers again, handed them back to Carlos, and waved us out of his shack. "Take the stairway to the right," he growled.

Marcos, the personnel manager, was a big man with close-cropped hair. "Well, well," he said as he looked up from our papers, "North Americans." I could read the unasked question—What the hell are you doing here?—in his eyes. He wanted to know if we spoke Spanish, what work experience we had in Cuba, and if we understood we would be treated just like any other Cuban worker. Union meetings were a must. Guard duty was from 6:00 P.M. to 6:00 A.M. once a month. You started work two hours later at 8:00 the same morning. The state provided health insurance, workers' compensation, and social security. The union never disagreed with the labor conditions set forth by the state, and union members never disagreed with their leadership.

We could begin working the next day, he said, but we'd have to be punctual and conduct ourselves like revolutionaries. The shop foreman, Mundo, was called in to show us around and fill in the details. Mundo was a short, plump man with a round face. Except for tufts of jet black hair around the ears, his head was cleaner than a cue ball. Mundo had started working at Sabates before the revolution. He had moved up from janitor's helper to shop foreman, and was damned proud of it.

"You had to pay kickbacks when I started working here," he said, glad for the chance to practice his English. "But for people with families and no job, half a day's pay was better than no pay at all. I was lucky. My uncle and cousin worked here. They managed to sneak me in."

Mundo led us up a narrow metal stairway that clung to the outside wall of the main plant like a giant serpent. We walked into a large, noisy room where aged stamping machines clanked out a tuneless rhythm while large, tired floor fans strained to stave off the stifling heat emitted by the sunbaked tin roof. The odor of raw soap hung in the air like fog. "Watch your step," said Mundo. "It's very slippery here."

"Hey," I asked, "what's this stuff all over the floor?"

"It's soap," Mundo answered. "Bits of it drop from the carts and the workers track it in on the bottoms of their shoes. It's always like this except at the beginning of the shift. But don't worry, you'll get used to it." I learned later those bits of soap had caused more than one accident. The floors and the outside stairway were absolutely unsafe.

As we advanced into the room, heads lifted and curious eyes fastened upon us. Then, with the grace of experience, three sweating janitors worked their way past us. One of them pushed a wide beaded scraper on a long stick and rasped away at the scraps of soap trampled into the concrete floor. The second skillfully thrust a large push broom at the dislodged shavings, swept them into tidy little piles, scooped them up in his dustpan, and deposited them in a wooden cart at his side. The third man, tall and muscular, backed slowly along the aisle swinging an enormous cloth mop in wide graceful strokes from one side to the other. He stopped only to wring out the mop and reposition his oversized bucket with a twist of his foot.

"This is the stamping and packaging department," Mundo said. "Both of you will work on these stamping machines. But right now, follow me; I want to explain to you about the soap."

Mundo led us to the windows at the far end of the building, where we looked down on a blacktop courtyard. A forklift unloaded large metal canisters from flatbed trucks and set them down beside a steaming vat sunk into the ground. Sweating, bare-chested workers wrestled the lids off the canisters and overturned them at the vat's edge. The air was heavy with the odor of rancid grease. The stuff in the canisters was tallow from the Soviet Union. It was melted down in the vats, then piped through metal tubes to the mixing room in the basement, where it was combined with other ingredients, cooked at high temperatures, dumped into portable molds to cool, and finally sent up to the cutting room. Mundo took us there.

Workers in sleeveless shirts guided the massive blocks of soap through the cutting machines, then loaded the neatly sliced bars on large wooden racks. One of the cutting crew adroitly slid the racks onto runners in a tiered, cage-like structure, and wheeled it into an open-sided cooling shed between the cutting department and the stamping and packaging area.

"Let's go back and meet some of the people you'll be working with," Mundo suggested.

Four identical stamping machines stood in the center of the

crowded, heat-filled room. Each machine had its own team of two. A male operator wrestled the heavy soap-laden racks into position and transferred the bars from the racks to the stamping machine, which stamped each bar with the logo BATEY. Then a female packer loaded the bars into thin cardboard boxes and placed the boxes on a conveyor belt that quickly whisked them to the basement.

The heat was suffocating, but everyone seemed accustomed to it. Mundo introduced us to the middle-aged operators and packers. Most of them had put in as much time at Sabates as Mundo had. A neat, well-ordered locker room reminded me of the YMCA. The attendant welcomed us with a big smile, clean towels, and face soap. "If you ever need anything," he said, "anything at all, just let me know."

We were at the factory bright and early Tuesday morning, eager to get started on our new job. Our first day of work was hectic. We learned how to maneuver the soap-laden carts into position next to the stamping machines without losing our footing or tipping the carts over. We also practiced feeding the bars of soap into the stamper, a job that was a lot harder than it looked. By quitting time that evening, we were exhausted and hungry, but ecstatically happy.

Later in the week, Mundo put James and me on a machine by ourselves. By Saturday noon, we had the routine down pat and could run the soap through without jamming the machines. Monday morning each of us had his own machine.

We felt we were riding a lucky streak. A week after starting work at Sabates, we enrolled in Spanish classes at night school in Old Havana. Our 6:00 P.M. classes gave us time to do voluntary work at the factory after the regular shift ended at 4:00 P.M. and still get to school on time.

The teachers, graduates of Havana's pedagogic schools, followed a standard methodology: The date in the upper right-hand corner of the blackboard, the topic in the center, and class objectives in the upper left-hand corner. The small classes, normally eight to ten people, were dynamic and instructive. I studied hard and never missed a class, but Spanish—its articles, genders, and pronunciation—continued to baffle me.

"I don't think I'm ever going to speak Spanish," I confided to James one evening after class. "I just can't seem to wrap my tongue around those double *r*'s."

"Me neither, and there ain't no way I'm ever going to learn the articles and pronouns."

"It's funny," I said. "I understand you when you speak Spanish and you understand me, but the Cubans don't understand either of us."

Between the factory, the school, and volunteer work on weekends, I had little time to spend with Diana. As a result, she spent most of her time in the streets looking for new experiences and excitement. "You can waste your life slaving for these people if you want to," she said one evening, "but I can't. I'm young, good-looking, and sexy, and I intend to get as much enjoyment out of life as I can."

Convinced the problems between us were more political than anything else, I simply said, "Right on, sister."

▼

GEO SPENT HALF HIS TIME AT THE HOUSE AND THE OTHER HALF with his many girlfriends. He didn't talk about the political work he was involved in with other exiles from his country, and I didn't think it was my business to ask. One evening he told me an American couple who were living and working in Cuba wanted to get together with me and talk. Their names were Margaret Randall and Robert Cohen. They were friends of Virginia Miller's and had been in Havana for several years.

I met Geo at the Coppelia ice cream parlor after class the next day and we walked to an apartment building on Línea Street. Each floor was a separate apartment. I remember Margaret as a well-built woman with dark eyes and a shy smile. She led us to the study, where Robert was waiting for us.

Bookshelves covered one wall of the study. Robert, tall, thin, and studious-looking, got up from his desk with a big smile. We sat around and rapped for a while. Then Geo asked if there wasn't any rum in the house. Robert went for a bottle and a bowl of ice. We sat around and made small talk about the Hijack House, the soap factory, and the language school for over an hour. Robert worked at Radio Havana Cuba, the island's main international radio station. Like everyone else, he also did guard duty and voluntary work with the Committee for the Defense of the Revolution, a voluntary civilian block organization dedicated to civil defense, political education, and social services. Among the CDR's many responsibilities was reporting regularly on foreigners, troublemakers, and people with criminal records living in their neighborhood. Then, too, there were always overzealous busybodies who thought their revolutionary duty was to inform on everyone they knew or came in contact with.

Margaret was also a CDR member. She worked with the Cuban Women's Federation and was writing a book about Cuban women. She and Robert had four children, three young girls and a teenage boy. Their three-year-old, Anna, woke up crying just as Geo and I stood up to leave. Damn, I thought, the kid's got the bluest eyes I've ever seen.

I began visiting Margaret and Robert's home several times a week. Their four kids and I got along well; occasionally we lost track of time and I stayed over. Margaret and Robert were very popular. Interesting people from leftist movements in the States, as well as from other parts of Latin America, hung out at their apartment. It was there I met Joan and Jim Shapiro, another couple from the States.

Joan taught English at the University of Havana, and Jim, I believe, worked at the Academy of Sciences. We got together often, sometimes at Margaret and Robert's, other times at their place. In time, the two couples made it clear to me they believed in and engaged in interracial and extramarital sexual relations. I assured them I was in full agreement with the practice.

One night Margaret had guard duty at the Women's Federation from eight to midnight. Joan decided to keep her company for a while. I had stayed over so Robert and the kids could help me with my Spanish. Shortly after nine the phone rang. It was Margaret. She and Joan had something important to discuss with me and wanted me to come over to the Federation building. When I arrived, the two women were sitting on the veranda drinking coffee and chatting away.

I sat down on the steps in front of them, wondering what this was all about. "Well," I said, "here I am. What do you want to discuss with me?"

They looked at me for a second, then at each other, and burst into laughter. I wondered what the joke was and hoped it wasn't on me. "I hate beating around the bush," Joan said, brushing a strand of hair from her forehead. "The truth is . . . well . . . we both want to make love to you and we wonder how you feel about us."

I was speechless. I sat there, looking from one to the other, a smile frozen on my face. Son of a bitch, I never even dreamed something like this would happen, I thought. Got to come up with something fast 'cause next they'll probably want me to choose between them, and I know whatever choice I make will be the wrong one.

"I must admit I never anticipated anything as personally pleasing as this," I said lamely. "I really don't know what to say. I feel honored beyond words. I like both of you very much and I can't think of anything I'd rather do than make love to each of you."

"You see," Joan said, "you have to nudge these strong silent types, but once they get started . . . look out."

"Which of us would you like to make love to first?" Margaret asked.

"You're asking me which of you I like the best," I said, "and I ain't about to cut my own throat by choosing one of you over the other. I'll go along with whatever decision you make between you."

They decided to flip a coin, and Joan won the toss. We sat around talking for a while, then took off for her place. "What about Jim?" I asked.

"It's his turn to sleep on the couch," she said matter-of-factly.

I spent the next few weeks making love to Margaret and Joan alternately. Neither Robert nor Jim showed the slightest resentment or jealousy.

One night, during dinner, Robert and Margaret invited me to move in with them. I accepted without thinking.

After class the next evening, I went to the house in Siboney to get some of my things and to tell Diana I was moving out. I knew she was into other men, including some of those at the house, so her reaction completely surprised me.

"I know all about the little white bitch you fooling around with," she said angrily. "She don't care nothing about you; she's just playing games, and as soon as she gets tired of you, she'll cut you loose without even thinking about it."

"Look, sister," I said, "you don't ask me how you should run your life, and I sure as hell ain't asking you how to run mine.

Now do us both a favor and don't go putting on your woman-in-love-about-to-lose-her-man act, 'cause you ain't in love with nobody but yourself and we both know it."

When I moved out of the house, Diana felt she was losing one of her many conquests. The thought didn't set well with her. First she sent me a note asking me to call her. She tried to guilt-trip me, so I hung up. Then she sent me a letter swearing her love for me, accusing me of breaking her heart, and predicting my new relationship wouldn't last. I didn't bother to answer. As for her words of undying love, she didn't write again, and eventually went back to the States, leaving her young son behind with his father.

I continued working and studying Spanish, but the heat, the unsafe working conditions, and the hard regimen of the factory caused me to give serious thought to my future as a worker in Cuba. I had no clear-cut idea or objective in mind. But one thing was certain: I sure didn't want to spend the rest of my time in Cuba working on these stamping machines. Joan was sent to Korea as a reward for helping to translate some of Kim Il Sung's works. When she returned, she had lost the hots for Bill Brent and refused to have anything to do with me. I was hurt, but quickly got over it. She and Jim soon packed up and went back to Baltimore.

One evening, Margaret and Robert invited me to attend a meeting with other Americans at the Foreign Residents' Union, an ICAP umbrella group for residents from Latin American and Caribbean countries and also from the United States. The Union of North American Residents—called the American Union—was part of the larger group.

Margaret introduced me to the other Americans as an ex-Panther and a skyjacker. She also told everyone how good I was with kids and how well I could cook and clean house, and gave them a general rundown on my work record in Cuba. By the time she finished, I felt as if I were a slave on the auction block.

The Union of North American Residents was made up of a small group of Americans and repatriated Cubans—about thirty people living and working in Cuba who wanted to express their solidarity with the Cuban revolution in an organized way. Some were members or supporters of the U.S. Communist Party. Others were New Left advocates. Still others just thought the Cuban revolution was a damned good idea that had found its moment in history. Their occupations were as diverse as their political backgrounds. Some, like Robert Cohen, worked in radio. Harold Spencer taught English at the University of Havana, and his wife, Alfreda Mahler, taught modern dance. Jane McManus, a longtime activist on the political left, was a multifaceted journalist (her work had appeared in *The New Republic, Time, Mademoiselle,* and the radical newsweekly *The Guardian*). She had recently come to Cuba to translate *Tricontinental* magazine into English for its publisher, OSPAAAL (the Organization of Solidarity of the Peoples of Africa, Asia, and Latin America). I was the first nonwhite and the first skyjacker to become a member of this union. The one thing we all had in common was our respect and unbridled admiration for Fidel Castro.

The union supported the Cuban revolution with words and deeds, held solidarity meetings with other unions, organized Marxist-Leninist study groups, and sent messages of support to political prisoners in the States.

Margaret and Robert wanted to take over and run things their way. Elections were coming up soon, and they felt their popularity among union members and their ICAP sponsors would easily win them the presidency and vice presidency, leaving a lesser office for me.

Unknown to them, other members of the union were also

making plans—which did not include those two as their leaders. Instead, Margaret and Robert were elected information secretary and solidarity secretary, respectively. Jane McManus was voted president, and Marge Emerson, organizing secretary. I was voted ideology secretary.

Margaret and Robert were crushed. Margaret was especially bitter toward Jane, calling her a privileged liberal who didn't know anything about Latin America or the Cuban revolution.

I liked Jane from the minute I laid eyes on her. Through our close contact and work on the union's executive committee, I found she opposed intolerance and injustice, had participated in the campaign to save the Rosenbergs, and had supported the idea of fair play for Cuba in the early sixties. She also supported the black liberation struggle and other progressive causes.

Much like me, she wanted to help the Cubans and their revolution. She was good people, to my way of thinking, and I felt comfortable talking to her and being with her. She felt the same way about me. One thing led to another—an invitation to dinner at her place, a goodnight kiss that became harder and harder to break off. Little by little we fell in love. It was the best single thing to happen to me in Cuba.

One evening I arrived at Jane's apartment for dinner and found her almost in tears. Her kitten, Florinda, had fallen down the air shaft and couldn't get out. It was crying piteously.

I offered to climb down on a rope and send the kitten up, but Jane was afraid I'd fall or wouldn't be able to climb out again. So I tied a bucket to the end of a rope, put a piece of raw steak in the bottom, and lowered it down the shaft. But every time the poor thing tried to get at the steak the damn bucket tipped over and frightened it away. Finally I laid the bucket quietly on its side. The kitten walked into it, and I quickly hauled the bucket and Florinda up to safety.

Florinda turned out to be a he. A male cat, I pointed out,

needed a good masculine name. I suggested Rufus. "Good," Jane said. "From now on we'll call him Rufus." She prepared me a wonderful meal.

When Rufus got a little older, we would let him out at night and he'd be back knocking at the door like a person the next morning. I remember how sad Jane and I were when he didn't come back one morning. I went out and looked for him in vain. We never found out what had happened to him.

Meanwhile, back at the Randall-Cohen household, things weren't going so well. Margaret and Robert no longer regarded me as a desirable tenant. They claimed I wasn't doing my share of work in the apartment and wanted me to start paying rent and add cleaning the floor in the girls' room to my share of the chores.

"Look," I said, "we agreed not only that the girls were old enough to clean up after themselves, but that the experience would help them form good habits. I suggest we stick to the agreement until I'm out of here."

Jane and I talked with Robert and Margaret to avoid ending up hating one another. They became even more inflexible and argumentative.

Jane understood my situation very well; there were no secrets about my background. She invited me to move in with her and Rufus. I gratefully accepted her offer of love, comfort, and sanctuary. I could never have imagined the tremendous positive influence Jane would have on my future.

9

HUEY IN HAVANA

VOLUNTARY WORK consisted of everything from sweeping and cleaning up your block on Sunday morning to picking coffee in the countryside on weekends or straightening nails and moving construction materials from one place to another at Havana's Talla Piedra electric plant at night. Union activities kept Jane and me on the move. Solidarity meetings with other unions were only part of our responsibilities. Organizing our own members to donate blood was relatively easy; getting them to put in extra hours finishing kitchen utensils in a factory outside Havana was another story. When the Venceremos Brigades came down, we were sometimes sent to their camp to give them a firsthand account of what life was like for Americans actually living in Cuba. And, too, some of the *brigadistas* occasionally visited a union meeting in Havana. The Brigades first came to Cuba in November 1969 to show support for the revolution by working in the fields. After their tours ended, many of the *brigadistas* wanted to stay and work. Only a few ever made it.

Union activities kept us so busy, in fact, I had to drop out of the language school. I was convinced the union was a positive political experience and was able to persuade James, Edna, and several other residents at Hijack House to join too. Other unions, like those of the Haitians, Peruvians, and Chileans, had each selected one of their country's fallen heroes as their union martyr. Robert and Margaret wanted George Jackson to be the martyr for the American union. Others thought it should be Wobbly labor organizer Joe Hill. Jane, James, and I convinced them the martyr who really represented our struggle in the sixties and seventies was Malcolm X.

The biggest disagreement within the union was over carrying the American flag in the annual May Day parade. Each union carried its country's flag. I was dead set against having the American union carry the Stars and Stripes. "In the minds of millions of people the world over," I argued, "the American flag has come to represent oppression, racism, injustice, invasion of other countries, murder of innocent people, genocide, and just about every other evil you can think of. In my opinion, the U.S. flag no longer represents the will of the majority of the American people, and I refuse to be associated with it."

"I agree some people have used our flag for their own selfish gains," said Harold Spencer, a former officer of the union, "but I think we should do everything in our power to restore its true meaning. The flag is not at fault; the people who carry it make the difference." A few of the members agreed with Harold. They didn't want to disown their flag, yet they realized that, for millions of people the world over, the Stars and Stripes was a negative symbol. The solution was a large, brightly colored banner with the words UNION OF NORTH AMERICANS RESIDENT IN CUBA emblazoned across it.

The union also had its share of personalities. One of the more colorful was Agnes, a middle-aged North American who had come to Cuba with her Cuban husband, Frank, a union leader who had been forced to leave the United States during the Mc-Carthy period. Agnes never learned to speak Spanish and made no effort to try. She insisted the Cubans should learn English if they wanted to talk to her.

Both she and Frank were heavy drinkers. He controlled his liquor well, but Agnes just didn't give a damn. She never came to a union meeting sober, and she often needed the support of Frank's arm to make it home after an outing. Nevertheless, everyone loved and respected her because she had given up a comfortable life in the States to be with her husband in a foreign country she would never understand.

▼

JANE HAD A USED VW BUG WE CALLED PUPU. SHORTLY AFTER we began living together, Pupu's carburetor developed a problem I couldn't handle. Fortunately, a neighbor introduced me to an all-around mechanic named José León Vidal—everyone called him Pepe—who lived just down the block. Pepe fixed the carburetor in nothing flat, and has been our close friend and mechanic ever since. Pupu took us everywhere. Jane was always cool and calm, as if she were riding in a Rolls-Royce. I did all the driving and was always a little anxious because spare parts were hard to come by and service stations were few and far between. I kept a tool kit and an extra can of gas in the trunk and a couple of bottles of Havana Club under the front seat.

We lived in a one-bedroom apartment on the second floor of a building on the corner of Fourth and Calzada Streets, in the Vedado district. The National Folklore Group was headquartered only two doors down, so we involuntarily sat in on their daily practice sessions. We were the only Americans in the neighborhood.

OSPAAAL had assigned the apartment to Jane rent-free as part of her contract. She paid for the electricity, gas, and telephone. The designation "foreign technician" also came with the contract and allowed her to shop at a special store and receive extra rations of canned goods, meat, and gasoline.

We woke up mornings to the aroma from the fish market on the first floor and the incessant chatter of the early birds gathering to mark their places in line. Cubans thought nothing of discussing personal matters as openly in the streets as they would at home. Conversations from the sidewalk to balconies and windows were commonplace.

People talked and played their radios as loud as they could. When Fidel made one of his many speeches, radios were turned up so loud everyone for blocks around heard him. Pictures of Fidel, Che, and Camilo Cienfuegos were in nearly every home and on the walls of schools, offices, and factories. To the Cuban people, their maximum leader wasn't Mr. President or Mr. Minister. He was Fidel. Cubans, as well as foreigners, quoted him religiously.

On one corner directly across from our building stood a mansion with colonial wrought-iron fencing, beautiful shrubbery, stately palms, and a number of mature fruit trees. It was the home of José Martí's descendants until the last one died, when it became a research center on topics related to his life and work. No matter who occupied it, the neighborhood kids found ingenious ways to climb over or squirm through the fence and snitch mangoes, oranges, and honeyberries.

Most of our neighbors in the building had lived there since before the revolution. A few had small children. In general, everyone was quiet, courteous, and friendly.

Our apartment was only three blocks from Havana's most popular gathering place: the Malecón, a drive, a promenade, and a wall, which protects the city from the enduring sea. Thousands of Havanans flock to the Malecón to smooch, stroll along the shoreline and bask in the wondrous beauty of a Cuban sunset, or just hang out. On calm days, fishermen sit patiently on its walls and dream of pulling in a big one. Youngsters dog-paddle and splash about below them.

One balmy Sunday evening, as I strolled leisurely along the Malecón enjoying the fresh air, I passed two young black men having an animated discussion in English. I could tell they weren't Americans or Jamaicans, so I stopped and asked them where they came from. It turned out they were Congolese and were in Cuba to take a special four-year course in Spanish for foreigners at the University of Havana.

We talked for a while and they assured me any foreigner could enroll. I checked with the university and found out the course would begin in less than a week. With a letter from my work center or from an official organization, I too could enroll in the special course for foreigners. All I had to provide in addition was a favorable report from my CDR and a valid ID card.

"Impossible!" Marcos, the personnel manager at Sabates, screamed when I asked him to change my work hours so I could attend the university. "I wish I could go to the university too, but there's too much work to be done here. We can't spare anyone right now."

"I want to continue working," I said apologetically. "All I'm asking is to be allowed to work half a day, from noon to four, so I can have time to study at night and go to classes in the mornings."

"I knew there would be trouble from the moment I saw you," Marcos said. "You don't belong here, because you don't understand what the revolution is all about."

"I know I'm not Cuban," I said, "and there are a lot of things I don't understand. But education, I was told by Immigration, is a right, not a privilege, and the work centers are required to help workers study and raise their educational levels."

We glared across the desk at each other for what seemed like hours. The huge picture of Fidel on the wall behind his desk seemed to be staring directly at me. Finally Marcos dropped his eyes, shuffled some papers, and said, "The best I can do is change you to the night shift. You will have plenty of time for classes during the day."

I knew this arrangement wouldn't work because I would have to work a full shift at night, get a couple hours sleep, and be in class by eight in the morning. This left me no time at all to study. Still, I decided to accept the straw boss's offer. I would also get a letter of sponsorship from ICAP, just in case problems developed later on. The first week at the university was one of settling in, learning the location of the classrooms, and getting to know the other students, the teachers, and the curriculum. Things got serious in the second week, however, and I realized I would either have to give up the night shift at the factory or drop out of the university.

Jane and I discussed the problem thoroughly. I could always get another job somewhere. But at my age I'd never get another chance at a university degree. I had to go for broke now or give up the opportunity and regret it for the rest of my life.

Jane was completely supportive. The decision was mine. I chose the university and didn't even go back to the factory to pick up my work clothes or my pay for the month. The straw boss complained to Immigration. I had abandoned my workplace without permission, he charged, and should be taken before a disciplinary commission. If sanctioned, I could receive a reprimand, a fine, or a jail sentence.

In Cuba, Immigration is a power unto itself. It has its own

laws, police, and jails. All foreigners (except the diplomatic corps) and all Cubans who travel outside the country fall under its incredibly bureaucratic control. We who had entered the country illegally were completely at the immigration officials' mercy; we had to do exactly what they ordered or be thrown back in jail without so much as a hearing. They weren't at all pleased with my decision to go to the university. But since I had ICAP as a sponsor and had officially enrolled, and also had a legitimate place to live and wasn't dependent on them for my livelihood, they decided to leave me alone and see what happened. It's a small victory, I thought to myself, but the taste is sweet to the tongue. Now comes the hard part. I can't bluff, con, or fast-talk my way through the university. This is going to take all the intelligence I can come up with and then some. Maybe I should have let well enough alone and just stayed in the factory.

With my skimpy knowledge of English grammar and syntax, I had to face up to the greatest challenge of my life: four years learning Spanish grammar, Latin, French, linguistics, phonetics, Cuban history, Latin American history, Spanish literature, and art appreciation. This wasn't about muscle and willpower, as in the cane fields and Plan Porcino; now I would have to use my intellect, and I wasn't at all certain I could handle it. I might fail, I thought, but I'm sure as hell going to try.

All classes for the international students were given in Spanish. My classmates came from Africa, Bulgaria, Czechoslovakia, Poland, and the Soviet Union. Not only were they younger than I, but they spoke the language better. (Many of them had completed an intensive one-year course in Spanish at one of the language schools in Havana, and their Spanish was excellent.) I studied basic Spanish at home at night and bugged Jane and the neighbors with lots of dumb questions, such as: "How come the words ending in *a* aren't all feminine and those ending in *o* aren't all masculine?" I spent a lot of time at the library. I had never realized how difficult studying could be.

I discovered I had to learn how to learn. My classmates Bitemo and Michelle kindly drew me into their study circles. With their patient help and encouragement, I began to feel a bit more comfortable in class. Whenever I began to falter, Jane was there to keep me moving in the right direction.

The university's College of Arts and Letters is a brick-fronted four-story building set among tall trees at the corner of Presidente and Zapata, about a twenty-minute walk from our house. A long, marble staircase leads to large classrooms. All university students—including us outsiders—received a stipend of twenty pesos a month. Bitemo, Michelle, and the other African students—two men and a woman—had government scholarships.

The Soviets and other Europeans in the class were either married to Cubans or related to foreign technicians working in Havana. The Cuban students loved to hang out and rap with us. I think they were fascinated by our different accents and the ways we spoke their language. Many of them thought our studying in Cuba rather than in our own countries was strange. The atmosphere was one of mutual curiosity and friendliness. On occasion, small groups of us got together and went to Coppelia for ice cream.

Jane and I lived within walking distance of several movie houses and theaters, but work and study didn't leave much time for socializing. Occasionally, however, we would force ourselves to take a break and catch a performance by the National Ballet Company at the García Lorca theater in Old Havana. We also enjoyed performances by the Rita Montaner theater group at the Bertolt Brecht theater in Vedado, and once we caught Leo Brower in a tribute to Charles Mingus at Vedado's Amadeo

Roldán theater. (The theater was destroyed by sabotage a few years later and has yet to be restored.)

Most times, I walked to the university to avoid the hassle of fighting my way onto, and off of, the always-crowded buses. Sometimes I took Pupu and always wound up having to give someone a ride home after classes. In spite of the help from my friends, I felt extremely uncomfortable at the university. As I later realized, years of cultural, economic, social, and spiritual abuse had conditioned me to believe I didn't really belong there.

First-year finals came. I had studied night and day to prepare myself, but I fretted over the exam for hours before finally turning it in. I wasn't even sure I had understood the questions, much less answered them correctly. I went home tired and depressed. Convinced I had flunked the exam and would surely get kicked out of the university, I spent the night dreaming I was the dumbest person in the world. A smiling Bitemo met me on the stairs of the Arts and Letters building the next evening. "Good news," he said. "Everybody got good grades; we all passed everything."

"Are you sure?" I asked.

"Of course I'm sure," Bitemo said. "The grades are posted in the hallway." My grades were among the lowest in the class but not as bad as I'd expected. Right on, I said to myself. Right motherfucking on.

My Soviet classmates came over and we all congratulated each other. Ana Ginsberg, a superintelligent Soviet student, had the highest marks of us all. "I've talked with some of the Cubans," she said. "They say we'll really have to study now because second-year Latin, grammar, and linguistics are always harder than the first year."

All my classmates from the Soviet bloc countries were women. Most of them were married to Cubans, and that naturally gave them a head start in understanding Spanish. They were warm and friendly and just as curious about the United States as I was about the Soviet Union. Other than language, there was no difference I could see between them and everyone else I knew. They had the same dreams of peace, prosperity, and happiness; the same need for love and understanding; the same desire to make something out of their lives. The Cubans have a saying for it: *"Todo el mundo quiere lo bueno"*—Everybody wants the good things in life. Some of these women, like their African and Cuban counterparts, were so concerned about getting good grades they copied test answers on their inner thighs in preparation for a test. "If you don't have the piece of paper with good grades on it," said Ludmilla, "you can't get a good job here or anywhere else."

The Africans, like the Cubans, were full-time students and always complained about the stipend they received. "Oh, Comrade Bill," Michelle said, "you can't imagine what we have to go through here. They don't give us enough food or enough pesos. I'm hungry all the time."

"I've lost so much weight my clothes don't fit anymore," Bitemo said. "I'm selling them to get food. Soon I'll have to come to classes naked."

"You'll be too thin to notice," quipped Michelle.

▼

I WAS ALONE IN THE APARTMENT ONE EVENING, TRYING HARD to memorize the differences in the painting styles of Rubens, Botticelli, Michelangelo, and Piero della Francesca, when someone knocked at the door. Oh fuck, I said to myself, the last thing I need right now is a visitor.

I pushed the books aside, strode angrily to the door, and flung it open. "Hi," a well-dressed young black man said. "Are you Bill Brent?"

"Yes, I am," I said brusquely. "What can I do for you?"

The stranger, whom I'd immediately pegged as American, told me his name was Denis Franklin. He was a California lawyer and wanted to talk to me, in private, on behalf of a mutual friend. I hesitated for a moment. Who could possibly have sent him? I invited him to take a seat in the living room and asked who the mutual friend was. Huey Newton, he said, taking out a pack of Dunhills and lighting up.

I was dumbfounded. Having spent more time in the immigration jail than in the Party, I hadn't given any serious thought to the Panthers or Huey in quite a while. Huey, Denis informed me, had been here for several months. He was living in the Capri Hotel and was anxious to get together with me. He hadn't contacted me before, because the Cubans didn't want him to get involved with any of the skyjackers here. Huey had insisted, and they finally relented. I agreed to come to the hotel the following evening at eight.

After Denis left, I went out on the balcony and stood there, lost in thought. I don't believe this, I said to myself. Huey Newton here in Havana and asking to see me. The idea of finally meeting in Cuba the man whose courage and audacity had inspired me to join the Panthers made me nervous. I wondered how we would react seeing each other after so many years.

The next evening, Denis was waiting for me in the hotel lobby. We got the required pass at the desk and went up to Huey's room. Another business-suited brother, a rarity in Cuba (except for diplomats), met us at the door. He looked me over suspiciously before letting us enter. Everyone in the room looked as though he'd just stepped out of a fashion magazine. Dressed in my customary faded blue jeans and a T-shirt, I felt like a bum. Huey got up from his seat in the center of the small but comfortably furnished room and walked over. We looked at each other for a few seconds, then shook hands and embraced.

"It's good to see you free instead of just talking about it, brother," I said. "I wasn't sure it would ever happen but I'm glad it did."

"People like you made it possible, brother," Huey said with a big smile. "We've heard nothing but good things about you from the Cubans. You've earned their respect."

"I respect the Cubans, too, and I'm grateful they decided to give me asylum. The system is different, but I'm learning to concentrate on all the good things going on here. I haven't had any problems since they put me on the street."

Huey took my arm and led me into the room where his pretty, brown-skinned young wife, Gwen, and two well-dressed brothers sat near the window. We shook hands all around and Huey suggested we would be more comfortable at the rooftop pool. A nervous-looking blond waiter hurriedly took our poolside orders. He probably thinks we're going to either steal the silverware or contaminate the water in the pool, I thought.

Huey looked young and healthy. His eyes were alert and intelligent, and his boyish smile constantly wrinkled the corners of his mouth. His relaxed manner put me at ease.

Huey expressed his sympathy for all the shit I'd gone through in the States and especially for the time I'd spent in jail in Cuba. In response to his questions about Cuba and socialism, I described the island's complete dependence on the Soviet Union for its development. I admitted I hadn't quite gotten a grip on socialism. What I'd seen so far was a small, underdeveloped agricultural society whose people were struggling like hell to survive without having to bow down to the U.S. government.

After a few shots of rum, the other brothers joined in the conversation. They brought me up-to-date on what was going on in the Panthers and the black movement in general. I was glad to have this input because most of my news came from Cuba's daily newspaper *Granma,* Radio Havana Cuba, and literature brought down by the Brigades or other visitors from the States. The few Panther papers I'd seen were months old by the time I got them.

Huey had really come to Cuba to avoid going back to jail on assault, tax evasion, and murder charges. His lawyers had advised him to leave the country until things cooled down, and Cuba was the only place he could be sure of being accepted. A private yacht had brought him and his wife as close to Havana as possible, he explained. Then the yacht's captain put them in a small boat with a 9hp motor, pointed them toward the lighthouse at the Morro Castle, and cut them loose. The sea was very rough, and about fifty yards from shore the boat capsized. Luckily, the waves washed them ashore, and they were picked up by the CDR. They suffered only minor cuts and bruises. That was on Thanksgiving Eve, 1974.

As I walked back home from the hotel, I was lost in amazement at the way time and circumstances had brought Huey and me together in the last place I could have imagined we'd meet. I wondered how long he would stay here and how he would react, in spite of privileged treatment from the government, to the Cuban reality. Two major questions kept buzzing around in my mind: Who was running the Party while he was in Cuba? And what would happen when he went back to the States?

I visited Huey at the hotel again about a week later. This time Panther lawyer Charles Garry was there. Huey told me he'd met some of the other brothers who'd come to Cuba illegally. Some said they'd had trouble with the police and had gone to prison for hustling dollars and dealing on the black market. They also told him the government was racist. He asked whether this was true and why so many of the brothers had such difficulty adjusting to the Cuban way of life.

"Part of the problem," I told him, "is they came with stars in their eyes, hoping the Cubans would train them in guerrilla warfare, arm them, and sneak them back into the States to engage in armed struggle, or help them get to Africa. It didn't happen and they're pretty pissed off about it. Also, they are a lot younger than I am and don't give a damn about going to jail, because they can afford to waste a few years behind bars. To them, it's all part of the game. In short, they don't want to be here. I do."

As for the racism, I told him I'd run into several racist Cubans, but I thought the wide racial mixing showed that the problem was more a lack of racial sensitivity than out-and-out racism. People referred to each other affectionately as *chino, negro, blanco,* without any overt racial overtones. Nevertheless, racism had existed before the revolution, and I didn't think fourteen years was enough time to wipe it out completely.

"Brother Bill," Huey asked unexpectedly, "how would you like to rejoin the Panthers?"

I was taken by surprise. "I really hadn't thought about the possibility. I don't know what to say."

"Just say yes, brother," Huey said. "I'd be proud to be able to say Bill Brent is still a member of the Black Panther Party."

I left the hotel with feelings of wonder at Huey's presence in Havana and happiness at his invitation to rejoin the Party. I had daydreamed of doing something outstanding to make the Panthers regret their decision to expel me and ask me to rejoin them, but I'd never imagined Huey Newton would be the one to do the asking. And, of all places, here in Cuba.

I had been unjustly accused by the Party of being a police agent. I had also been made to question my own sanity and ability to judge right from wrong. So I accepted Huey's offer, not only because it cleared my name with the black movement, which I still loved and wanted very much to be a part of, but because it allowed me to feel good about myself again. I think I wanted that almost as badly as I wanted to be back struggling beside my people in the States.

The government gave Huey, Gwen, and her children an apartment in Santa Clara—some three hundred kilometers from Havana. We didn't hang out together in Havana, but Jane and I did drive out to visit them. When we got to their apartment, we found Huey and Gwen in a quandary. They had been given a live chicken as part of their monthly rations and neither of them had the slightest idea what to do with it. I was surprised to find the leader of the Black Panther Party didn't know how to wring the neck of a chicken and cook it for dinner.

Huey worked at a Santa Clara garage as a mechanic's helper for a while. He couldn't speak or understand Spanish, so I can imagine what the experience must have been like. I think Gwen had more success teaching English at a local hospital. Her children, Jessica and Ronnie, had a ball going to school with Cuban kids and learning Spanish. Between shifting locations—Havana for half a year, Las Villas for another half, back to Havana for a year, then another six months in Alamar—Huey spent some two and a half years in Cuba. He maintained almost constant contact with the Party through long-distance phone calls and a seemingly endless string of visitors from the States, including Party officials, lawyers, and Hollywood personalities. On the day he and his family left for home, Jane and I went to say good-bye in the lobby of the Riviera Hotel. He knew what he had to face up to and was determined to see it through.

After Huey left Cuba, I had no further contact with him or the Panthers. I did hear about some of his alleged misdeeds— beating up Party leaders and kicking them out of the Panthers, among other things. I hoped the stories weren't true and somehow Huey would be able to pull himself and the Party together again.

▼

ONE OF JANE'S FAVORITE THINGS WAS TO PACK A PICNIC LUNCH and, with a few close friends, head for one of the beautiful East Havana beaches. We did this at least twice a month. Jane was like a fish in the water, while I couldn't even dog-paddle. But, like most of the Cubans, I had just as much fun wading and splashing around in the shallows.

Cubans and foreigners alike loved to get invitations to receptions and other political functions at ICAP or the Chinese, Vietnamese, and Korean embassies, mainly because there was always plenty of good food and drink. Most times, the speeches were long and drawn out, but the goodies made listening worthwhile.

Each year, with our UNION OF NORTH AMERICANS RESIDENT IN CUBA banner waving high, we participated as a bloc in the May Day parade in La Plaza de la Revolución—Revolution Square. I had coordinated my union activities with my studies and, to improve my ear and pronunciation, listened to Cuban news programs and most of Fidel's speeches. I especially liked the way he rolled his *r*'s when he wanted to emphasize a point.

On January 28, 1974, Leonid I. Brezhnev, general secretary of the Soviet Communist Party, began a one-week state visit to Havana. The American union, along with everyone else, was organized to participate in a mass mobilization in Revolution Square to hear Brezhnev speak. The night before the big day an immigration official came to our apartment to notify me that a bus would come by the next morning to pick me up—just me, not Jane. I wasn't under arrest or charged with anything, but if I didn't catch the bus, I would be picked up and put in jail.

I guessed the reason and felt more hurt and disillusioned than angry. Jane was furious. She got on the phone immediately and started calling everyone we knew. There was nothing anyone could do. The Soviet general secretary was too important to take chances with. The Ministry of the Interior was rounding up everyone they thought might cause trouble and holding them in a safe place until the activities at Revolution Square were over. I obediently climbed on the nearly full bus the next morning. After a few more pickups along the way, we were driven to a beachfront social club surrounded by armed guards. Inside the comfortably furnished clubhouse I saw other Americans from Hijack House, and quite a few Latinos dressed in their militia uniforms or white doctor's or nurse's smocks. A few were silently crying.

An immigration official called us to order, took the roll, and explained this was a necessary security measure that in no way implied we were considered dangerous or threatening to the revolution. He expressed confidence that the government could continue to count on our support and cooperation. He also called on several of us to express our views of solidarity with the Cuban revolution.

I don't remember exactly what I said, but I know my heart wasn't in it. After the speeches in Revolution Square were over, we were taken back to our homes. The incident was widely talked about and heavily criticized for a few days and then forgotten as we all fell back into the rhythm of our daily routines. There were similar pickups from time to time, but I wasn't included in them.

The foreigners' unions were gradually phased out as Cuba began to reestablish diplomatic relations with many of the Latin American countries it had been at odds with over the years.

By the time I reached my fourth year at the University of Havana, I could read and understand Spanish quite well and I no longer felt intimidated by exams. I not only knew what books to ask for at the libraries, I also knew how to use the information in them, how to do research, and how to work collectively to solve difficult problems.

I graduated from the University of Havana in November 1981 with a bachelor's degree in Hispanic languages. "I never dreamed this day would come," I said to Jane. "I've had a lot of help, but I did it."

Immigration's policy toward the people who had entered the country illegally changed drastically during the four years I spent at the university. They selected several of the brothers and sisters from Hijack House and gave them ration books and a house of their own. Stateside lifestyles, however, didn't meet the approval of the CDR in their zone, and trouble developed. The neighborhood watchdogs complained about the Americans' long hair and loud music, and, above all, about the number of young Cubans hanging out at their house. Immigration officials began hassling the Americans and their visitors.

The brothers fought back by writing a long letter that detailed what they considered unjust treatment and smuggling it out of the country. After the letter was published in a U.S. newspaper, Cuban officials took it as a criticism of the revolution. Before long, the authorities began transferring the hijackers to shoddy rooms in several cheap Havana hotels. Some of the women had young children to care for, and at one point they brought their plight to the attention of the American union. They said the living conditions in those hotels were degrading and the food was less than adequate, especially for the kids. They also said Immigration had made it difficult, if not impossible, for them to get jobs, and their monthly stipends didn't cover their needs.

The union was sympathetic but unwilling to interfere in Cuba's policy toward the hijackers. Shortly after the meeting, many of the hijackers were rounded up and shipped out to the provinces. In early October 1978, Jane and I received a telegram, signed by James, from Manzanillo, in Granma Province. It said he had been there for three weeks and asked me to find out from immigration officials how long they planned on keeping him there without money or a job. I immediately went to Immigration and talked with the people in charge of the hijackers.

"The problem is being taken care of," they said. "Don't worry about it."

The following week, we received another message from James, saying he still hadn't received any help from the people in charge of him. I knew it would be a waste of time complaining to Immigration again, so I went to ICAP. They were sympathetic, but they couldn't interfere in official government policy. There was nothing I or anyone else could do.

My reply to James was as encouraging as I could make it. I told him the people at Immigration had said everything was being taken care of. I urged him to hang on and keep after them from his end. Yet, I had to admit, Immigration's hard-line policy toward skyjackers had me exceedingly worried.

10

▼▼▼▼▼▼

EACH ONE
TEACH ONE

▼▼▼

I BEGAN TEACHING English in the William Soler Junior and Senior High School in Los Sitios, one of the poorest districts of Havana. The school was named to honor a fourteen-year-old who was assassinated while working with the underground movement in Santiago de Cuba. My starting salary was 170 pesos a month—about double the average pay for most Cubans.

"He has no teaching experience, and his Spanish is awful," the municipal personnel manager for schools complained when I applied for the job.

"He'll do just fine," Irene, the municipal methodologist, said. "He's a native English speaker and a university graduate. Besides, he's here to teach English, not Spanish."

The school covered a full city block on Belascoáin, a main thoroughfare where the traffic seldom slowed down. The four-story school building resembled a bombed-out relic from the Second World War.

For the first few days, I sat in on several English classes to get the hang of the teaching methods. I had the good sense not to let my bad Spanish stop me from asking questions when I didn't understand. After several days, department head Luis Alonso assigned me two seventh-grade groups.

Two of the students in my first class decided they would put me to a test of their own. They refused to answer roll call, made fun of my Spanish, pretended they didn't understand me, and kept whispering and laughing during most of the class.

When class was over, I ordered the two troublemakers to stay seated. Then I closed the door, collared each one, and shoved them against the wall.

"If you two are looking for trouble," I said angrily, "I'll give it to you. Here in the classroom or outside after school. If you don't want to learn, don't come to my classes. Okay?" The shocked youngsters understood me perfectly.

"Okay, okay, *profy*," one of them said, "we don't want no trouble with you."

I don't recommend this method, but at the time I couldn't think of anything else. I knew my authority in the classroom was being challenged. If I didn't come down fast and hard on these two, others would follow their example, and I'd never be able to establish order in my groups or teach them anything. Word got around fast: The new English teacher didn't play. As a matter of fact, for the first month I played it hard and didn't laugh or joke even with my fellow teachers.

The following week, Luis Alonso gave me one more group in seventh grade and three in eighth grade. Each class averaged about forty students jammed into cramped and stuffy class-rooms. The thin plaster walls, some with large holes punched through them, gave no relief from the constant street noise or the din from other classrooms.

The government guaranteed every Cuban child the right to an education. But the classrooms were always overcrowded.

English was required, and it was the only foreign language taught at the junior-high level in Havana. Most students found the pronunciation especially difficult. All the English teachers had strong Spanish accents and were prone to converse in their native tongue rather than in English. Of the seven teachers in the English department, four had graduated from an English-language school. The others were still studying.

I shared seventh and eighth grades with another teacher, who helped me prepare my classes. Everything we did or said had to be written down in a class-planning notebook. "We always plan a week in advance," my colleague said, "so's not to get caught by the surprise inspections."

The methodologist was a frequent visitor to our classes and teachers' meetings. The teaching of a foreign language, she always emphasized, should contribute to the political, scientific, patriotic, and moral education of the students, and to the reaffirmation of their ideas of socialism and proletarian internationalism. We all took notes and nodded in agreement. I, for one, accepted every word she said.

I asked why Spanish was spoken in English department meetings.

"It's easier for us to think and communicate in Spanish," a teacher next to me replied. "We can deal with concepts and ideas much more easily in our own language."

"I love to speak in English," another teacher added, "but as soon as I make a mistake I get nervous and go back to Spanish."

The methodologist explained: "We encourage all the teachers to speak English, but it's more important for them to master the teaching methods and the technique of class planning. Their English will improve with time."

The principal and assistant principal of William Soler were young black women. Both were working mothers, and they did guard duty and voluntary work and participated in the CDR. They also kept a close watch on my progress and my relations with the students and other teachers.

I busied myself with the teaching methods and class planning, asked a million questions, and read everything I could get my hands on. I made a special effort to befriend and help my students. I also spent more time learning from the other teachers than my pupils did.

"You have to take it easy," Luis Alonso told me. "There's a lot to learn and it takes years to digest all this stuff."

The majority of the students wanted to learn and never caused problems in class, but some didn't really give a damn and frequently got into trouble. Each time a student started acting up in class, I saw a reflection of myself when I was that age. I recalled how I'd wanted help but hadn't learned how to ask for it. I also remembered I was a stranger here, and kids always challenge a newcomer. There were days when I spent much of my class time criticizing unruly students or sending them to the principal's office.

I was at a loss for a solution, when I suddenly remembered how embarrassed I'd felt when a teacher came and told my mother I was messing up in school. I decided to visit a few homes and found that the parents believed their kids were doing well in school because no one had told them differently. They thanked me for coming and promised that their kids would behave in the future. There was a marked improvement in discipline in my classrooms for the next few weeks.

I ran into my first real problem with Luis Alonso at the next departmental meeting. "The main objective of the school," he said, "is retention and promotion of students. The administration handles the retention, and we, as educators, handle the promotion. Every time we fail a student on a test, we fail in our objective. For that reason the principal has committed us to a promotion rate of 94 percent. That means each of you has to guarantee the promotion of all your groups. We will have collective reviews in each grade, with special emphasis on the objectives of each unit and class."

I waited until Luis Alonso and I were alone and told him I doubted my groups could get such high promotions. He told me not to fret, that everything would come out just fine. "Stop worrying," he said. "We never miss a promotion quota."

I knew he had more experience in education. I also knew my groups had serious problems. Most of my students didn't know Spanish grammar, much less English. On the way home that evening, I thought about Luis Alonso's words: "The main objective of the school is retention and promotion."

The only way to get 94 percent promotion out of that school was by giving students the answers or tampering with their test papers. I didn't intend to do either.

The testing went smoothly. I went through my best group very carefully. Just as I'd expected, nearly a third of them did poorly.

"Leave everything with me," Luis Alonso said. "I'll go over this and see that you're grading the answers correctly." I felt like a complete failure at teaching. I walked into the department the next day to find that all my groups had done very well and the English department had come out of the tests with exactly 94 percent promotion.

"You were taking too much off for spelling and punctuation mistakes," Luis Alonso said authoritatively. "It takes a while, but don't worry, you'll get the hang of it."

▼

THE GOVERNMENT'S SCHOOL-GOES-TO-THE-COUNTRYSIDE PRO-
gram demanded that Cuban students and their teachers spend
from fifteen to forty-five days a year working in the countryside. The program was designed to give city kids experience at
working in agriculture and teach them the importance of farmwork for the country's economy. The kids liked camp because
there were no classes.

I understood the thinking behind the program, but I wasn't
convinced that forcing kids to leave their homes and families to
do farmwork was a good idea. I also resented the fact that it was
mandatory for teachers as well. Learning socialism was one of
my reasons for being in Cuba, but I wasn't too enthusiastic
about going off to supervise kids doing agricultural work for
over a month.

Nevertheless, I knew that if I refused to go for anything other
than medical reasons, I could forget about a teaching career. Jane
drove me to the school on the departure day. The area resembled
an overturned beehive. Students and families crowded the
streets and kept up a deafening chorus of noises. For the kids,
this was a yearly happening, another phase in their revolutionary socialist development—and a chance to get away from home
for a while. The parents accepted the separation and the hardships it entailed without question.

Finally, the long-distance buses swallowed students and
teachers and sped off. The luggage—homemade wooden suitcases crammed with food—had the owners' names and destina-
tions painted on the sides. It would follow by truck later in the
day.

We hadn't gotten two blocks from the school before the students started singing, dancing in the aisles, and beating out Afro-

Cuban rhythms on anything that would make a sound. They were already enjoying their new-found freedom.

It took about three hours from Havana to the city of Pinar del Río and another forty-five minutes or so to the camp. The campsites were isolated barracks with outside toilets, cold water, and few lights.

Most of the women were deathly afraid of the frogs and lizards that inhabited the outdoor showers. Some of the men and boys were equally frightened, but would die before they'd admit it.

"The food is . . . how do you say in English . . . lousy," one of the teachers had commented before we left, "and the kids are always into some kind of mischief. But we all work very hard and somehow always wind up having fun."

The barracks turned out to be a large, ramshackle tobacco shed divided by thin plywood boards—one side for the boys, the other for the girls. The 60-watt bulbs trying to hold back the darkness, the shabby rows of sagging wooden bunks, and the smell of dust and dampness reminded me of the cane camp. The rear of the building housed the kitchen and mess hall, which also served as the indoor recreation area. Two other teachers and I would supervise the boys' side of the barracks.

Lunchtime finally rolled around. The trucks hadn't arrived and the kitchen brigade hadn't had time to set up, so Spam sandwiches and tap water substituted for a regular meal.

The campsite was a disaster, with weeds and trash everywhere. We spent the rest of the day cleaning, putting the compound in shape, and preparing for our first day in the fields. Everyone cheered when the trucks finally arrived with the luggage. The kids would be munching all night.

The next morning, we started working in the tobacco fields. At this stage of the harvest the work consisted mainly of weeding and thinning out the tobacco plants. I had forgotten how tough and stubborn weeds could be.

I started out supervising a group of teenage girls who knew a lot more about agricultural work than I did. Cuban women, as a rule, are very open, friendly, and flirtatious. When I tried to compare them to American women I came to the conclusion that they simply were not afraid to express their true feelings. If they liked you, you'd know it. If they disliked you, you'd know that too. I had experienced their coquettishness in the classroom; but here, in the nearly complete freedom of the countryside, I was hard pressed not to take advantage of their natural expressions of warmth and friendliness and do something stupid.

The girls in my group always greeted me with a hug and a kiss on the cheek. They took turns holding my hands going to and from the fields. They were very sympathetic to my lack of knowledge about the work. They taught me the difference between weeds and young tobacco plants, and patiently explained that weeding had to be done by hand and in such a way that the plants were not damaged. Furthermore, they said, if the rows weren't completely cleaned of weeds, the field boss wouldn't give us credit for completing our daily quota. One of my favorite students, a petite, almond-eyed brunette named Julia, helped me keep the other members of our group in order, gently corrected my Spanish, and made me dream of being young again.

To me, our assigned work area appeared to have more weeds than tobacco plants. On workdays, we got up with the chickens, had breakfast, walked to the fields, and worked until noon. Lunch back in camp usually consisted of boiled beans, white rice, and bread. We hit the fields again by one o'clock and worked until five. Dinner was more varied and tasty: soup, meat or fish with a sauce, white rice, and sometimes custard or rice pudding.

Anticipation, excitement, and joy pervaded the camp soon after the evening meal on Saturdays because Sundays were visiting days and made up, in part, for the hardships and bullshit we had to endure during the rest of the week. Relatives and sweethearts began arriving before dawn to vie for choice picnic sites. Then they waited patiently for the camp to come alive and the visiting to begin.

The Ministry of Education welcomed family visits but did not provide transportation. Each family—often at tremendous personal expense and sacrifice—had to get to the campsite on its own. Sometimes they managed to save a few coins by hiring group transportation. Whatever the situation, they never complained, and always came with enough extra food to replenish their children's stores. The students depended on those visits to supplement the frugal camp diet. Cuban *socioismo* (sharing among friends) took care of the teachers and students who didn't receive visits.

The work was divided according to the stage of development of the tobacco plants. Some students spent their first week weeding; others worked at fertilizing or irrigating. When the tobacco leaves matured enough to be picked, everyone joined in the harvest.

The more experienced girls worked in the drying sheds sewing the green leaves together and stringing them on poles to dry. A few teachers worked in the administration of the camp, but most of them supervised brigades of students. The brigades competed to become the best. Everyone in camp protested the high quotas, but pride and self-esteem inspired them to fight hard to meet them. One brigade leader, a bad black street brother affectionately called Chapapote (Tar Baby), made a lasting impression on me. Chapa was a born leader. He was good with his fists, sensitive, and intelligent. His group followed him to the fields every day on the double, and under his leadership

they always met their daily quota. Everyone in the camp respected Chapapote and his brigade.

I stayed awake every night until sheer exhaustion forced the
last restless kid to fall asleep. Then, after shaking out my bed-
clothes to get rid of any bugs, and amply dousing myself with
insect repellent, I managed to get a few hours' sleep before
dawn. None of this bothered me as much as the nagging feeling
that I wasn't cut out for the work. When I had to chastise kids
for not working hard enough, or write out a report on one of
them, I felt like an overseer working slaves on a plantation.
Everyone else took it in stride, but it bothered the hell out of me
because I remembered all the horror stories my relatives had
told me about working for pennies on white folks' farms in the
South.

The evening before my last workday in camp, Jane drove out
with her grandson John, who was down from Massachusetts for
a two-week visit. Jane thought it would be a good idea for
Johnny to meet Cuban kids his age who were working in agriculture as part of their general education.

Johnny, an awkward fourteen-year-old, was an immediate hit
with the girls. They crowded around him and searched for English words with an enthusiasm they never showed in the classroom. Their main request was for Johnny to sing "Hotel
California."

Johnny and Jane spent the night at the camp, she in the girls'
dorm and he in the boys' dorm with me. Next morning, we got
up at dawn, had our coffee with milk and a thick hunk of bread,
then went to work in the fields with the others.

After two hours of pulling weeds, I decided Jane and Johnny
had had enough hands-on socialist realism. We washed up, said
good-bye, piled into Pupu, and took off for the sleepy little
town of Viñales. We had reservations at Rancho San Vincente,
located some twelve kilometers away in the hills. We arrived

early in the evening. After we checked into our rooms, I went to the tourist shop for cigarettes, toilet articles, a tucked Cuban dress shirt called a *guayabera,* and some fruit juice and Havana Club. Back in the room, Jane mixed drinks and I began to relax for the first time in over a month. After a while, Johnny, wise beyond his age, decided to go swimming to give Jane and me some time alone. We fell into each other's arms as soon as the door closed.

At one-thirty the next morning, Johnny came down with a severe asthma attack. He had brought some special medication along, but nothing he took did any good. Jane and I were frantic. The hotel manager recommended that we take Johnny to the town's clinic, several miles away.

We threw everything into the car and took off down the narrow, winding mountain road with an asthmatic youngster in back gasping for breath. To make matters worse, there were no road lights in the mountains. Our headlights worked only when they felt like it, and I wasn't at all sure Pupu's brakes would hold up under the strain. Outwardly calm, but knowing a mistake could be fatal for us all, I concentrated on the job at hand. After what seemed like hours—leaning into the curves, cursing and praying—we reached Viñales, got directions from someone on the street, and raced on to the clinic with our hearts in our throats.

The hotel manager had called ahead. The doctor and her assistant were waiting for us. They helped Johnny into the emergency room and calmly went to work. Jane was quiet and composed on the outside, but I knew she was holding back the tears with all her strength.

I really needed a drink once we had made it down the mountain, but I was so shaken I couldn't remember what I'd done with my last bottle of Havana Club.

The doctors placed an apparatus similar to a gas mask over

Johnny's face and fed him an atomized mixture of oxygen and a special asthma medication commonly used in severe cases. Before long he was sitting up, a shy smile on his flushed young face.

Jane rushed over and gave him a big hug. I went out to the car and found my Havana Club. We thanked the doctors profusely for their wonderful service, piled into Pupu, and headed back to Havana.

I returned to the classroom with a changed attitude about the School-Goes-to-the-Countryside program. The students appeared to be more relaxed and natural in the countryside than in city classrooms. There was a marked difference in the way they related to each other: They were friendlier, more tolerant, eager to help one another. Despite hard work, miserable living conditions, and poor diet, camp was easier than school for most of them, I felt, because it presented a physical rather than an academic challenge.

Finals came and Luis Alonso reminded us of the 94 percent commitment. Final exams were graded by a special commission of teachers headed up by the municipal methodologist. My students didn't do as poorly as I'd expected. At the end of my first year of teaching, the teachers' union awarded me a certificate for 100 percent attendance, punctuality, and proficiency.

▼

THE MUNICIPAL METHODOLOGIST TRANSFERRED ME TO THE Protesta de Baraguá Junior High School. (In Baraguá in 1878, General Antonio Maceo, one of the most celebrated black generals in Cuba's first war for independence, rejected a peace treaty with the Spanish, El Pacto de Zanjón, that other Cuban officials had signed. This act of resistance became known as La Protesta de Baraguá—hence the school's name.) I welcomed the move because the new school meant smaller groups. There was more interest in learning here because the student organizations were more active and played a major role in student discipline and organization.

My new department head gave me six seventh-grade groups. I found the students at Protesta de Baraguá much more receptive to my teaching efforts. I'm certain the peer pressure from the highly politicized student groups and the broad participation by parents contributed to this improvement.

Using simple phrases and sentences illustrated with pictures or gestures, I managed to get a large percentage of the students to use more English in the classroom. I was truly proud every time one of my students greeted me on the street: "Hello, teacher, how are you?" (with a marked accent, of course, but with confidence). My new students consistently got good grades on their own, and there was no pressure on me to meet unrealistic promotion quotas.

At the end of the year I was transferred back to William Soler, which had been renamed Ignacio Agramonte in honor of another of Cuba's famous independence war generals. This time I would teach tenth graders. The move meant an automatic raise in salary and required that I learn a new method for teaching high school students. The basic objectives remained the same— retention, promotion, and heavy emphasis on reading and interpreting texts. I didn't mind because it gave me the chance to gain more experience and know-how in the classroom.

In my fourth year, a political decision made on the ministerial level sent most high school students to permanent boarding schools in the countryside. High school teachers would have to seek employment in junior highs, with less pay, or transfer to the permanent high schools in the countryside, miles away from their homes and families.

Through the grapevine, fellow teachers Eva and Fifi and I heard of possible openings at the prestigious Vladimir Ilich Lenin Vocational School on the outskirts of Havana. We piled into Pupu and rushed to check it out. Sure enough, three English teachers were needed to fill positions in the tenth, eleventh, and twelfth grades.

Evita got the tenth-grade slot, Fifi got eleventh, and I, because of my university degree and my status as a native speaker of English, got the coveted twelfth-grade position.

The Lenin School had been inaugurated in January 1974 by Soviet general secretary Leonid Brezhnev and Fidel Castro. It was organized by units, each with its own language labs, recreation areas, and hierarchy. The hospital, gym, sports field, theater, and mess hall were communal. It had some of the best teachers in the Havana area and was the school that parents concerned about their children's education preferred.

The idea was that only those students with the best grades, the correct political orientation, and a revolutionary attitude toward work and study would gain admittance. The truth, however, was that parents in important positions could use their connections to get their children enrolled.

I couldn't wait to get on the basketball court in the big, well-appointed gym, do a few laps around the manicured athletic field, and dive headlong into the Olympic-size swimming pool.

Matía, general director of the English department, assured me the school had excellent parent-teacher relations. Irregularities in class were discussed immediately with the students and their teacher. Matía also explained the school's basic philosophy: Children who grow up without knowing how food is grown and harvested or how goods are produced will grow up deformed. So classes alternated with agriculture and light industry—with students making flashlight and radio batteries or cutting and sewing uniforms in the garment factory. These activities also helped pay the school's overhead. Everything was organized on a rotating basis, so each student got the same work experiences.

Matía introduced me to Nancy, acting head of the English department. Nancy welcomed me by having me sit in on one of her twelfth-grade classes.

"This will be your new English teacher," she said. "His name is William Lee Brent and he's North American." I took a seat in the rear to observe both Nancy and the students.

During her class, Nancy spoke English and used lots of pictures and gestures. Her students were well behaved and showed a real interest in what she did and said. After class, I asked her what the secret was.

"This is their final year," she said. "They know that the technical, scientific, and medical textbooks all come in English at the university level. So at least they need to know how to read and interpret English."

I spent a lot of time visiting classes and talking with the teachers and the students. I studied twelfth-grade class plans and workbooks. Jane and I practiced giving classes at home until I thought I had invented teaching. Little by little, my efforts began to earn the respect of my pupils and fellow teachers.

I had been there a little over a year when the administration began demanding a higher rate of promotions. Teachers with low promotions would have their salaries reduced. I didn't like what was happening, but I wasn't thinking about giving up teaching. I worked hard and spent a lot of time with the few problem students I had.

In the meantime Jane was making plans to travel around the island. Pupu was too uncomfortable and unreliable for such a venture, so she bought a new 1983 Lada. It was the first new car either of us had ever had. We kept Pupu, of course, but the Lada was our pride and joy and turned out to be more reliable than I'd imagined it would be.

My relationship with the teachers and students at the Lenin School was good. I enjoyed teaching but felt limited at the high school level. Routine took over and the job lost its magic. I began to feel a compelling need for a significant change, for something more challenging and rewarding. I hit the job-hunting circuit again. This time my goal was to land a university teaching job.

For almost three years I made every possible effort to get a position in higher education, but since I had no juice, no connections in high places, my efforts were in vain. Reality finally sank in. I had gone as far as the system would allow me to go in teaching. I could either stay where I was or learn a new profession.

I began putting out feelers. After a month, I got an offer. A friend at Radio Havana Cuba, the island's principal international radio station, came to the house one evening and offered Jane and me jobs at the station as scriptwriters and announcers. We didn't know a damn thing about radio, but my friend assured us that, as native English speakers who had lived in Cuba for years, we wouldn't have any trouble.

Jane refused the offer because she preferred the job she had—translating and writing about tourism. But I was so excited I could have turned flips. I quickly agreed to a job interview at the station.

"You will have to go through a ninety-day trial period," the station director said. "A percentage of your pay will be in U.S. dollars—about fifty dollars a month. After a year you're entitled to a paid vacation of two weeks."

I had searched for a way out of education and here it was. I didn't hesitate to accept the conditions. The director sent a letter to the Lenin School asking that I be put on loan to the station for an unlimited time.

I liked the idea of working with other Americans, especially with benefits I would never get in education even at the university level. My transfer came through in a matter of days. I couldn't wait to get started.

11

FLIGHT WITHOUT END

W HEN I JOINED
Radio Havana
Cuba in Janu-
ary 1986, it was in its twenty-fifth year of operation. In February 1961, a small group of revolutionaries had begun daily
two-hour shortwave broadcasts from Havana in both Spanish
and English. The purpose was to promote international solidarity and counteract the vicious lies and half-truths the U.S. and
foreign press were spreading throughout the world about the
Cuban revolution. Three months later, Radio Havana Cuba was
officially inaugurated to celebrate Cuba's recent victory at the
Bay of Pigs. Prensa Latina—the Cuban version of AP and
UPI—also came into being at about that time. Within a matter
of months RHC was broadcasting news, interviews, political
analysis, and music twenty-four hours a day, with programs in
Arabic, Creole, English, French, Guarani, Portuguese, Quechua,

and Spanish. Each language had its own department and native speakers.

The head of the English department, Santiesteban, was an overweight and ruddy-skinned Cuban with a gravelly voice and an authoritative manner. His main function was to make sure the English programs that went on the air had the correct political content reflecting Cuba's socialist character. He spoke good English and was completely devoted to the station and to the revolution. The department itself was a mixed bag of English-speaking Cubans, a heavy-drinking Canadian, and a diverse group of American movement people hastily recruited from the Venceremos Brigades.

Santiesteban's girl Friday, Portia Siegelbaum, a dark-haired New Yorker, was one of the first recruits. She was married to a Cuban and supported the Cuban government without reservation. When I started working at RHC, everyone was outwardly friendly, yet I sensed an undercurrent of tension and formality that made me uneasy. Santiesteban was courteous enough when I walked into the office, but I got the feeling he wasn't at all glad to see me. He acted a little upset because I had been hired through the director's office and not by him. In fact, his attitude and tone reminded me that, prior to my joining RHC, Robert Cohen had worked there for years. Since he and Margaret were at odds with Jane and me, it was quite possible they had bad-mouthed us to Santiesteban before they left.

After passing a typing and translating test, I spent my first week reading scripts, learning to translate news clips, listening to the others broadcast their programs, and getting the feel of the station. Finally I was assigned to translate news clips from Prensa Latina. This was a brand-new challenge for me, because I didn't type well, and translating Spanish to creditable English took more knowledge and skill than I had at the time.

About two weeks after I started working, Santiesteban announced that he had hired another American, named Mike Finny. I'd known him at Hijack House as Macheo. Since then, he'd had several brushes with the law, gone to a Cuban prison for allegedly trafficking in U.S. dollars, and, quite recently, returned from Jamaica, where he had hoped to receive political asylum or find an undercover route back to the States.

The Cuban government hadn't prevented him from leaving and had even permitted him to return after he narrowly escaped arrest in Jamaica and certain extradition back to the United States. He typed well, spoke excellent Spanish, and was a good translator. I had no doubt that he would fit right in at RHC because he also had an ego big enough for three or four people his size. I hadn't known Mike in the States, but, curiously enough, his stepfather, lawyer Frank Brand, had represented me after the shootout in San Francisco. Mike and I weren't close friends, but we respected each other. That, to me, was more important than anything else. He started off at RHC the same as I had: reading scripts and translating news clips. Within a month, he was broadcasting news while I was still struggling with translating it. Santiesteban had promoted Mike over me without even bothering to explain why. When I asked him why he hadn't promoted me as well as Mike, since both of us were to be trained as broadcasters, his excuse was that I had a voice problem and he didn't think I should go on the air representing RHC.

I was mad enough to chew nails. I felt that he had finally shown his true colors—or, more precisely, his prejudice against me. I asked him to tell me exactly what was wrong with my voice so I could work on improving it. His response was "It just doesn't sound right."

True, I knew nothing about broadcasting, but neither did most of the others. Everyone in the department was learning. What I did know, however, was that I had a good voice for both singing and speaking. I had proven that many times as a spokesman for the Panthers and as an English teacher in Cuban schools. As I saw it, the basic differences between Mike's voice and mine were cultural and educational. I sounded black and he didn't. Santiesteban's answer, as far as I was concerned, meant only one thing: thinly veiled racism. I remembered my conversation with Huey about the difference between individual and institutionalized racism. Oh well, I said to myself, not even a successful revolution can wipe out these things overnight. Okay, so I'll practice. Time is on my side. RHC needs native English-speaking broadcasters. Santiesteban will have to use my voice whether he wants to or not.

My thoughts turned out to be more prophetic than I could have imagined. The tensions and formalities I had sensed at first were, in fact, indications of a power struggle going on in the English department.

Several months passed. The station sent Santiesteban to a broadcasters' conference in the States. He returned to find his job in the hands of a younger, less experienced person. After several weeks of office infighting and intrigue, a former *brigadista* named Gail Reed was appointed head of the English department. Gail had worked at the station for several years. A Columbia University School of Journalism graduate, she was married to a Cuban and had a young son.

All English-language broadcasts were directed primarily toward the Americas, especially the United States and its Cuba supporters. Now, with Gail at the helm, innovative approaches to radio programming and broadcasting were introduced. Everyone in the department was assigned to prepare programs based on interviews, eyewitness reports, cultural and sports events, and even personal experiences that reflected the socialist goals of the Cuban revolution. Taped phone calls to well-known political figures in the States and other countries became a vital part of RHC programming. Voice training and classes in radio broadcasting were better organized. Mike left news broadcasting and took over jazz programming. Under the name Bill Beaumont, I became host of a daily music and information program called Tour Radio Taíno, directed mainly toward English-speaking tourists visiting Havana and the provinces.

Most of the American music we broadcast had been brought down by *brigadistas* and other visitors. The station's music library, however, was up-to-date with the latest Cuban and other Latin sounds. As a result, my programs would intersperse tourist tips on the most popular hotels with the sounds of Mongo Santamaría's "You Better Believe It" or the Eagles' "Hotel California." After running down a list of the best floor shows in town, I might treat my listeners to Los Van Van's latest hit or something by Earth Wind and Fire. Aretha Franklin contrasted with Omara Portuondo; Rubén Blades was followed by Michael Jackson or Stevie Wonder. Kool & the Gang shared the spotlight with Willie Colón of Panama, or Brazil's Antonio Carlos Jobim. My program played them all, from the Rolling Stones to Bob Marley. On occasion, I even threw in a little gospel or country and western.

All of the departments were required to send representatives to the provinces to get on-the-spot narratives that could be turned into programs. I learned to do interviews, write them up as programs, and tape them for incorporation into the regular broadcasts. Other native English speakers in Cuba worked in the department on a part-time basis. Jane, for instance, did a very popular series of programs on tourism.

I am an early riser. My eyes automatically pop open between four-thirty and five o'clock every morning, and I can neither go back to sleep nor just lie in bed doing nothing. Most days, I started work around six. I had my program ready for editing and recording before any of the others showed up for work. Since I arrived and finished early, I felt justified in leaving early.

One day Gail told me I would have to stop leaving the station early. When I asked for a reason, she said it was hard to keep my time card straight, and sometimes one of the other broadcasters needed an additional voice or a producer and there was no one there to help out. "We never know when you might be needed. So, it will be better all around if you just come in and leave at the regular time like everyone else."

I had learned a long time ago that you didn't argue with the boss unless you were ready to get your hat. I conformed to the new rules even though I didn't agree with them. I was learning something new and enjoying the work. It felt good to know that my voice was being heard all around the world and that I was contributing to the revolution. Why should I blow the whole thing because of changed work hours?

Most of the journalists at the station loved out-of-town assignments because they gave us a break from the everyday routine and allowed us to travel to places we probably wouldn't otherwise visit. These assignments also allowed one to learn something about other areas of Cuba. For example, Santiago is known as the "cradle of the revolution." It is also the site of the Moncada garrison, where Fidel and his small group of rebels struck the first major blow against the Batista dictatorship. Trinidad is one of Cuba's oldest villas and the most perfectly preserved colonial city on the island. For much of the 1800s, its wealth came principally from sugar and slavery.

All of the out-of-town assignments were interesting, but the one that sticks in my mind was the visit to a maximum security prison in Santa Clara. Jane and I had visited Huey and Gwen in Santa Clara during their stay in Cuba. This time, the occasion was filled with gloom. Three other RHC reporters and I were picked up at our hotel the morning after our arrival in the city and driven to the prison, several kilometers away. It was easily recognizable by its high barbed-wire fences and desolate landscape. I began to empathize with the prisoners as soon as I saw it. I could imagine how they must have felt when they saw it for the first time, knowing that vital years of their lives would be wasted behind those walls.

We were ushered into a neat, well-organized prison reception room, where a young lieutenant, who looked like a Chicago Bears linebacker in a military uniform, shook hands with each one of us. This was a maximum security men's prison that received prisoners from all over the island. Some women also were housed here while going to court, or while in transit to a women's prison.

The structure had been built before the revolution. Living conditions were deplorable then: The guards were corrupt and abusive, violence was an everyday occurrence, and the prisoners—many of them political—were denied all civil and human rights and were treated like animals.

Now, according to the lieutenant, this was a model prison. The prisoners were not beaten or mistreated in any way. Their food was clean and well prepared; medical and dental care was guaranteed. The revolution paid prisoners for the work they did so they could help support their families on the outside. Some prisoners were talented at handicrafts, and all of them could learn a trade such as carpentry, furniture and mattress making, and upholstering—things that supposedly would help them adjust to society when they were released. The products they made were sold to other institutions. The only difference between this system and the ones I'd gone through in Lancaster, Quentin, and Tehachapi was that here it was run in Spanish and by the revolution. I neither saw nor heard anything that made me think these prisoners would be any better off when they were released than they had been when they came there.

The semidark cells, although spotlessly clean and orderly, were old, and they were permeated by the smell of closed quarters without running water or flush toilets. The main-line cells reminded me of overcrowded county jail dayrooms with double bunks. A few two-man cells were reserved for trusties. Freshly painted fifty-gallon water drums occupied one corner of the shower and toilet area. It didn't take much effort to imagine how uncomfortable these cells must be when they were crowded with restless, sweating human bodies.

The guards took us to the work area, where the daily activities had slowed as the curious prisoners waited to see the visitors. Tape recorders at the ready, we immediately split up and selected the prisoners we wanted to interview. I picked out a group of five young black men who were shellacking chairs in the center of the large workroom. As soon as they saw me walking toward them they stopped working. I spoke politely, saying I was from RHC and wanted to interview them. They told me that other reporters had talked with them and they'd never heard from them again, or read anything in the papers about their interviews. I assured them I would broadcast as much of the interview as my bosses allowed me to.

They agreed that the living conditions were pretty good. The cells were kept clean, the food was decent, they had television and movies, and medical and dental care. All kinds of people were allowed to come there and talk with them. They emphasized that most of the guards were sympathetic. Furthermore, the prison paid them for their work and allowed conjugal visits.

I asked about racism. They said the cells weren't segregated but most prisoners preferred to be with their own people whenever they could. Sometimes there were problems between individual blacks and whites, but they didn't feel that racism was the cause.

A small, rustic mattress factory brought vivid images of my days at Lancaster when I was nineteen years old. The equipment